Other Books by Trailer Life

Trailer Life's RV Repair & Maintenance Manual, Fourth Edition
Bob Livingston

This revised edition presents recreational vehicle owners with all the up to date practical knowledge needed for diagnosing problems, making repairs, and communicating with mechanics. Filled with detailed troubleshooting guides and checklists, hundreds of comprehensive illustrations and photographs, and easy to understand step-by-step instructions for repairing, replacing, and maintaining systems.

8½ × 11, 500 pages
ISBN: 0-934798-70-2
$34.95 plus $3.95 shipping and handling

10 Minute Tech – The Book

Here are hundreds of easy-to-do, money savings tips taken from Trailer Life Magazine's "10-Minute Tech," the most widely read and talked about self-help column for RVers. This handy book features clever ways to help you improve your RV's livability, plenty of towing tips, procedures for cleaning and maintaining your rig, user-friendly tips on fixing your appliances, great ideas for storage and much more. Filled with easy to follow illustrations that will help turn RVers into savvy do-it-yourselfers.

7¾ × 9½, 219 pages
$29.95 ISBN: 0-934798-59-1

Complete Guide to Full-time RVing: Life on the Open Road,
Third Edition
Bill and Jan Moeller

This best-selling how-to-do-it book covers a broad range of subjects of interest to fulltimers, those considering a full-time lifestyle, or seasonal RVers. New and expanded chapters include working fulltimers, remodeling your RV for full-time living, and widebody RVs, in addition to chapters on costs, choosing the right RV, safety and security, and more.

7⅜ × 9¼, 548 pages
$29.95 ISBN: 0-934798-53-2

The Best of Tech Topics: Volume I
Bob Livingston

Over the years, thousands of RVers have corresponded with Bob

Continued

Livingston through his monthly "Tech Topics" column in Highways magazine. The Best of Tech Topics includes their most important and most asked questions, along with no-nonsense answers and solutions to pressing RV problems. Whether you are working on your own RV or in the RV trades, you'll find the job-tested information you need right here.
5½ × 8½, 98 pages
$12.95 ISBN: 0-93478-55-9

100 Miles Around Yellowstone Park
Jim and Madonna Zumbo

This book is a comprehensive guide that focuses on the sights and activities within a 100-mile radius of Yellowstone National Park. It is a valuable guide for travelers who choose Yellowstone as their destination, but don't want to miss out on the many sights and activities nearby. Particular emphasis is made on RV travel and information in this area.
7⅜ × 9¼, 368 pages
$34.95 ISBN: 0-93478-52-4

Please Don't Tailgate the Real Estate:
Scouting the Back Roads and Off Ramps to Find True Love
and Happiness
William C. Anderson

A hilarious collection of insights, observations, and travel adventures of noted author and Hollywood screenwriter, William "Andy" Anderson, gleaned from more than thirty years of RV travel with his wife and family in their rig, Rocinante. Andy is a rare combination of gifted humorist and warm-hearted observer whose hilarious accounts of the twists, turns, quirks, and challenges of life on wheels comes from his own personal experience.
5½ × 8½, 224 pages
$16.95 ISBN: 0-934798-51-8

These books are available at fine bookstores everywhere. Or, you may order directly from Trailer Life Books. For each book ordered, simply send us the name of the book, the price, plus $3.95 per book for shipping and handling (CA, CO, IN residents please add appropriate sales tax).

Mail to:

Trailer Life Books,
64 Inverness Drive East,
Englewood, CO 80112

You may call our customer-service representatives if you wish to charge your order or if you would like additional information. Please phone, toll-free, Monday through Friday, 6:30 A.M. to 6:30 P.M.; Saturday, 7:30 A.M. to 1:30 P.M., Mountain Time;
1(800) 766-1674.
OR, Visit us online at www.tldirectory.com

THE RV HANDBOOK

Third Edition

Bill Estes

TRAILER LIFE BOOKS

Trailer Life Book Division

Editorial Director: Bob Livingston
Production Director: Ann Emerson
Production Manager: Brian Fitz-Gerald
Editorial and Design Coordinator: Denise Coin
Technical Illustrations: Miyaki Illustration
Cover Design: Gary Grettor

Printed and bound in the United States
by Ripon Printers.
9 8 7

ISBN: 0-934798-66-4

The RV Handbook

TABLE OF CONTENTS

Using an RV with little knowledge of how the various systems work seems similar to traveling without a road map. You'll probably get there, but the trip may be less predictable and more expensive.

This book is at least a partial road map for RVing, ranging in coverage from ways to improve fuel economy and performance to living without hookups—from vehicle handling and stability to propane safety. Just as different kinds of maps are available to help us locate travel destinations, there are different kinds of books to explain and illustrate the various aspects of RVs. *The RV Handbook* is designed to help you understand a wide variety of RV topics, rather than to tell you in step-by-step fashion how to make repairs. That's the approach taken by another book, *Trailer Life's RV Repair & Maintenance Manual*. The two books are designed to complement each other, with *The RV Handbook* taking the more theoretical approach.

As one of my early mentors said many years ago when RVs first caught my interest as excellent adventure-travel vehicles, "If you know how it works, you can fix it." While that's obviously an oversimplification, it is indeed difficult to repair or modify a mechanical device or system unless you know how it works. Of course, it's impossible for us to include specific data on each and every mechanical aspect of RVs in this book.

Based on more than more than three decades of contact with the readers of *Trailer Life* and *MotorHome* magazines, I have selected topics that I know are of interest to RV owners—topic coverage that readers of these magazines have repeatedly requested. I trust that you will find information here that you did not discover anywhere else and that it will help you enjoy your RV. The RV hobby easily becomes a lifestyle, and more expertise means more enjoyment. On the practical side, being able to diagnose problems not only reduce hassles, it can cut costs.

Trailer Life's Towing Guide, which is recommended as a supplement to *The RV Handbook*, is a unique collection of data that has been in heavy demand for many years. Not only does the guide contain official trailer-weight ratings for tow vehicles, it includes suitability data on compact cars and light trucks for towing behind motorhomes. Also, there are specifications on motorhome chassis.

As a dedicated long-term RV tinkerer—one who enjoys the mechanical aspects almost as much as rolling along the open road—it's my best hope that this book will help you find a new, heightened level of RV mechanical expertise that will make your RV travels more enjoyable.

Chapter 1

HOW TO BUY AN RV

Figure 1.1
Shopping several dealerships is essential not only in making a well-researched RV choice but in determining the best price.

In most respects, buying an RV isn't all that different from other purchases. Whether it's a car, an article of clothing, a new sofa, or a washing machine, four basic steps are needed in making an intelligent selection:

1. Establish or recognize a need. Among the most common errors made in an RV purchase is selection of a unit that does not meet one's needs. Attitudes may change during the period from shopping to ownership, but more often the prospective buyer didn't closely evaluate intended uses for the RV.

2. Set a dollar range of how much money can be spent. You may have champagne tastes and a beer budget, and it's necessary to be realistic or you may end up with a financial burden that takes some of the fun out of using the vehicle.

3. Make a decision on the character of the item. If you need a new pair of pants,

you will probably decide ahead of time whether they will be summer or winter weight, dress or casual. You might even decide what color you want before you ever go shopping. And so it is with a new RV.

4. Shop around before making the purchase—visit several dealer lots (Figure 1.1). Make sure the necessary legwork is done so you know what is offered in the type, size, and cost of the RV that you have identified as suitable. It's not comforting to buy a unit only to find out a few months later that a friend or neighbor got one you like better or bought an identical model to yours at a considerably lower price. Unfortunately, people regularly fail to get the best prices, and the dollar amounts that can be saved by comparing prices offered on the same or similar units by two or three different dealers can be very substantial.

THE PURPOSE

Initially, it's necessary to decide how you will use an RV—defining your needs that specifically relate to the RV. For those of us who already own an RV but want a new one, the question of how it will be used may be virtually settled, unless we're planning a major change of lifestyle. Folks with little or no RV experience are in a more difficult position, however. They are not only faced with learning about RVs, but with trying to relate them to their potential use. Following are some questions that might assist you in deciding how you will use an RV.

Why Do You Want One?

The answer might be as simple as being "tired of tenting," or as unfocused as a desire to spend more time in the great outdoors. But it can help to give some thought to actual use. Will you be traveling extensively or taking short trips to local attractions? Will you just be using it on weekends, or are you in the enviable position of having lots of free time? If you have a fairly good feel for how you will use an RV, it will be much easier to envision how an individual model will fit into your plans.

What Kind of Camping Do You Enjoy?

Will it be primitive, Forest Service-style campgrounds, or commercial RV parks with full hookups? Do you prefer hunting and/or fishing in remote locations with no formal camping facilities? This will have a bearing on the type and size of RV that will be appropriate, as well as the degree of self-containment needed. If you are not familiar with the different types of camping facilities available, take a weekend to look at the different types available in your area. Check out some RV parks, the campgrounds at state and county parks—and campgrounds operated by federal agencies if they exist in your area. Not only can this give you a good idea of the kinds of destinations you prefer, it will identify the style and size RV favored in these locations. It also offers a fine opportunity to talk with RV owners. Most RV people enjoy answering questions about their rigs and the reasons they selected them.

How Many People Will Be Going on RV Outings?

Some thought needs to be given to the number of children and adults. If there are children, try and think a few years ahead as well as considering immediate requirements. Children grow up, and either require more space or, in the case of teenagers, no space at all because they tend to have more pressing engagements than going camping with Mom and Dad. It's important to differentiate between occasional and regular users who will require more room for dining, bathing, and storage. The occasional user or guest can generally be squeezed into existing space for a short duration without dictating a larger, more expensive RV.

Can You Satisfy Additional Needs with This Purchase?

Items to consider might be using an RV or tow vehicle as a first or second car, or as a guest bedroom at home, or even as a replacement for a cabin at the lake. Any of these considerations could have major financial impact on how much you can afford to spend on an RV. For instance, if the RV can serve as a second car, it could mean selling or trading in a vehicle that appreciably changes the total price.

Using an RV as guest quarters might require a bit of planning and construction, such as a level parking spot at your home, plus electric, sewer, and water hookups, but this is considerably simpler and cheaper than building on an extra room or trading houses to gain space. An existing or proposed vacation cabin or home might be replaced with an RV that can be used at the same location as well as thousands of other locations across the country.

Where Will You Store the RV?

Answer this question before you begin serious shopping. How much room is there at home to store it? Is it legal to keep an RV in your driveway, yard, or on the street? If you will have to put it in a storage yard, how much will it cost?

By knowing answers to the five questions discussed in the preceding pages, you are in a much better position to evaluate any RV in terms of your own needs.

BUDGET CONSIDERATIONS

After you've defined how a new RV will be used, establish how much you can or want to spend on it. There are numerous ways to finance a new or used RV, and a good way to insure selecting the best method for your needs is to shop around before you sign on the dotted line. Since dealers have a vested interest in getting you good financing, most keep pretty close track of the best deals available, and the larger dealers not only check lenders in other cities but in other states. Some lenders specialize in RV loans, and dealers are in a position to know about these deals. Some RV manufacturers offer financing, as does the Good Sam Club (800-234-3450). Don't forget to check with your bank or credit union. If you need to finance your RV purchase, the cost of financing can have a bearing on which RV you will be able to afford.

INSURANCE

The cost of insurance should be figured into the overall cost of owning an RV. Rates will vary with locale. City dwellers typically pay considerably higher rates than do residents of less populated areas. Rates usually are determined by postal ZIP code.

Shop several agencies for the best rates for equivalent coverage, and be sure to check into the Good Sam Club's insurance program, which typically is very competitive on rates. If you plan to use a storage yard, check specifically for coverage on theft of equipment from the RV while it's in storage. Coverage for an RV may be less expensive than you might expect if the vehicle is not used for daily transportation. Coverage for trailers and campers usually is especially economical because liability coverage is included with the insurance on the tow vehicle.

TYPE AND SIZE DECISIONS

The next task is deciding, in general terms, what type and size unit will meet your needs and finances. One of the initial decisions regarding the type of RV is whether you want to drive or tow your new RV. In part, it's a matter of personal preference, but if you want to tow a boat or other type of trailer, the question is pretty much settled before starting. You will need an RV you drive, not tow, except in states that allow towing a conventional trailer behind a fifth-wheel trailer. Motorhomes, camping van conversions, and pickup campers fall in the category of RVs you drive, while conventional travel trailers, folding camping trailers, and fifth-wheel trailers are towed. Following are the pros and cons of the different types of RVs and how each type might fit individual situations.

Slideouts

The use of slideouts has created the most dramatic change in RVs during the past decade. Slideouts offer the buyer more space, comfort, and convenience without more exterior length or width while traveling. Indeed, slideouts have encouraged many purchasers to choose shorter RVs, which are more maneuverable.

Many fifth-wheel trailers are equipped with three slideout units, and Class A motorhomes often have two, one of them a large single slideout that houses either a dinette/sofa arrangement or the motorhome's full kitchen.

Except for low-cost models, purchase of slideouts in all types of RVs is so popular that the purchaser of a non-slideout model may have to sacrifice resale value when the time comes to sell or trade the unit.

TYPES OF RVS

Motorhomes
As their name implies, motorhomes must at least include a motor. But there is an incredible range of vehicles classed as motorhomes. Some portion of the vehicle must be set aside

Figure 1.2
Class A motorhome

for driving, which will somewhat reduce the overall living space. But this is also one of the motorhome's major virtues. With living and driving space combined, it means the living space is accessible from the driving space. Slideouts have extended the available living space (when parked), making motorhomes even more attractive.

Class A Motorhomes
Price Range: $50,000 to $900,000

At the very top of this group is an almost separate category of luxury Class A models, characterized by diesel pusher engine configurations and costing from about $150,000 to $900,000 for the largest bus conversions. These are the crème de la crème of RVs, but if price is no deterrent, they are incredibly luxurious and incorporate all the latest features.

Just below this group of highliners is a huge selection of units ranging in price from around $50,000 to over $125,000 (Figure 1.2). Most units in this group are front-engine gasoline-powered models; the higher prices usually reflect the use of a diesel pusher engine, although some diesel pushers have dropped below $100,000 due to introduction of lighter weight, less expensive chassis. Sizes for this overall motorhome category run from around 25 feet to 40 feet. Slideouts are offered in virtually every model lineup.

The driver's seat in a Class A unit usually sits high and slightly outboard of the conventional driver position in a car, with the windshield stretching the full width of the motorhome, which may make it somewhat intimidating to drive at first. But acclimation comes quickly. Class A motorhomes offer a great deal of luxury, both on the road and when set up in camp.

Class B or Camping Van Conversions
Price Range: $35,000 to $65,000

Camping vans utilize the existing van body and provide basic amenities for living in very compact quarters (Figure 1.3). Interior space is at a real premium. Yet, for two very friendly people, the arrangement can be workable. Obviously, they serve very well as second cars since exterior dimensions in most cases are the same as those of full-size vans except for height. With the right combination of engine and axle ratio, they are capable tow vehicles. For a couple who like to intersperse nights in a motel with camping out, a van conversion offers the best of both worlds in many respects. Camping vans make excellent traveling vehicles.

Class C or Mini Motorhomes
Price Range: $45,000 to $70,000

Most Class C motorhomes (Figure 1.4) are built on cutaway chassis with a manufactured

Figure 1.3
Camping van conversion

cab and driver and passenger doors. A sub-group in this category consists of an RV body built on a cab-and-chassis pickup truck (without the truck bed). Such vehicles usually are equipped with four-wheel drive. For both types of vehicles, nearly all the automotive parts are standard and available at dealers across the country. To most drivers, a Class C feels more carlike than a Class A the first time it is driven because the full width of the coach (96 to 102 inches—same as most Class As) is behind them.

In the past, the permanent bed over the cab section, in large measure, accounted for the reduction in size, and to some degree, price, compared to Class A models. A certain amount of agility is required to get in and out of this bed, and as a consequence some people don't care for the arrangement.

With the introduction of higher-rated chassis, Class C motorhomes have grown to lengths in excess of thirty feet, offering floor plans more akin to those of Class A motorhomes, featuring full-size beds in addition to the cabover bed.

Figure 1.4
Class C motorhome

Figure 1.5
Pickup camper

Pickup Campers
Price Range $4,500 to $22,000
Pickup campers are available to fit nearly any pickup, from 6-foot pop-top versions for small import trucks to large 11-foot units for full-sized pickups (Figure 1.5). They range from units with minimal living accommodations to models with full baths, elaborate galley facilities, plus dinette and beds for four to six, air conditioning, and a built-in AC generator. Living space in a camper has been relatively compact because even the largest units must conform to the dimensions of a pickup box. However, slideouts are being used in some models to dramatically increase living space and comfort. For the outdoor person, the camper-hauling pickup can be purchased with factory four-wheel drive, making the combination ideal for back roads and primitive campsites.

Trailers

While motorhome owners must tow a smaller vehicle (dinghy) for auxiliary transportation, the trailerist simply unhitches the trailer and uses the tow vehicle for transportation. The tow vehicle and trailer can be bought and/or sold separately, which can be a major economic consideration. A trailer is usable only when stopped or parked, while occupants can move around

Figure 1.6
Folding camping trailer

inside a motorhome while driving, although it's best to remain seat-belted at all times.

Folding Camping (Tent) Trailers
Price Range: $3,500 to $12,000

Folding camping trailers are relatively inexpensive, yet they offer a pair of double beds, and the dinette makes up into a double bed in most models (Figure 1.6). They feature minimum cooking facilities, with a two- or three-burner stove, sink, and an icebox or optional small refrigerator. More expensive units can be equipped with a furnace, toilet, shower, and other similar amenities to self-contained travel trailers. A few folding tent trailers utilize hard sidewalls. The living area is quite pleasant, with an open and spacious feeling because of the many large vinyl windows in the canvas sides. Setup requires ten to twenty minutes. Tent trailers are inexpensive to buy, store easily, and can be towed with just about any size car, truck, or sport-utility vehicle. Hooked to a four-wheel-drive vehicle, tent trailers make excellent back-country RVs. Their primary use, however, is by families who want the feeling of the tent along with the convenience of camping "off the ground."

Travel Trailers
Price Range: $8,000 to $75,000

Small trailers may weigh less than 2,000 pounds and can be pulled with a wide selection of compact vehicles (Figure 1.7). The ease of towing, combined with their relatively low purchase price, makes them an excellent first RV. Facilities are very compact, but completely suitable for short-term use. Self-containment is minimal and usually the beds are all convertible models, either a sofa and/or dinette that makes into a bed.

Medium-sized travel trailers range in weight up to about 5,000 pounds before supplies and fluids are added, and in price from about $10,000 to about $20,000 (Figure 1.8). These are the most popular travel trailers, the majority requiring some planning in selection of a tow vehicle. Many models are suitable for towing with properly equipped full-size cars. Most models offer a high degree of self-containment, with full bath, galley, and dining facilities. In the smaller sizes, the beds are usually convertible models, a couch or dinette by day and a double bed by night. But even the smaller models can be fitted with stationary beds and are able to handle four adults or a family

Figure 1.7
Small travel trailer

Figure 1.8
Medium-sized travel trailer

with two or three children in reasonable comfort. As size and price increase, facilities improve—full-time beds and a division of the living spaces into bedroom, bath, galley, and a lounging or living room area. Slideouts expand living space considerably without adding to trailer length, and have grown in popularity.

Large travel trailers range up to about 9,000 pounds and vary in price from about $15,000 to $60,000 (Figure 1.9). Depending on the floorplan, these units can be suitable for large families or extended use by two people. Ranging in size from about 25 to 34 feet, a wider selection of floorplans is available. Many of these trailers, equipped with slideouts, make suitable full-timer abodes.

Some of the options are aimed at the large family, with separate bunk-house-style rear bedrooms, while others are aimed at couples. The larger models provide generous living accommodations. Even when a new tow vehicle is fac-

Figure 1.9
Large travel trailer

tored in, the range of prices for the most expensive trailers is well below the higher-priced motorhomes. Most of these units will require a pickup truck, or a truck-based vehicle such as a Suburban or a full-size van for towing. All of these vehicles, including a pickup, if a shell is added, are suitable for hauling a small boat atop. These large trailers offer a lot of living space at a realistic price. For budget-conscious buyers who want to spend extended periods of time traveling or live full time in an RV with a small boat included, a large travel trailer is an excellent choice.

Fifth-Wheel Trailers
Price Range: $12,000 to $110,000

Fifth-wheel trailers range from about 8,000 pounds to over 18,000 pounds, plus the weight of fluids and personal effects (Figure 1.10). In the more compact fifth-wheelers, a major difference between conventional models is sleeping accommodations. The small fifth-wheel models all provide a full-time bed in the raised forward section, which can be a real advantage when compared to a convertible bed. Headroom varies considerably, but most compact fifth-wheels require stooping while using the front section. Most of these models provide adequate living accommodations with little wasted space. As with any fifth-wheel trailer, they require a pickup truck for towing. But owing to the relatively small size of these units, a wide range of trucks is suitable.

The larger (26- to 40-foot) fifth-wheel models are the hot setup for anyone seeking maximum living space—the RV of choice for full-time living. Most include up to three large slideouts and standing room in the front bedroom; the larger models are available with a wide range of appliances including built-in washer/dryer, dishwasher, and entertainment centers with surround sound. The larger fifth-wheel units require the beefiest dual-rear-wheel pickup trucks as the tow vehicles, or specialized conversions of medium-duty trucks. It is important to match the size and weight of a new fifth-wheel to the tow vehicle, or, select the fifth-wheel first and then order a truck of adequate towing capacity.

By this time you should have at least some idea of the RVs that will fit your needs. The next step might be attending an RV show or getting a copy of Trailer Life's annual *RV Buyer's Guide* to further examine the different types and sizes. At a show you are able to see one RV after another, which can make comparisons easier than traveling from dealer to dealer. A show should also give you a good idea of actual prices and help make the decision on what size and type you can afford, and whether you will want to buy new or used. Don't be reluctant to compare show prices with those of your local dealer; in some cases show prices can be high. It's important to have at least some knowledge of price ranges for a particular RV before attending a show if you might make a spur-of-the-moment purchase.

Figure 1.10
Fifth-wheel trailer

Figure 1.11
Fiberglass insulation is commonly used in a variety of RVs. Properly applied, it is effective. Frame construction of this unit is of aluminum.

EVALUATING A NEW RV

The following are a few points to be aware of when evaluating a new or used RV.

Weight Capacity

See Chapter 5 for a discussion of RV weight capacity, which is a very important item of consideration when buying a new or used RV. It is essential that the RV have the capacity to haul or tow the weight that you expect to add, and not all do. The unwary buyer may encounter tire problems and poor handling if weight capacity is not adequate.

Construction

Whether the RV is new or used, another purchase consideration is type of construction. While the type of construction is important, equally important is the degree of quality control employed when the RV was built. Closely inspect cabinet interiors and underneath the unit. Check under the sink and see how propane and water lines are routed. Are they all neat and tidy or just allowed to hang and take up storage space? Pull the drawers all the way out and check how they are made and how the drawer guides and runners are made. Are they just stapled together or fitted and glued in place? Check inside exterior storage compartments. Are they finished and clean? This is also a good place to see the type of framing used and check the quality of workmanship. Examine wiring in hidden locations in the exterior and interior cabinets. Is it secured? If a manufacturer didn't take the time to do these little items correctly, chances are good they didn't take a great deal of care with parts that are completely hidden. Check the roof, which will reveal a lot about workmanship.

Framing can be wood, aluminum, steel, or a combination of these materials. Various insulation materials are used by different manufacturers. Fiberglass, similar to the type used in most homes, is very common and effective if it is attached so it doesn't settle (Figure 1.11).

Structural Styrofoam, which comes in solid sheets (Figure 1.12), must be cut to size and fitted into the spaces between the framework. It doesn't settle with use and can add to the structural integrity of side walls, roof, or floor. Another type is polyurethane foam, which is sprayed in place, and then it expands and hardens.

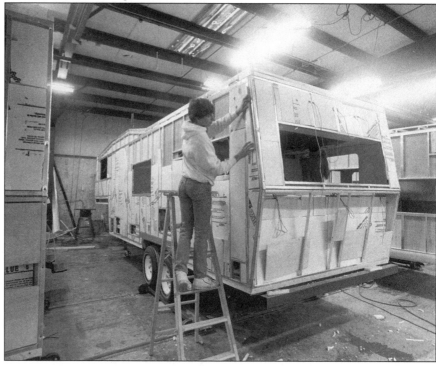

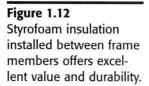

Figure 1.12
Styrofoam insulation installed between frame members offers excellent value and durability.

Aluminum still is widely used as exterior covering, but fiberglass panels are now the dominant material. Aluminum is less expensive, lighter weight, and easier to repair, but fiberglass resists small dings and scrapes better.

Wood is the least expensive framing material from a manufacturing standpoint and the most widely used. If used correctly it is a completely acceptable method of construction for trailers that are not occupied during travel. The frame is built of wood, then insulation is added and interior and exterior coverings are attached. The only real liability of wood is that it rots if leakage allows water inside the sidewall.

A more expensive method is lamination (Figure 1.13). A framework is assembled (it can be wood, aluminum, or steel), then insulation is added, usually block foam. At this point, the interior and exterior coverings are glued and bonded under pressure to the frame and insulation. This makes a strong and rigid wall, ceiling, or floor since the coverings become part of and enhance the strength of the frame. All-metal framing is generally considered the best and the most expensive to build. Laminated or all-metal frames are more expensive to repair because they require special equipment and tools.

For motorhomes, steel is the frame material of choice, for obvious crash-durability reasons. Steel also holds up better if the vehicle is subjected to exceptionally rough roads. It is impervious to rot but not to rust. Water can generally wreak havoc when it gets inside walls, ceiling, or floor.

Shopping

Once you have established that you are going to purchase an RV, decided about how much money you can spend, and settled on a size and type RV that will meet your needs, then you are ready to start serious shopping. Early in your shopping, whether at a dealer's lot or an RV show, you will come up against the harsh reality of current RV prices. If prices for the size and type RV you want are reasonably close to what you have decided you can afford, you're in great shape. If the prices are way over your self-imposed spending limit, you will have to make some compromises.

For any given type and general size class of RV there can be a sizable range of prices; in many cases it can amount to thousands of dol-

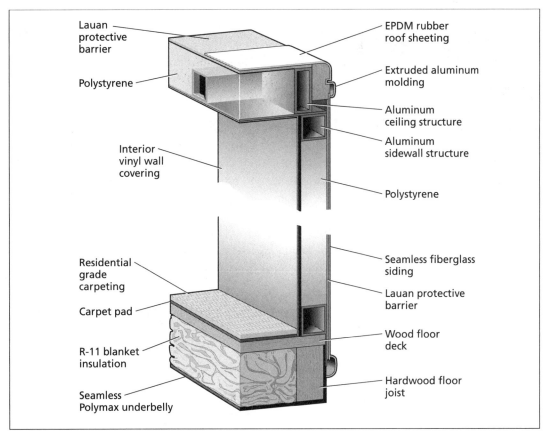

Lauan protective barrier

Polystyrene

Interior vinyl wall covering

Residential grade carpeting

Carpet pad

R-11 blanket insulation

Seamless Polymax underbelly

EPDM rubber roof sheeting

Extruded aluminum molding

Aluminum ceiling structure

Aluminum sidewall structure

Polystyrene

Seamless fiberglass siding

Lauan protective barrier

Wood floor deck

Hardwood floor joist

Figure 1.13
Lamination is a popular construction method in all types of RVs, offering high strength and relatively low weight. In this example, the sidewall and roof contain aluminum frame members and polystyrene foam while the underfloor is insulated with fiberglass.

lars in price difference. Besides selecting a model toward the low end of this price range, there are a number of other ways you can keep prices within your reach. You might go to a smaller unit or skip some of the more expensive options. Many of the options can be done without or added at a later time, such as a roof air conditioner, an AC generator, or a microwave oven. You might consider getting a used RV instead of a new one. Up to this point the steps are pretty much the same whether you select a new or a used unit. This includes looking at new units to get a feel for prices and various floorplans that you like.

To get the most out of your shopping, there is definitely a right and a wrong way to go about it. The wrong way is to go to the dealer's lot or an RV show, wander around looking at different RVs, and then go home.

Usually after the tenth or fifteenth unit looked at, they start to run together in your mind, and you might know there was one you really liked, but not be sure just which one it was, or even where it was. The right way to do your shopping is to have a clear-cut objective.

Carry a note pad and a pen or pencil. You might even want to list in the front of the notebook the type, size, and price range of RV you are shopping for. Referring to this during your expeditions can help keep you on the right track and help eliminate non-productive excursions into fantasyland.

When you find a model you like, collect the literature on it, but also make a note of the brand, model, size, and price in your notes. Write a few descriptive comments, and list everything you like and don't like. This

RV Interior Checklist

✔ Look for evidence on ceiling and sidewalls of water leaks.

✔ Check especially where walls and ceiling join. Look along all ceiling seams, around vents and roof air conditioner for signs of leakage (brown or yellowish stains). Water leaks can cause dry rot which is expensive to repair. Be suspicious of a ceiling that has been repainted; it may hide water damage.

✔ Check inside cabinets and under built-in furniture and the dinette, again looking for signs of water leakage as well as general condition.

✔ Examine upholstered surfaces and carpets carefully, looking for wear and damage.

✔ Check condition of house battery(ies).

✔ Appliances—tests performed by buyer or service center.

✔ Check function of all appliances.

✔ Refrigerator—run for six hours alternately on 120-volt AC power and on propane.

✔ Water pump—check function.

✔ Check for odor in water lines, indicating poor maintenance.

✔ Run water heater.

✔ Check furnace function.

✔ Roof air conditioner should be checked for cooling performance.

should get you down to two or three units that meet most or even all of your requirements.

SHOPPING FOR USED UNITS

If you are shopping for a used unit you will certainly want to check what the local dealers have, but you can also buy a used RV from a private party. In many respects finding a good buy in a used RV is more difficult than buying a new one. Basically you are trading time for money; the time you spend finding just the right unit, in good shape and at a good price, can provide a large saving over buying a new unit. In some cases, many thousands of dollars will be saved. But you must exercise caution in

selecting the unit you will be living with for a good number of years.

The best time of year to purchase any RV is late fall and during the winter months because sales are down at that time of year, and most sellers are willing to deal, with the exception of dealers in sunbelt areas who cater to full-timers. Buying a used RV from an established, reputable dealer is the safer course. The savings might not be as great as you could possibly find from a private party, but there is less risk. A good dealer will have conducted full-system tests to ensure the RV is in good operating condition. Quality dealers will perform complete safety checks on motorhome chassis. It's a good idea to include mechanical

RV Exterior

General

✔ Check overall condition, looking for dings or repaired damage.

✔ Look for warpage or other irregularities in sidewalls, indicating delamination. Press against walls to feel if outer skin has separated from substrate.

✔ Examine outside storage areas.

✔ Check that doors operate properly. Do they lock and are there keys? Check storage compartment doors for smooth operation.

✔ Check spare-tire condition.

Roof

✔ Check for separation of seal material from roof surfaces around roof vents and other fixtures. Bad seals indicate poor maintenance and probable roof leaks that may be causing rot that is yet undetected.

✔ Check for any indication of sagging around an air conditioner (indicates possible water damage).

✔ Check for rubber-roof chalking. White streaks indicate the need for regular roof maintenance. Rubber-roof bubbling indicates misuse of cleaning materials formulated with petroleum distillates.

✔ Make sure all roof vents, plumbing vents, and refrigerator vent are in good condition. Cracked or broken vents can indicate water leakage.

Other

✔ Check for any sagging of the body at the rear of the unit or along the outside portion of the floor (indicates frame damage and is expensive to repair). Jump up and down inside the RV; if the floor gives, there may be structural damage.

✔ Check water and plumbing systems for proper function.

✔ Check all exterior lights for operation (trailer will require electrical hookup to a tow vehicle if the dealer does not have suitable testing equipment).

✔ Check function of trailer brakes.

breakdown insurance in the deal, or purchase it separately.

In some cases the dealer will offer a form of warranty—especially true on late model RVs. It could be 30-, 60- or 90-day coverage, possibly stipulating that the buyer might pay for parts and the dealer pay labor or some form of a shared-cost arrangement. A dealer might also be able to offer a service contract as insurance against future repair costs.

Checklist for Buying an RV Chassis

TRAILERS AND MOTORHOMES

✔ Springs: Check for any broken or damaged leaves. Have overload springs or extra leaves been added? (May indicate overloading in past.)

✔ Axles: Check condition of wheel bearings and seals.

✔ Tires: Check for abnormal tire wear, which may indicate improper alignment or underinflation/overloading. Check for cracks or weathering. Make sure the tires are rated for the particular RV.

✔ Wheels: Check wheels for rust or rim damage.

MOTORHOMES ONLY

Ask for any maintenance records and have a mechanic check the following items:

✔ Engine

✔ Cooling-system condition

✔ Cylinder compression/leakdown

✔ Spark plugs, for signs of excessive oil consumption

✔ Oscilloscope check of electrical system

✔ Alternator and starter operation

✔ Exhaust system, especially for signs of leaking exhaust manifold (may be cracked)

✔ Fuel system, fuel pressure, and filters

✔ Transmission: Check condition of fluid on dipstick; brown color, burned odor indicates overheating.

✔ Brakes: Hydraulic system and condition of front/rear brake pads/linings and rotors/drums

TRAILERS ONLY

✔ A-frame: Check for damage or rust.

✔ Springs and shackles: Look for elongated bolt holes in spring shackles, broken leaves.

✔ Coupler operation: Make sure the locking lever works freely.

✔ Tongue-jack operation

✔ Operation of trailer brakes

A dealer can be a big help with financing a used unit. But it will still pay to shop around for the best interest rate and terms. Many banks have a limit on the age of RVs they will finance, usually seven years. Regarding price fairness, ask the dealer to show you the *Kelley Blue Book* or *N.A.D.A. RV Guide* prices (if your dealer refuses, ask your banker or credit union). It's possible to find a good, clean, low-mileage unit. Motorhomes with 7,000 miles or less per year of age can be considered low mileage.

When you find a unit that looks promising, the inspection begins. The first step may be obvious, but it's important. When you first enter the RV, it should look good and smell right to you. If it passes this test, then you can start using the Checklists for Buying a Used RV.

SERVICE CENTER TESTS

* Fill water and holding tanks, checking for leaks.

* Test 12-volt DC and 120-volt AC electrical systems.

* Check battery specific gravity, or open-circuit voltage.

* Check converter and battery-charge circuit.

* Check AC and DC power delivery.

* Test propane system for proper pressure and leaks (manometer test).

* Pressure-test water system.

THE PRICE

By the time all the bases have been covered in shopping for a new RV, you should have two or three quotes on the one or two units that you feel meet your needs. Getting several quotes is very important because, unlike cars and trucks, most RVs have no manufacturer-provided window stickers indicating retail price, and there are no published lists of wholesale prices as for cars and light trucks.

This means that you may pay too much for the RV if you have not comparison-shopped. As a rule, don't pay more than your bank will loan on the unit—or would loan even if you plan to pay in cash. Extensive shopping and checking with your bank are your only assurances that you will not end up paying more than the unit is worth.

After you have inspected all the items possible on the list, and you are still interested, it's time to talk price. There are several books that list used RV prices. Two of the most popular are *Kelley Blue Book* and the *N.A.D.A. RV Guide*. All banks that offer RV financing will have one or both of these price books and should be able to tell you the low and the high book figures for the unit in question. They both list odometer mileage (for motorhomes) and add-on figures for major accessories. Private individuals tend to stick closely to the retail figure, but will usually deal on the final price. Dealers nearly always use the retail figure or one that is even higher when pricing clean used RVs. It's difficult to compare used RVs with similar units on another sales lot down the street.

Once you have settled on price, it should be made contingent upon having the RV checked out mechanically and having all the system checks performed. When you make a deposit on the unit, it should be stated in writing who will pay any repair costs shown to be needed by the service center that checks the unit. It should further be stated in writing that if neither condition is met you will get your deposit back. You will be required to pay for the inspection, which may cost a couple of hundred dollars. While it's well worth making a small investment before buying the RV, take a close look before deciding to have it inspected at a service center. That way you'll be less likely to waste money during the buying process. If the dealer or private party won't cooperate, walk away.

Selecting a new or used RV should be fun because it's easy to conjure up all sorts of daydreams about places you'll want to go. But take your time, define your needs, and find the right unit at the right price.

Chapter 2

SELECTING A TOW VEHICLE

Homework is the key to selecting a tow vehicle that will perform and handle properly with the trailer of your choice. Homework is necessary because, in most cases, salesmen will pressure prospective buyers to take whatever is on the sales lot at the time, whether or not it is properly equipped. All too often, the salesman has not read the manufacturer's towing brochure. Thus it's fully up to the buyer to make the right choice.

Most motor-vehicle manufacturers offer a considerable amount of specific information on vehicle types and how they should be equipped in the form of trailer-towing guides. However, selecting a suitable used tow vehicle involves some additional guesswork. It's not always possible to find a used vehicle equipped with specialized towing options, even if the buyer knows which towing options were available when the vehicle was new.

Trailer Life's Towing Guide contains ratings designed to solve that problem—ratings for passenger cars, light trucks, vans, and sport-utility vehicles, beginning with the most recent model year and dating back five years. The *Towing Guide*, combined with the information provided in this chapter, offers you the ability to make an intelligent, accurate tow-vehicle choice.

SELECTING YOUR VEHICLE TYPE

Consider the following points when choosing among a car, truck, sport-utility vehicle, or van for towing:

- Evaluate your needs and desires. How many people will accompany you? Where do you like to drive? Regardless of what might work best, do you prefer a passenger car, truck, or van? If you prefer a car, is your trailer too large and heavy to be towed by the model that interests you?

- Make sure the vehicle's overall size and wheelbase are adequate for the trailer in question. Check *Trailer Life's Towing Guide*. Evaluate the drivetrain in view of

the ratings. Engine performance and axle ratio, which are critical elements in determining if the vehicle will adequately tow your trailer, must be appropriate to handle the weight of your trailer.

- Tires should have adequate capacity for the weight of passengers and supplies in the vehicle, as well as for that portion of hitch weight carried by the tow vehicle. (A load-distributing hitch distributes hitch weight to all axles of the tow vehicle and trailer, with the tow vehicle carrying about two-thirds of the hitch weight and the remainder transferred to the trailer wheels.)

- Suspension components should also be adequate for the load. The vehicle should have a heavy-duty radiator, which usually is standard if the vehicle has factory air conditioning. If a new vehicle is being purchased, the manufacturer's trailer-towing package, which includes special heavy-duty cooling options, should be ordered.

- Evaluate the mechanical condition of the vehicle if it is used.

NEW TOW VEHICLES

Covering all the bases in selecting a new tow vehicle may sound like quite a project. And it would be without the benefit of manufacturers' trailer-towing brochures (Figure 2.1). A purchase should not be made before you read the appropriate brochures for the vehicles you are considering.

All domestic manufacturers and most foreign companies offer towing guides in one form or another. Some guides are abbreviated, while others are extensive and educational, even beyond simply listing specifications for the brand in question.

The most comprehensive guides are published by Ford and Chevrolet/GMC, which also have developed the most extensive option packages for towing. Chrysler Corporation does a good job in trucks and vans, but does little

Figure 2.1
Manufacturers' towing guides offer detailed advice on equipment selection and trailer weight limits.

with passenger cars. Among Japanese manufacturers, Toyota, Nissan, and Mazda offer trucks with ratings ranging from 5,000 to 7,200 pounds, and a variety of Japanese SUVs will tow trailers up to 5,000 pounds. Many Japanese cars are rated for maximums of 2,000. In the absence of a towing brochure, check the vehicle owner's manual.

Specific options usually are required or recommended for trailer weights above 3,500 pounds, which is the weight level separating the companies that are serious about towing from the companies that don't give it much consideration.

When you visit a dealership, you should already know what the manufacturer recommends for the weight of your trailer with full water and propane tanks and all your supplies aboard. That weight can be calculated by adding the amount of weight you anticipate taking on trips to the UVW (unloaded vehicle weight) listing for your trailer. If your trailer was built prior to 1996 and does not have the RVIA weight label introduced during that year, which lists the UVW, note the dry weight of

the unit and calculate the amount of weight you will add.

To estimate the weight of what you will add:

Water   8.3 pounds per gallon
Propane 4.5 pounds per gallon

If your trailer's sticker does not include a UVW number, add the weight of one or two batteries because, prior to the change in weight-listings format during 1996, trailer manufacturers generally did not include them in their dry-weight figures. (Batteries weigh 50 to 60 pounds each.) If you already own the trailer, weigh it on a commercial scale (see Chapter 5).

While examining vehicle manufacturers' literature, take particular note of two recommended weight limits:

1. Maximum gross trailer weight
2. Maximum gross combination weight

Maximum gross trailer weight is the maximum weight of the trailer and all its contents. Maximum gross combination weight is the maximum weight of the trailer as well as the tow vehicle and all their contents. This includes fuel, water, supplies, and passengers.

In order to calculate the actual gross combination weight of a tow vehicle and trailer, actual weight of the tow vehicle must be determined. With a new tow vehicle, ask the dealer to check his reference books for the base curb weight, which is the weight of the vehicle with a full tank of fuel and standard equipment. The dealer also can supply listings for weight of specific options, which are important to add because their weight can be substantial, especially in the case of an optional diesel engine.

With reasonably accurate weight figures in hand, choose a tow vehicle that is rated to handle about 10 percent more than the calculated weight, as a margin of safety. RV owners hardly ever underestimate the weight of their vehicles. The ratings are the keys to safe towing and adequate performance, and they also have a bearing on fuel economy.

If you're buying a new or used travel trailer, pay particular attention to the proportion between hitch weight and gross weight because this denotes the trailer's balance and is the key to how well it will handle. Insufficient hitch weight often means mediocre or poor handling. If you already own a trailer with minimum hitch weight (10 percent of gross weight or less), or have found one like that with a floor plan you simply can't resist, you'll need to select a tow vehicle that has as much

inherent stability as possible. That means a truck or van with maximum wheelbase length and minimum rear overhang.

With a good understanding of the weight situation, you're ready to shop for the proper tow vehicle. The trailer-towing brochures will offer detailed information. The highest trailer-weight rating for domestic passenger cars is 2,000 pounds, which limits them to lightweight towing. Many cars, including the Ford Crown Victoria, are more capable than that—and were previously rated higher—but manufacturers have chosen to de-emphasize passenger-car towing. Trucks, sport-utility vehicles, and vans are more suitable than cars as tow vehicles for medium to heavy weight because of their larger engines, numerically higher axle ratios (higher numbers mean better pulling power), improved engine cooling, heavier suspensions, and longer wheelbases (in some cases).

AXLE RATIOS

The choice of engine size versus axle ratio often is difficult for the tow-vehicle buyer. The axle ratio is the relationship between driveshaft revolutions and wheel revolutions (see Figure 2.2). For example, in a vehicle with a 3.50:1 axle ratio, the driveshaft revolves 3.5 times for each revolution of the wheels. As you can see, more driveshaft revolutions for each wheel

Figure 2.2
Selecting the proper axle ratio is important to performance and fuel economy. The ratio indicates the proportion between the pinion shaft and axle shaft revolutions.

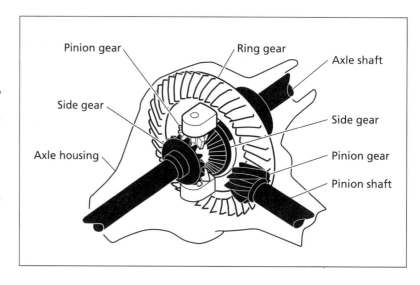

revolution mean more torque multiplication. Ideal axle ratios for driving without the trailer are numerically high, such as 3.08:1. They keep engine rpm at minimum levels for best possible fuel economy. But they are not well suited to moving large amounts of weight. Typical axle ratios for light trucks range from 3.25:1 to 4.56:1.

The choice of axle ratio for a tow vehicle is a compromise between fuel economy in solo driving and performance while towing. Numerically high ratios are better for power and worse for mileage, and numerically low ratios are just the opposite. Fortunately, four-speedautomatic and five-speed manual transmissions in cars and light trucks have reduced the penalty of this compromise. Their overdrive top gears give the vehicle a "tall" solo cruising-gear ratio even if a "torquey" axle

ratio such as 3.73:1 or 4.10:1 is chosen in the interest of good towing performance in mountainous terrain.

CHOOSING AN ENGINE

Engine selection may seem confusing because more than one may be suitable for your trailer weight. The manufacturers' towing ratings are designed for typical driving conditions, which assume medium to low altitude. An engine loses about 3 percent of its horsepower for each 1,000 feet of rise in elevation. Thus, at 10,000 feet elevation, about 30 percent of the available horsepower has been lost (Figure 2.3). When a considerable amount of travel at high altitudes is planned, the vehicle's towing rating should be reduced by

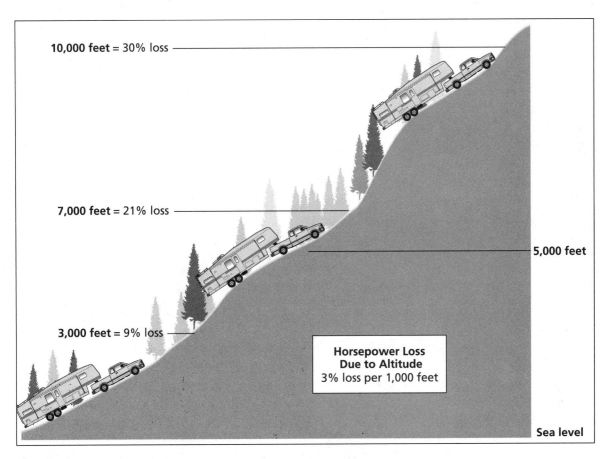

10,000 feet = 30% loss

7,000 feet = 21% loss

5,000 feet

3,000 feet = 9% loss

**Horsepower Loss
Due to Altitude
3% loss per 1,000 feet**

Sea level

Figure 2.3
Atmospheric pressure drops as altitude increases, reducing performance of naturally aspirated engines.

about 2 percent per 1,000 feet in elevation above sea level.

Typically, buyers are torn between the smaller engines for fuel economy and the larger engines for performance. When trailer weight is in the middle to upper middle of the weight-rating category for a given engine/vehicle combination, the midsize engine is valid for good performance. When trailer weight approaches the maximum, the prospective buyer must examine his or her travel habits and priorities very closely.

For example, a trailerist has a 32-foot fifth-wheel trailer that weighs 8,000 pounds, loaded for a trip. He is considering a Chevrolet C2500-series truck either with the Vortec 5700 (5.7 liters) or 7400 (7.4 liters) gasoline engine, and is having trouble deciding between the two. The differences: The 5700 should get better fuel economy during solo driving but have substantially less muscle for climbing grades than the 7400. The decision should favor the 5700 if most towing is in low elevations, and the buyer is not heavily performance oriented. The 7400 is preferred if considerable mountain travel is planned and/or if the buyer wants to maintain a relatively fast pace. One buyer's definition of "adequate" performance may be quite different from that of another, so personal preferences are important factors.

TOWING OPTIONS

Manufacturers of tow vehicles that receive serious attention by trailerists offer special trailer-

---

Used-Vehicle Evaluation Checklist

Engine Condition Cylinder compression is very important. Compression should not vary more than 10 percent from one cylinder to another. Check spark-plug condition (look for evidence of oil consumption). Black, wet-looking soot on spark plugs indicates that the engine uses excessive oil. If possible, have a qualified shop perform a cylinder-leakdown test, which will give an even better indication of the condition of piston rings and valves.

Cooling-system Condition If the vehicle is not equipped with factory air conditioning, it probably does not have a heavy-duty radiator. Such a vehicle is more liable to overheat when used for towing, particularly if the trailer weighs more than 3,000 pounds. Beyond the size of the radiator, the condition of the cooling system is crucial. If the system has not been maintained, not only may the radiator be partially blocked by corrosion, but flow of coolant through the engine block may be restricted as well. A thorough check of the cooling system should be performed by a mechanic, including inspection of the radiator tubes for partial blockage.

Transmission While driving the vehicle, pay close attention to shifting characteristics. The transmission should shift smoothly and without delay. It should downshift automatically when the accelerator pedal is pressed to the floor. Remove the dipstick and check the color and odor of the transmission fluid. (New fluid is red and has clarity.) If the transmission has been overheated, the oil will be darker than new fluid and will appear cloudy. It may also have an odor that is distinctively different than new fluid. Overheating causes transmission fluid to oxidize and lose lubricating ability.

Brakes Inspection should include the condition of pads and shoes, as well as a check to see if the rotors or drums have been machined excessively to make up for damage, towing-equipment packages, which usually are good values. The packages may range from very simple, possibly including only a wiring harness and a few other minor items, to a large package priced at several hundred dollars that includes a hitch receiver.

The prospective buyer should order the towing package and closely analyze the option list for other items that might be ordered, some of which are essential to towing performance and others that are merely for convenience and comfort. For heavy towing the list should include:

- Heavy-duty radiator

- Heavy-duty transmission-oil cooling

- Engine-oil cooler (for the higher weight

categories; external cooler is not offered by all manufacturers)

- Hitch receiver

- Heavy-duty shock absorbers

- Front stabilizer bar

- High-output alternator

- High-capacity battery

- Cruise control

- Increased fuel capacity

- Positive-traction differential

- Trailering wiring harness

- Extended mirrors

meaning you may have to replace rotors or drums when the brake work is next needed.

Tires Inspect closely for large repair plugs that would indicate the tire has been punctured by a large object. Check for bubbles or other irregularities that would indicate ply separation. Check for irregular wear, such as ripples in the tread. Once established, irregular wear is nearly impossible to correct.

Shocks and Suspension Components A road test will provide an indication of the condition of the shock absorbers. However, worn-out shocks are the least expensive replacement item. Have a mechanic check the suspension components, such as ball joints and struts, for wear. Use high-quality gas-type replacement shocks if a change is needed.

Air-conditioning System Conduct an air-conditioner performance test during your test drive, if weather permits. If not, have an operational check performed at an air-conditioner service shop.

Fuel Sensitivity Operate the vehicle at full throttle for several seconds in a safe area, preferably while climbing a hill, to see how the engine handles heavy loads at medium to high rpm. Ask the owner what grade of fuel is being used. You should hear no rattle or knocking from metal parts or any spark knock (ping). If the engine pings, either the initial spark advance setting is too high or the engine is oversensitive to regular grades of fuel. If spark is too far advanced, you'll have to retard it for towing (to prevent ping), which will reduce performance. If the engine pings and the spark is set to manufacturer's specifications, it means you'll have to use premium grades of fuel to prevent knocking.

Some of these items may be standard equipment, depending on the vehicle model, while some may be options included in special towing packages.

External engine-oil cooling is available only on a few large V-8s in trucks and vans and is a worthwhile option if offered. Some companies offer factory-installed auxiliary transmission-oil coolers, while others increase the size of the transmission-oil cooling tank inside the radiator. In the latter situation, it's often wise to add an auxiliary transmission-oil cooler if the vehicle will be used for heavy towing in mountainous terrain.

The hitch receiver usually is an aftermarket item but also can be ordered from the factory. In fact, trailer-towing packages usually include the hitch receiver.

It is wise to order heavy-duty springs in passenger cars and half-ton trucks and vans. In ¾- and 1-ton vans and trucks, ordering heavy-duty springs usually results in an excessively stiff ride, although some of the motor companies specify heavy-duty springs in their towing packages, especially for fifth-wheel towing. The only situation in which heavy-duty springs are needed in a ¾- or 1-ton van or truck is when hauling substantial amounts of weight in the vehicle in addition to towing a trailer.

The problem with ordering excessively stiff springs is that the owner is stuck with the stiff ride. If, having ordered slightly lower-rated springs, the owner determines that additional suspension help is needed, air springs can be added.

Data books supplied to dealers can help you select the proper gross vehicle weight rating (GVWR), which dictates spring ratings, depending on your specific anticipated loading of the vehicle.

A high-capacity alternator is important only if your trailer is equipped with a refrigerator that is operated on 12-volt DC power while traveling. Otherwise, the standard alternator will suffice. Cruise control theoretically is a convenience item, albeit one that most of us feel we cannot do without. Increased fuel capacity is essential because of the adverse effect of towing on fuel consumption. A positive-traction differential is not necessary for towing but is generally helpful if the vehicle is to be driven often on slippery surfaces. Extended mirrors can be added later, but the ones that come from the factory may be of higher quality and usually are mounted more securely.

OIL COOLING

If your vehicle is equipped with the optional factory-installed towing package, which includes high-capacity transmission-oil cooling, and if you are within the manufacturer's recommended trailer weight maximum, it should not be necessary to add an auxiliary (external) transmission-oil cooler.

USED VEHICLES

The manufacturer's recommendations serve as the primary guide in choosing vehicle type and drivetrain equipment for new vehicles. If you're in the market for a used vehicle, check the manufacturer's ratings provided in *Trailer Life's Towing Guide* to give you an idea of the engine sizes and axle ratios suitable for various trailer weights, along with the types of special equipment recommended or required by the manufacturer, and check the vehicles you're considering for similar equipment. Using the engine/axle ratio recommendations as guidelines, while not a guarantee of satisfaction, will usually get you closer to a proper choice than mere guesswork.

If the vehicle is being purchased from a private owner who has used it for towing, the owner's assessment of its performance may be helpful, although it should be taken with a grain of salt, since an optimistic description of the vehicle's towing prowess may help make the sale.

A thorough mechanical evaluation of a used vehicle by a reliable mechanic can also be helpful, if the vehicle's current owner will permit it.

Whether your choice of tow vehicle is new or used, the time you spend on research can pay off in good performance and trouble-free towing.

Chapter 3

MOTORHOME CHASSIS SELECTION

Chassis Types ∎

Gasoline Versus Diesel ∎

The opportunity to choose a specific chassis for one's new motorhome traditionally has been limited to gasoline-powered units; many companies offer buyers either Ford or Workhorse (formerly the Chevrolet Class A) chassis. However, builders of diesel-pusher motorhomes usually offer only one choice for each motorhome model.

This belies the fact that proliferation has occurred in the pusher chassis market, with manufacturers offering more sophistication in powertrain as well as suspension, while also introducing smaller units designed for lighter-weight coaches. The lightweight chassis have allowed manufacturers to introduce coaches that compete head-on with gasoline-powered units.

It's wise to take note of chassis design, suspension type, and engine specifications in order to make a well-informed chassis choice, if one is offered, or to recognize the level of chassis design sophistication if one is not. To that end, *Trailer Life's Towing Guide* contains specifications on most chassis, including load ratings.

Motorhome chassis overloading has been a problem for decades but became more prevalent in the early 1990s with the advent and increasing popularity of so-called basement storage. The amount of storage space in most basement-style motorhomes is voluminous, and few of these units have such high load ratings as to be virtually immune to overloading by an owner who makes no effort to understand that every vehicle has a specific load limit. However, the RV industry began using more specific weight labeling in 1998, which has made inadequate load capacity more obvious to prospective buyers and has put more pressure on individual manufacturers to provide adequate capacity.

It is essential for prospective buyers to determine a new motorhome's cargo carrying capacity (CCC) before making a purchase decision (see Chapter 5). If CCC is inadequate, overloading is likely, which compromises safety.

Motorhome chassis are built by these companies:

- Workhorse Chassis Company (Class A chassis formerly produced by Chevrolet Motor Division of the General Motors Corporation)

- Chevrolet Motor Division of the General Motors Corporation (Class C chassis only)

- Country Coach

- Ford Motor Company (Class A and C)

- Freightliner Custom Chassis Corporation

- Foretravel, Inc.

- Magnum Manufacturing Division of SMC Corporation

- Roadmaster Division of Monaco Coach Corporation

- Spartan Motors, Inc.

Chevrolet, Ford, Freightliner, Spartan and Workhorse supply chassis to the RV industry; the remaining companies build chassis only for their own coaches.

Following are descriptions of the varying chassis design elements and how they relate to performance and to the quality of on-the-road motorhoming.

CHASSIS TYPES

Three basic chassis types are offered:

- Class C (cab and chassis)

- Class A rail, front or rear engine

- Class A semi-monocoque, rear engine

The type of chassis selected by the coach manufacturer is determined by the price level and the type of motorhome the manufacturer intends to build. Thus, the buyer may in some cases choose from among the different chassis types only by changing motorhome model/brand selection, at least in low- and midpriced motorhomes.

Ford and Chevrolet Class C chassis consist of basic truck-type front-engine rail chassis fitted with a van-type cab (Figure 3.1). The chassis' backbone consists of two C-channel rails to which axles, drivetrain, and all other components are attached.

Class A chassis also use the rail approach, without the manufactured cab, up through the motorhome lineup, including some luxury

Figure 3.1
Ford Class C chassis

coaches. The Class A rail is available in front engine gasoline (Figure 3.2) and diesel-pusher configurations (Figure 3.3). Front diesels are available only in Class C chassis.

The Class A rail consists of two large C-channels plus outrigger frame members to which all suspension components and engine/transmission are attached. The primary attributes are simplicity and low manufacturing cost, balanced against the disadvantages: intrusion of the rails into under-floor storage space, higher

coach center of gravity, and less-sophisticated suspension arrangements.

The most sophisticated chassis design is semi-monocoque (Figure 3.4), which is exclusive to high-line coaches. The design consists of a tubular steel structure that supports loads and stresses that otherwise would be concentrated in chassis rails. This design is exceptionally rigid, yet low in weight, and houses the coach as well as under-floor storage bays with minimal intrusion of the frame.

Figure 3.2
Ford Class A chassis

Figure 3.3
Freightliner Class A
diesel chassis

Figure 3.4
Country Coach semi-monocoque rear diesel chassis

In addition to its structural rigidity and high strength to weight ratio, the semi-monocoque also permits the use of more effective outboard mounting of air suspensions and shock absorbers. A few rail chassis also use outboard mounting of air bags and shock absorbers.

Suspension Selections

Several types of suspension systems are available on motorhome chassis. Suspension selection is limited on the Class C and Class A rails, but for highline coaches many innovative systems offer features that improve ride quality as well as handling.

Types of springs include:

1. Coil-front/rear-leaf springs

2. All leaf springs

3. Air springs

4. Air springs with independent front suspension (IFS)

Type 1 is found on Ford and Chevrolet Class C and on Workhorse Class A chassis. The Workhorse chassis includes air springs inside front coil springs for auxiliary assist, and motorhome manufacturers may add aftermarket auxiliary air springs to the rear. But the air assists are auxiliary; the basic suspension type is steel coil and leaf springs.

Ford uses an I-beam front axle on its Class A chassis while Workhorse uses an independent A-arm front suspension. Both Ford and Chevrolet use independent front-coil-spring and rear-leaf-spring suspensions on their Class C chassis.

Coil springs generally offer a smoother ride than do leaf springs, since they have less internal friction when the axle moves through its range of travel. However, coil springs have a greater tendency to bottom out on rough road surfaces if shock absorbers are not effective or if the suspension is overloaded.

Type 2, an all-leaf-spring suspension, is a very common truck-type suspension used widely in the motorhome market. Leaf springs formerly were synonymous with rough ride,

Figure 3.5
Independent front suspensions offer better road feel and more resistance to bump steer.

but manufacturers have reduced friction with the use of nylon inserts between leaves, have lengthened the springs, and have redesigned the spring stacks to successfully bridge ride-quality barriers while affording good roll resistance (stability).

In situations where the coach builder adds an air-spring kit on the rear suspension of the coach, it is intended to prevent rear sag. The owner has the ability to inflate the left and right springs at different pressures to compensate for marginal side-to-side weight imbalances. These springs do not increase the chassis GVWR. Suspension stiffness is increased when the springs are inflated normally (60 to 90 psi).

Type 3 full-air suspensions are normally found on highline coaches and include automatic-leveling features. Large air springs used as the primary suspension method with beam-type front axles offer a soft, smooth ride with excellent resistance to bottoming out. As the suspension is compressed, the air pressure rises rapidly to resist suspension travel.

In the most advanced semi-monocoque chassis, two air springs are used per wheel for the capability of using lower air pressure, which enhances ride quality. The springs, as well as shock absorbers, are mounted outboard—as near the wheels as possible—for maximum stability. Coupled with high-quality shock absorbers, the air-spring suspension offers the ultimate in ride quality and sophisticated road handling.

Type 4 suspensions consist of air springs on all wheels but with independent front suspension (IFS) in place of the traditional I-beam (Figure 3.5). Most high-line motorhome manufacturers offer some IFS models and more are moving in that direction. IFS offers improved steering control and road feel, ride quality, and resistance to bump steer; enhanced roll stability also is claimed, although that is subject to debate.

Bump steer is a tendency of the suspension and steering system to feed road impact up through the steering column to the driver. It is more pronounced with some chassis than others, which makes a thorough test drive essential prior to purchase.

Brakes

Four brake design approaches are common:

1. Vacuum-boosted hydraulic disc or disc/drum brakes (some Class C chassis)

2. Hydraulically boosted hydraulic disc or disc/drum brakes (Class C and Class A)

3. Air-assisted hydraulic disc or drum brakes (higher load-rated Class A chassis)

Advantages of Diesel-Engine Power

Durability The engine is designed to operate continuously under severe conditions at full power. For owners who plan to keep a motorhome for many years and roll up lots of miles, diesel is the obvious choice.

Torque Diesel-engine horsepower ratings may appear low when compared to gas engines of the same displacement, but torque is the overriding performance factor in heavy vehicles. Torque is defined as twisting force applied to the driveshaft and hence to the wheels, propelling the coach. Higher torque means more energy applied to the wheels. Diesels produce high torque at low engine rpm, providing a strong, steady driving force.

Economy A gallon of diesel fuel contains more energy than a gallon of gasoline, and the diesel engine makes better use of it via higher compression. Diesels get better fuel mileage than gasoline engines under the same weight and road conditions. Of course, the buyer must pay more for the diesel engine at the outset, which must be amortized by the fuel savings.

Resale Value A diesel-powered coach usually holds its value better than a gasoline-powered unit, reflecting the diesel's durability and fuel efficiency and its higher purchase price.

---

4. Full air brakes, disc or drum (higher load-rated Class A chassis)

Some chassis makers use all-wheel disc brakes while others use drum brakes or a combination of disc and drum brakes. The typical consumer bias is in favor of disc brakes because they are universally used in cars and light trucks. However, many heavyweight motorhome chassis equipped with large drum brakes provide very effective braking capacity due to the ample size of the brakes—ranging up to 16½-inch drum diameter and 10-inch brake-shoe width. Beyond brake size, such chassis are fitted with speed retarders that reduce the driver's reliance on service brakes while descending steep grades.

Anti-lock Braking

Anti-lock braking systems (ABS) are widely used in motorhome chassis. ABS functions effectively in preventing wheel lockup on slippery surfaces, but drivers tend to react automatically to brake-pedal pulsation and other ABS characteristics by partially releasing pedal pressure or by pumping the brake pedal, thereby preventing the system from performing properly.

To avoid this pitfall, drivers should test the performance of their ABS systems in a safe area on wet or otherwise slippery pavement so they can become familiar with ABS brake performance and feel, as well as memorize the need to resist old habits. When an accident is imminent, it's necessary to apply constant heavy brake-pedal pressure while attempting to steer around obstacles. Drivers have a tendency to forget that steering often is possible on slippery surfaces while standing on the brake pedal.

GASOLINE VERSUS DIESEL

The choice between gasoline- and diesel-engine types is limited to Class C coaches because gasoline engines are not offered in larger, heavier

Disadvantages of Diesel-Engine Power

Cost The cost to manufacture a heavy-duty diesel engine is several times that of a gasoline engine because compression in diesel engines is very high (20:1). Another factor that raises the price of diesel coaches is the additional cost of a heavier-duty transmission, which is necessitated by the higher torque output of the engine. Made by Allison Transmission, the units have four, five, or six speeds, depending on the torque output of the engine.

Noise Diesel engines produce a higher level of noise than gas engines, although while traveling, the noise is isolated from the driver and passenger in rear-engine motorhomes. This noise may be difficult to tolerate for some, but it's music to the ears of others.

Braking Diesel engines do not offer as much compression braking force (drag) as gas engines do, and speed retarders are fitted either to the engine or transmission. The engine-mounted units are exhaust brakes, essentially turning the engine into a compressor, and the transmission-mounted units retard speed hydraulically.

Maintenance Diesel fuel produces more combustion byproducts than gasoline, and the crankcase usually contains more than twice the oil capacity of a gasoline engine, raising the cost of maintenance. The price of engine components is higher for diesels than for gas engines, as is repair work; neglecting maintenance can be very expensive.

---

coaches, which require the high-torque output of diesel engines. Coaches with GVWRs less than the 20,000-pound range are offered almost exclusively on gasoline-powered chassis.

Illustrating the step up from a gasoline-powered Class A to a diesel-powered unit, torque output of gasoline engines used in motorhomes is limited to about 425 lb-ft, whereas the output of the Cummins ISB 260 engine commonly used in competitively priced pusher diesel Class A units is 550 lb-ft.

Even though the name of the game for acceleration and hill-climbing is torque, diesel-engine models commonly are identified by horsepower ratings—i.e., the popular Cummins ISB 5.9-liter engine is an inline six-cylinder 24-valves-per-cylinder power plant available in horsepower ratings from 185 to 275. Gasoline engines are identified by displacement—i.e., the GM (used by Workhorse) Vortec 7400 (7.4-

liter) V-8 and Ford's 6.8-liter V-10.

In Class C chassis, both Chevrolet and Ford offer optional diesels—Chevrolet, the 6.5-liter turbodiesel, and Ford, the PowerStroke 7.3-liter. They are capable engines but torque output is limited to 425 lb-ft for the PowerStroke, which is the stronger of the two engines; the 6.5-liter engine has been replaced by GM's new Duramax 6600 (6.6-liter) turbodiesel engine. Chassis-load ratings peak at 14,050 pounds for the Ford.

Ford and Chevrolet supply the following fuel-injected, electronically controlled gasoline engines:

Ford: 6.8-liter V-10 (Class A and Class C chassis), 305 hp @ 4,250 rpm, 420 lb-ft torque @ 3,250 rpm; 5.4-liter V-8 (Class C only), 255 hp @ 4,200 rpm, 350 lb-ft. torque @ 2,500 rpm.

Chevrolet: 5.7-liter Vortec 5700 V-8 (Class C chassis only), 250 hp @ 4,600 rpm, 330 lb-ft torque @ 2,800 rpm; 7.4-liter Vortec 7400 V-8, (Chevrolet Class C and Workhorse Class A chassis), 290 hp @ 4,000 rpm, 410 lb-ft torque @ 3,200 rpm

8.1-liter Vortec 8100 (Chevrolet Class C and Workhorse Class A chassis), 340 hp @ 4,200 rpm, 455 lb-ft. torque @ 3200 rpm.

Ford and GM diesel engines:

Ford: 7.3-liter PowerStroke turbodiesel V-8 (Class C chassis), 215 hp @ 2,700 rpm, 425 lb-ft torque @ 1,800 rpm

GM: Duramax 6.6-liter turbodiesel V-8 (Class C, introduced as a 2001 model), 300 hp @ 3100 rpm, 520 lb-ft torque @ 1800 rpm.

Beyond those offerings in the light- and medium-GVWR categories, individual chassis makers purchase engines from four sources for chassis that extend from the most economically priced diesel pushers to the most luxurious 45-foot bus conversions:

- Cummins
- Caterpillar
- Detroit Diesel

Cummins, which is largely responsible for popularizing diesel power in motorhomes, provides power for the lower end of the diesel pusher range as well as the high end.

For the lower-priced motorhomes, the electronically controlled ISB 5.9-liter engine is available in ratings from 185 to 275. In the midrange is the electronically controlled Cummins ISC 8.3-liter engine, available in horsepower ratings up to 350. At the high end of the Cummins line, powering the heaviest, largest coaches, is the Cummins ISM 11-liter engine rated at 500 hp. Caterpillar and Detroit Diesel also compete in the high-weight range.

Caterpillar covers the full chassis GVWR range as the front-runner in the conversion of diesel engines to electronic controls, which are necessary to meet ever-tightening emissions regulations.

The Cat 3126 engine is the most popular example, rated at 300 hp in its most popular motorhome usage. The Cat C-12, rated at 425 hp, also is used in motorhomes. These two engines utilize two microprocessors to control critical engine functions such as metering and timing of fuel and control of emissions. Fuel injectors are hydraulically powered and electronically controlled to provide high pressures at low rpm.

The electronic controls allow coach manufacturers to depart from the use of mechanically operated throttles and cruise-control units, while supplying a variety of data including fuel consumption, road speed, oil pressure, and coolant temperature. The system also provides electronic self-diagnosis of problems, plus storage of operational, maintenance, and diagnostic data.

Navistar has long provided diesels for the trucking industry and became a household word among pickup-truck owners by providing the first diesels for Ford pickups. What began as a normally aspirated 6.9-liter V-8 diesel in the early 1980s was transformed into the PowerStroke 7.3-liter turbodiesel, used in Ford Class C chassis.

Diesel engines carry specific warranties that go well beyond the warranty coverage of the chassis itself (see *Trailer Life's Towing Guide*) and prospective motorhome buyers are fortunate to be offered a broad range of engines that perform well and have excellent service and longevity records.

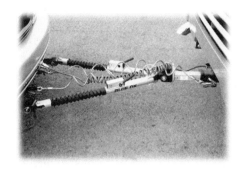

Chapter 4

DINGHY TOWING

Towing a dinghy vehicle for auxiliary transportation adds so much convenience, mobility, and versatility to motorhome travel that the majority of motorhomes can be seen towing a small car, truck, or sport utility vehicle. The advantages are compelling: Not having to move your coach for sightseeing, shopping, and side trips, not to mention the security afforded by a back-up vehicle in the event of mechanical difficulty with the motorhome. It's especially important while traveling little-known byways where service facilities are few and far between.

There are a few disadvantages. One, of course, is cost. Motorized vehicles are expensive to own, operate, and insure; towing a vehicle adds to the cost of owning and operating a motorhome. If you already own a vehicle that is suitable for towing, the initial cost is significantly less.

Many RVers choose the motorhome mode of travel because they prefer not to tow a travel trailer. However, connecting a vehicle to the rear of a motorhome creates a towing situation that requires hitching and unhitching. Reduced maneuverability is a dinghy-towing drawback, particularly when negotiating turns in tight spaces. Backing up with a dinghy in tow is often impossible except for short distances in a straight line, making it necessary to unhitch the dinghy and individually drive each vehicle out of the difficulty.

If you are considering a towed vehicle, make sure the total weight of the motorhome, vehicle, and necessary hardware, such as the dolly, trailer, or tow bar, does not exceed the motorhome chassis manufacturer's gross combination weight rating (GCWR).

TOWING RATINGS

Controversy has surrounded dinghy towing for a number of years because, until recently, most manufacturers of compact cars and trucks recommended against it. Some still do. The only reliable guide to the dinghy-tow suitability of a vehicle—new or used—is the specific owner's manual for the vehicle. Those suitability ratings are summarized in *Trailer Life's Towing Guide*. The guide lists the latest recommendations on dinghy towing by the various manufacturers. Fortunately, many of them have specifically addressed towing, and the number of approved vehicles—including several automatic-transmission cars that are approved for flat-towing—is increasing.

Flat-towable with automatics are the 1995-2000 Chevrolet Cavalier and Pontiac Sunfire, the 1997-2000 Chevrolet Malibu and Oldsmobile Cutlass, plus Saturn models. A number of other cars, trucks, and SUVs are towable with manual transmissions.

Those four-wheel-drive vehicles with automatics that are approved for towing are in that category because they are equipped with transfer cases that can be placed in neutral, preventing rotation of any components in the transmission. Read owners manuals carefully; restrictions apply to some vehicles with automatic-locking hubs.

WEIGHT RATINGS

Although even a relatively small motorhome may be able to tow a heavy car, the questions are how far, how well, and how safely. Weight limits prescribed by manufacturers of motorhome chassis are intended to ensure adequate performance and braking for the motorhome. Applying these limits to one's personal situation requires knowledge of the motorhome's curb weight and the chassis manufacturer's GCWR, which is the maximum total weight of the motorhome, towed vehicle, and all their contents. With knowledge of the motorhome's weight loaded for travel (including passengers), it's possible to calculate the weight allowance for a towed car or truck.

GCWRs of motorhome chassis vary from one manufacturer to the next and sometimes are changed on short notice. Thus it's necessary to consult the chassis manufacturer for the rating on your specific chassis. In general, GM and Ford allow 3,500 to 5,000 pounds for a dinghy vehicle or trailer, and the high-line chassis manufacturers allow 5,000 or more. Most specify that any dinghy or trailer over a specific

Figure 4.1
"Flat towing" with a tow bar is the most popular dinghy-towing method.

limit—usually 1,000 or 1,500 pounds—must have automatically actuated dinghy brakes.

Lighter loads—towed or hauled—mean better performance, better fuel economy, and improved braking, which suggests that motorhome owners should choose to tow the lightest vehicles that suit their needs, preferably 3,000 pounds or less. Popular exceptions are compact four-wheel-drive vehicles such as the Ford Explorer and Jeep Cherokee, which weigh 3,500 to 4,000 pounds. Even when the gross combined weight is within the manufacturer's limit, the ability to keep speed in check on steep downhill grades may require more braking capability than the motorhome can produce from the combined effect of downshifting the transmission (engine-compression braking) and application of service brakes.

TOWING EQUIPMENT

Beyond maintaining a realistic weight situation, the choice of towing equipment is important to safety and convenience. Vehicles can be successfully and legally towed three ways: on their own four wheels utilizing a tow bar (Figure 4.1), with two wheels on a dolly (Figure 4.2), or with the entire vehicle on a trailer.

Trailers are uncommon due to the difficulty of fitting them into sites in RV parks. But one of the advantages of a dolly or a trailer is the availability of brakes (surge or electric),

Figure 4.2
A towing dolly supports the front axle of the dinghy vehicle and can be ordered with brakes.

although the motorhome owner should make sure that the extra weight of a dolly (350 to 700 pounds, depending on brand and model) or trailer (700 to 1,000 pounds) does not cause gross combined weight to exceed the motorhome chassis manufacturer's rating.

Dollies became popular with motorhome owners when only a few manufacturers of small front-wheel-drive cars approved of their vehicles being towed, even those with manual transmissions. Many motorhome owners prefer automatic transmissions in their towed cars, limiting them to General Motors models or to towing a nonapproved car on a dolly. A dolly immobilizes the front (drive) wheels of the car, eliminating any concern about transmission damage while towing.

Dollies basically are small trailers equipped with ramps that haul one axle of a vehicle. The dolly will tow either end of a car. For example, a rear-wheel-drive car can be backed onto the dolly. However, at least one manufacturer recommends against towing a car backward due to the possibility of sway (yaw) that may occur if the car's front suspension has worn components or is misaligned. Either hydraulic or surge brakes are offered.

Most owners prefer flat-towing with a tow bar. In any case, proper choice and installation of equipment is important—especially so with tow bars since they are mechanically attached to the towed vehicle, whereas a dolly or trailer is hitched to the motorhome and only requires that the towed vehicle be secured.

For motorhomers who want to flat-tow but do not own an automatic-transmission vehicle that is recommended for it, a special pumping system may be used to circulate lubricant even while the dinghy vehicle's engine is not running. Also available is a device that permits one axle of a front-wheel-drive car to be mechanically unlocked. Both are available at RV supply stores and from Camping World.

Hitch Platforms and Ball Height

Whether the towing method is a tow bar, dolly, or trailer, the height of the hitch ball is important to proper handling and safety. Ball height will vary with the road clearance of the vehicle or trailer, which means that there is no precise ideal ball height; however, the average will be around 18 inches. The proper ball height is one that places the tow bar or A-frame of the dolly or trailer in an approximately level attitude. When the ball position is too high, coupler damage may be possible if the motorhome is driven into an unusually high position relative to the towed vehicle; the coupler may pop off the ball.

A proper hitch receiver is mounted as close to the bumper as is practical. If the ball is positioned at the level of the receiver, it may be too high or too low depending on the towed vehicle's height. Ball mounts of different configurations are used to create proper ball height regardless of the position of the receiver (Figure 4.3).

Figure 4.3
Ball mounts of different configurations can be used to create correct ball height to assure that the tow bar is fairly level.

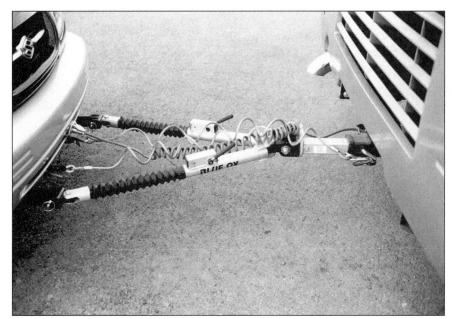

Figure 4.4
Safety cables or chains are required by federal law.

The hitch platform attached to the motorhome must be clearly rated for the total weight of the car and car/dolly or trailer to be towed. Ratings usually are stamped on hitch receivers and on ball mounts. Likewise, couplers must be clearly stamped with load ratings that are sufficient for the weight being towed.

Beyond the ratings, use a mechanic's creeper to get under the motorhome and check the integrity of the hitch attachment to the motorhome frame. The hitch platform should be bolted securely with grade 5 bolts and lockwashers or locking nuts, or by using Loctite thread sealant. Check all nuts for tightness. Welding is not recommended because the quality of the welds varies from one shop to another.

In their original length, some motorhome chassis are not long enough to extend fully to the bumper of the motorhome. Thus coach builders sometimes add frame extensions. It is to these extensions, sometimes hastily welded to the chassis, that the hitch platform is attached. Periodic inspection of the quality of the welds is important.

Hitch-Ball Choices

Hitch balls are available in various quality levels and types. The ball should be stamped with a load rating equal to, or in excess of, the entire weight of your towed vehicle—and dolly or trailer if either is used. If the ball is not stamped with a rating, discard it and buy one that is. The ball should have a stem that allows the coupler full flexibility of movement. Don't use a ball without a stem because the coupler could be forced off the ball when the motorhome and towed vehicle are at odd angles.

Safety Chains

Federal law requires the use of safety chains or cables, regardless of the towing method (Figure 4.4). Two chains or cables should be attached to the motorhome frame and they should be rated for the equipment involved; Class 2 and Class 3 chain or cable should be rated for 3,500 and 5,000 pounds capacity, respectively.

Installation of Tow Bars

A variety of tow bars is available, ranging from universal units to late-model telescoping, self-aligning bars that offer additional flexibility while positioning the towed vehicle for hitching. Some telescoping bars are designed to remain with the dinghy vehicle (Figure 4.5) while the trend is toward those that are folded

Figure 4.5
Many telescoping tow bars are designed to be stored temporarily on the dinghy vehicle.

Figure 4.6
This telescoping tow bar can be locked in place parallel to the motorhome bumper when not in use.

flat with the rear of the motorhome (Figure 4.6). All tow bars should be identified with ratings for maximum vehicle weight. Make sure your vehicle's curb weight does not exceed the tow-bar rating.

Locking pins make many tow bars easily removable so they can be stowed in the vehicle or with the motorhome until needed. All tow bars utilize a triangular structure for rigidity, whether the structure is steel tubing, flat steel-bar stock, or two lengths of chain that form triangular support for a telescoping center bar. Rigidity is necessary because heavy stress can be exerted on a tow bar during sharp turns or when traversing uneven terrain.

Most small trucks and four-wheel-drive vehicles present no significant installation

Dinghy Towing Inspection Checklist

It's important while traveling that the motorhome owner visually inspect the tow bar every time the vehicle is stopped. The owner should perform a walkaround that covers these visual inspection points:

- ✔ Coupler secured on hitch ball

- ✔ Tires appear to have normal inflation pressure

- ✔ Pin (or bolt) securing coupler in locked position

- ✔ Hitch-ball nut tight

- ✔ Ignition key positioned so steering column is unlocked

- ✔ Transmission shift lever and/or transfer case shift lever (four-wheel drive only) still in desired position

- ✔ Hand brake in "off" position

- ✔ All bolts, nuts, and pins on tow bar and baseplate tight

- ✔ Wiring harness connected and lights operating properly

At least once a week while traveling, additional points should be covered. This inspection takes less than a minute, and includes the motorhome's tires and a quick look underneath the chassis for signs of oil or coolant loss:

- ✔ Inspect all bolts underneath vehicle or otherwise out of sight that are used to attach tow-bar baseplate to the vehicle. Inspect vehicle body or frame for deformation caused by stress on the bolts.*

- ✔ Inspect bolts securing hitch platform to motorhome.

- ✔ Check wiring for chafing or damage.

- ✔ Inspect all tow-bar pivot points for excessive wear.

* All bolts should have several threads protruding beyond the nuts. Fewer threads protruding provide a danger signal without having to retorque each nut with a wrench (although that should happen periodically). Deformation of metal components indicates improper design of the baseplate.

challenges for tow-bar manufacturers. These vehicles have body-on-frame designs, offering a system of steel girders in the front of the vehicle for attachment of the tow-bar baseplate (mounting platform). Ideally, the tow-bar manufacturer should supply a baseplate (mount) designed specifically for the vehicle so that few, if any, additional holes must be drilled in the vehicle's frame. The baseplate generally is bolted into place utilizing grade 5 bolts, lockwashers, and Loctite thread sealant as added insurance against loosening (or locking nuts may be used).

The design of baseplates for cars with unibody construction presents a real challenge because such cars do not have conventional frames. The sheet-metal body itself provides the vehicle's rigidity, and the engineers do not allow stress loads of engine and suspension mounts to concentrate too heavily at single points. Unfortunately, front ends of unibody cars typically are not designed with tow-bar attachment in mind, and the tow-bar-baseplate designer faces a real challenge. Care must be taken to distribute stress loads properly. Failure to do so can result in the baseplate mounting bolts being pulled out of the body. Or, in extreme cases, major front-end sheet metal components may be torn off the car.

While a baseplate can be custom built, it's best to choose a dinghy vehicle for which a prefabricated baseplate is available, assuring the buyer that design expertise and experience have been applied.

Lights

Most states require the motorhome's light system to activate the towed vehicle's legal tail, brake, and turn-signal lights. Even in states that don't have the requirements, a full lighting system is necessary for safe towing. Dollies and trailers are fitted with appropriate lights by their manufacturers, and a four-wire plug can be installed at the rear of the motorhome to include the necessary lighting circuits.

The motorhomer who tows a vehicle on its own wheels with a tow bar must either use the towed vehicle's taillights or add a light bar, which is an independent tail/signal-light system. When utilizing the towed vehicle's lights, the common wiring method is to splice three wires from the motorhome (tail, left turn, and right turn) into the wiring harness leading to the towed vehicle's rear lights. The splice point may be in the engine compartment or slightly to the rear, under the floor.

Electrical feedback problems can occur with vehicles utilizing transistorized ignition systems. Current from the motorhome may feed back through the towed vehicle's lighting system into ignition components or other control systems. This can be prevented by using a taillight wiring kit that includes diodes (one-way electrical valves). Such kits are available from a variety of sources, including at least one manufacturer of widely used tow-bar products. Light bars require a simple four-wire hookup that is identical to the system used for a dolly or trailer.

Motorhomes using turn signals that are separate from brake lights require the use of a solid-state converter to provide compatibility with the conventional lights of a dolly or trailer in which the same bulb is used for brakes and turn signals. Such converters are available from the same companies that make light bars and wiring kits.

TRACKING

Some compact cars and trucks track better than others while being towed, due to differing steering geometry. If a vehicle does not track well, have an alignment shop set the front-wheel caster to the maximum factory-recommended setting. Maintain maximum air pressure in the tires to help reduce tread wear.

In the few cases in which the towed vehicle's front wheels have a tendency to reverse steer (crank all the way in the wrong direction) in driveways, it may be necessary to use a stretch cord to anchor the steering wheel to a point behind the driver's seat so the wheel cannot make a full revolution. This is not ideal because it accelerates tire wear, but it will prevent an annoying lockup situation in driveways and on other uneven terrain. Most late-model vehicles do not exhibit this steering problem.

While maneuvering the motorhome, avoid sharp turns at slow speeds. Motorhomes have long rear overhangs, and sharp turns cause rapid lateral movement of the hitch ball that tends to drag the towed vehicle sideways. When driving with a tow bar or dolly, avoid backing up during turns as well as in any straight distance greater than several feet. The car or dolly will not steer in the motorhome's intended direction, and may be dragged sideways. Be sure transmission lubricant is kept up to the recommended fill level.

BRAKING

With extra weight tagging along behind, it's always best to allow more stopping distance than normally would be required, especially if the dinghy vehicle, dolly, or trailer is not braked. Any motorhome towing a vehicle should always have the capability of making an emergency stop on a downhill grade even after the brakes have been used intermittently to retard speed. However, extensive use of the service brakes can result in brake fade, which is caused by overheating of brake pads, shoes, drums, and rotors to the point where friction between the two is partially or fully lost. Although the brake pedal may feel firm, little or no reduction of speed occurs.

Downshifting to a lower gear can be an effective way of avoiding brake fade, by instead relying on engine compression-braking to slow the coach. This braking force can be further amplified by using an exhaust brake (Figure 4.7) or retarder, allowing the coach/dinghy combination to descend steeper grades before significant use of the service brakes becomes necessary. This saves wear on service brake components, and can also be utilized when the coach is being driven solo. Unfortunately, the need to downshift in order to obtain sufficient braking tends to diminish a retarder's usefulness during sudden, unplanned stops. This contrasts with tow dolly and dinghy braking systems, most of which can deliver maximum stopping power almost instantaneously.

Tow Dolly Brakes

Most dolly brakes are of the surge variety, in which a hitch-mounted master cylinder is connected to hydraulic brakes on each dolly wheel. Whenever the motorhome is braked, the dolly "surges" forward on the hitch, actuating the master cylinder to pressurize the brake lines and create brake actuation.

Figure 4.7
Exhaust brakes such as this Pacbrake model can improve safety and reduce wear on service brakes.

Brake Actuation for Dinghy Vehicles

For brake actuation of dinghy vehicles, several schemes are currently used. Surge-operated systems employ a hitch-mounted master brake cylinder connected directly to the dinghy's hydraulic brake lines, much like on a tow dolly. Vehicle manufacturers recommend against modifying their brake systems, and installation of these systems may be complicated by the presence of ABS on some cars. Also, if the tow bar is removed for storage, care must be taken to prevent brake fluid leaks or the introduction of air into the dinghy's brake lines.

A variation of this scheme uses forward motion of the tow bar to operate a cable connected either to the dinghy's brake pedal or the emergency brake cable (Figure 4.8). Although this eliminates any connections to the hydraulic system, it still presents an installation challenge on some vehicles, particularly if holes must be drilled through the firewall to route the cable to the brake pedal. Also, versions that connect to the emergency brake cable may suffer from reduced performance associated with only braking two wheels.

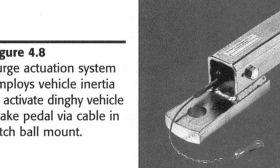

Figure 4.8
Surge actuation system employs vehicle inertia to activate dinghy vehicle brake pedal via cable in hitch ball mount.

Another approach to dinghy braking employs an air- or electrically powered solenoid or servo that presses the dinghy's brake pedal (Figure 4.9). Usually, the solenoid is disconnected and moved out of the way (or removed entirely) before driving the dinghy, although one variant has the solenoid permanently mounted between the dinghy's vacuum booster and master cylinder, thereby leaving the passenger compartment free of system components. Most solenoid-operated systems use electronic controls to moderate the applied braking force. With some products, the braking controls are adjustable from the motorhome driver's position; in others, the system is entirely self-contained inside the dinghy.

Aside from the safety benefits obtained with a dinghy braking system, there are also legal advantages. Most state vehicle codes that declare a braking requirement for trailers do not specifically mention towed vehicles, but a few lump both into the same category. Although there has been no significant enforcement in most states, the general trend is toward strengthening both the language and execution of these codes.

The reason why dinghy towing has grown so popular is obvious: It adds greatly to the convenience and adventure of motorhoming. With proper equipment, maintenance, and precautions, the motorhome owner can be reasonably well assured that towing will be trouble free.

Figure 4.9
Servo solenoid depresses brake pedal in response to input from control unit in motorhome.

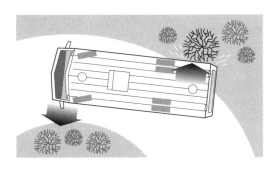

Chapter 5

WEIGHT, HANDLING, AND SAFETY

By nature, most RVs are larger and bulkier than the family sedan and cannot be expected to handle the same way. In particular, towing a trailer requires new skills and judgment because a tow vehicle/trailer combination is an articulated vehicle; that is, segmented or joined.

New criteria and some adjustments in driving habits are necessary to graduate from a car or truck to an articulated vehicle or a motorhome. It isn't difficult, and few problems occur unless a driver fails to realize that tow vehicles and motorhomes aren't as agile or as powerful as cars and light trucks alone. What's more, violation of their weight limits can have serious consequences.

The major factors that must be considered for safe RVing include:

- Visibility—forward and side- and rear-view mirrors

- The vehicle's length, width, and height

- Turning circle

- How the vehicle tracks while turning

- Braking ability

- Stability during emergency maneuvers

- Stability on curves

- Stability in crosswinds

- Acceleration for passing

- Loading and load ratings

- Weight distribution

MIRRORS AND VISIBILITY

Good forward and side visibility are needed in any motor vehicle, particularly in one that is larger and more difficult to handle than a typical car or truck alone. The levels of visibility we tend to accept as adequate may not be very good; visibility often can be improved.

Few vehicles have poor forward visibility even though some may have relatively small windshields that restrict the upward scenic view. In motorhomes, side vision sometimes is restricted by excessively large corner posts between the windshield and the side windows, and by mirrors that are positioned too high. Little can be done about corner posts after the fact, but it's a point of consideration while shopping for a new unit. Side visibility in motorhomes may be restricted by window frames—particularly those that block the view through mirrors (Figure 5.1). The solution is either to move the mirror to a more advantageous position or to modify the side window. Moving the mirror usually is the easiest solution.

Figure 5.1
The view through side-mounted mirrors sometimes is partially blocked, requiring repositioning.

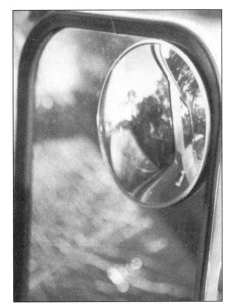

Figure 5.2
Stick-on convex mirrors can help eliminate a "blind spot" to the right rear of the vehicle.

Figure 5.3
Large motorhome mirrors offer excellent combination of conventional lens with adjustable convex lens.

Figure 5.4
A convex lens may be attached to the frame so it does not block the lens of a conventional towing mirror.

Mirrors themselves are an area of poor visibility, which can lead to accidents. Mirrors on a tow vehicle or motorhome should be 10 × 7 inches to offer an adequate field of vision. On tow vehicles, door-mount positions are far better than fender mounts. Fender-mounted mirrors don't offer a good rear view due to their size and their distance from the driver. Also, a convex right-side mirror, which helps the driver monitor his or her "blind spot," cannot be used as a fender mount. The solution for cars is a set of good door-mounted mirrors, with a convex mirror added on the right side. On trucks and vans, extensions may be used to move some mirror heads outward, or a replacement set of extended mirrors may be purchased. Extensions and replacement mirrors are available at RV supply stores.

While trucks, vans, and motorhomes usually have larger mirror heads, the owner still must make sure visibility is not restricted by window frames or by an insecure mirror mounting that causes excessive vibration, blurring the reflected images. Most right-side mirrors of pickup trucks and vans do not have wide-angle lenses, which must be added to the face of the mirror (Figure 5.2). On motorhomes, the side-mounted mirror often is about two-thirds conventional view and one-third wide angle (Figure 5.3). This combination is acceptable but tends to restrict the driver's ability to see the area around the rear tires, which is helpful to keep from running over curbs while making tight turns, as well as checking for exhaust smoke or an errant wheel cover. The preferred arrangement is a convex mirror that is outside the conventional mirror. Add-on convex mirrors are available at RV supply stores and those that sell equipment to truckers. These mirrors should be positioned immediately below or above the primary mirror (Figure 5.4). The preferred location is the one that offers maximum visibility.

VEHICLE SIZE

Most of us drive passenger cars or light trucks more frequently and graduate to our RVs only occasionally. Thus, it's always necessary to make a mental transition and keep the size and handling characteristics of the larger rig in mind. Failing to do so may result in a tendency to make turns too tightly, run over curbs, hit stationary objects, or crowd other traffic. It may take some concentration for the novice RV owner, but acclimation happens fairly rapidly. The get-acquainted period may be difficult to get through without minor dings and scrapes, but traffic accidents are unusual, even though the new driver may not have fully adjusted to the particular characteristics of handling an RV.

The best defense against problems associated with the vehicle's size is practice. All too often, we encounter a tight turn into or out of a campground site or service station and are tentative about our ability to make the turn. Practicing tight maneuvers will improve our judgment, reducing the chance of embarrassing situations. Practice also helps improve our judgment in making sure we don't hit overhanging tree limbs and other such obstacles. It's helpful to measure the actual height of the vehicle and list this figure somewhere on the dash for reference when driving under structures that are marked for road clearance. If you're uncomfortable driving under unmarked overhangs, exit the vehicle and check clearance if the situation permits. Soon you'll have a clearer mental picture of your RV's height.

Tailswing is an RV handling characteristic that causes quite a number of dings and scrapes. It occurs during tight, slow-speed maneuvers when the rear of a trailer or motorhome swings opposite the direction you are steering (Figure 5.5). Tailswing can be monitored in the mirrors of a motorhome or truck camper, allowing you to avoid costly conflicts with lampposts and other obstacles. But with a tow vehicle and trailer, you're blind on the right side during left turns. Also, while backing to the left, we can see where we're going on that side, but we can't see the right side of the trailer. Pulling forward sharply to the left and then straightening the wheel can swing the trailer's rear to the right—into a post, tree, or other obstacle if it happens to be your misfortune. The best defense is to practice in a parking lot and observe how the vehicle's rear changes position. With a tow vehicle and trailer, have someone else drive while you watch what happens in tight turns.

ON-THE-ROAD PERFORMANCE

RVs are like most other vehicles that are larger and heavier than cars and light trucks in that they must be driven differently. We can't expect to pass other vehicles with the same authority in a 16,000-pound motorhome as we do a car. However, it is possible to pass. Drivers of 18-wheelers do it, but they wait for enough clear highway.

While passing, don't hesitate to use the full rpm potential of your engine when necessary. This means holding the accelerator pedal to the floor, causing the automatic transmission to downshift and allowing it to determine the upshift point. With V-8 engines, the transmission is programmed to upshift at 4,000 to

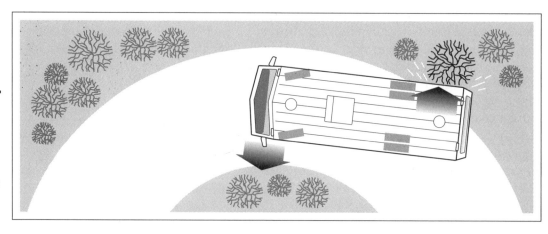

Figure 5.5
Tailswing creates the danger of a collision when the rear of a motorhome or trailer swings in the opposite direction of the turn.

4,500 rpm, depending on the engine; these levels are not excessive in short bursts.

ROAD MANNERS

RVs are heavier than cars, and they climb hills more slowly than other private passenger traffic, as do 18-wheelers. But fast traffic seems more tolerant of slow 18-wheelers than of slow recreational travelers, which makes courtesy an important safety factor. It's best to frequently monitor rear-view mirrors and be aware of vehicles behind us. When a vehicle is tailgating and trying to pass, drive slightly to the right to give the other driver a better view of the road ahead, even if a passing opportunity does not exist at the time. Use turnouts when possible, and don't follow another vehicle so closely that the vehicle passing you cannot return to your lane. Failure to display courtesy to other drivers can affect your own safety by causing angry reactions and poor judgment in other motorists.

MANEUVERING

While all RV drivers must acclimate themselves to longer vehicles that require more care while maneuvering, some RVs track differently than others in turns. With the exception of very large motorhomes, all the self-propelled RVs are relatively easy to handle in turns. With the large ones, the driver must take extra care to swing as wide as possible in tight turns. The techniques are to keep the vehicle as far away from obstacles as possible, and proceed as far as possible into the area of a turn before beginning the turn.

Trailers require more practice and more visualizing because it's necessary to learn how the tow vehicle and trailer respond to steering input. Small- to medium-length travel trailers will follow closely in the tracks of the tow vehicle in turns, so the tow vehicle needn't be steered exceptionally wide in turns. A long travel trailer will track moderately on the inside of the turn, requiring more space. A fifth-wheel trailer tracks considerably farther to the inside of the turn (Figure 5.6), so a turn that is not taken rather wide will result in the trailer's tires climbing a curb. The reason for this is that a fifth-wheel trailer's hitch point is directly above the rear axle of the tow vehicle, whereas the pivot point of a travel trailer is 4 to 5 feet behind the tow vehicle's rear bumper. The tow vehicle's tailswing tends to make a travel trailer follow closely in the tow vehicle's

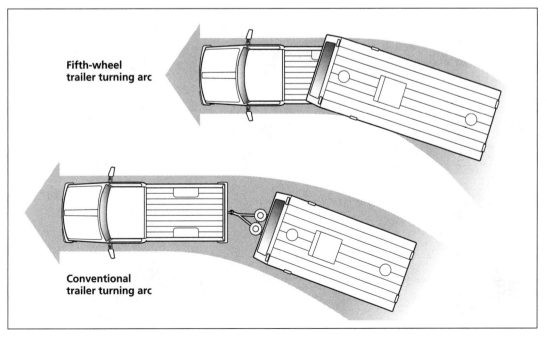

Fifth-wheel trailer turning arc

Conventional trailer turning arc

Figure 5.6
Ball-type trailers track closely with the tow vehicle, but fifth-wheelers track to the inside of the turn.

tracks. But tow-vehicle tailswing does not steer a fifth-wheel trailer, so it tracks farther to the inside of the turn. As fifth-wheel trailer length increases, more care must be taken during turns.

TRAILER BACKING

With conventionally hitched trailers, ease of backing increases with trailer length, which is the opposite of what most novices often assume. A utility trailer is much more difficult to back; its short ball-to-axle distance causes it to react swiftly to tow-vehicle steering input, while a longer trailer will react gradually. Fifth-wheel trailers are more difficult to back than conventional trailers, requiring more practice. Techniques for backing differ widely.

Here are some general guidelines for backing all types of trailers:

- When you are ready to begin backing, place your hand at the bottom of the steering wheel. Then move it in the direction you want your trailer to go (Figure 5.7). This is more effective with conventional trailers than with fifth-wheelers, which require more turning of the steering wheel.

- Hand-held two-way radios, available at low cost, can allow an assistant to relay backing instructions to the driver more effectively.

- After arriving at a site, inspect it for the final position of the trailer and lay a length of white cord (clothesline) along the intended path. Begin laying the line a few inches to the left of where you want the left rear wheel of the trailer to be. Lay the line out to about where the left front of the tow vehicle will be when the trailer is in position, and continue with the line along the intended backing path so the line can be seen in the left rear-view mirror. Backing to the left is easiest, but this method can also help while backing to the right.

Backing Fifth-Wheels
When backing fifth-wheels, follow these procedures:

- Watch your outside mirrors and when you see the trailer moving where you don't want it to go, turn the steering wheel in that direction. For example, while looking in the left mirror, if you

Figure 5.7
While backing a trailer, steer from the bottom of the wheel and turn in the direction you want the trailer to go.

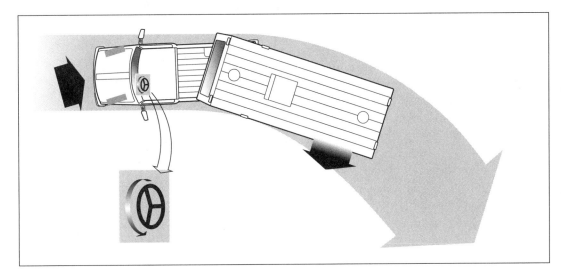

Figure 5.8
If a fifth-wheel trailer moves in an undesirable direction while backing, turn the steering wheel in that direction to straighten out.

see the trailer moving toward that side and you don't want it to go in that direction, turn the wheel to the left (Figure 5.8). Position someone near the rear of the trailer, in the driver's view, to watch for obstructions.

- Remember that you have no tailswing leverage to help you steer the fifth-wheeler while backing, as one has with a conventionally hitched trailer. Therefore, the tow vehicle must be at a significant angle to the trailer before any turning occurs. This does not necessarily mean that extreme winding of the steering wheel is required, but it does mean that turns must be started before you get to the slot into which you're trying to move. The trick is figuring how much earlier. Each time you pull out of a slot, observe the path the trailer wheels make, and pay particular attention to the surprisingly long way you go before the trailer is aligned straight behind the tow vehicle. That is the magical point at which you should start to turn if you were to reverse the process and back into that slot.

Backing All Types of RVs

Before backing an RV, be sure to inspect the site, decide where you want the wheels to be,

and lay a line of white cord or place "targets" on the ground—small rocks, pieces of wood, and such—along the path that the wheels must follow to end up where you want them. When the wheels are directly opposite the target, they serve as guides not to back up too far.

No matter what the type of rig, practice is the answer. Regardless of the techniques the driver and his or her helper may use, there is no substitute for repetition of backing maneuvers until they become almost second nature.

BRAKING AND BRAKE FADE

While RV brakes are adequate for most situations, care is necessary to avoid overheating, which can lead to brake fade. When brakes fade, friction has raised the temperature of brake pads and linings to extremely high levels, resulting in temporary loss of braking. The brake pedal is still firm, and its height is normal, but heavy foot pressure on the pedal produces little or no braking action. This is a frightening situation, caused by excessive use of brakes to retard downhill speeds on long, mountain grades. Beyond use of top-quality brake components, the cure is prevention—downshifting to a gear range that is low enough to retard speed sufficiently that brakes need not be used more than occasionally. This way, enough braking performance is reserved to make an emergency stop if it becomes necessary.

The proper way to use brakes is to apply them intermittently, with moderate pressure, to scrub off speed. Then release the pedal to allow the brakes to cool. Do not ride the brake pedal for long periods.

If brakes fade prematurely—which means an emergency stop cannot be made effectively on level highway even though brakes have not been preheated—or if braking is not sufficient for more than moderate reduction of speed on a downhill grade, the brake system should be checked for glazed brake pads and linings. Top-quality semi-metallic brake pads and linings should be used.

When a trailer is involved, action of the electric trailer brakes should be apparent to the driver and sufficient to take care of the trailer. The controller should be adjusted so maximum braking action does not cause trailer-wheel lockup. If the driver can not feel the action of the trailer brakes, he or she has no way of monitoring whether or not they're functional.

Many RVs have relatively high centers of gravity, which complicate the use of brakes while traveling curving roads. By staging test situations, it should be possible to determine the vehicle's response to braking action on curves. Handling deficiencies such as a tendency toward excessive body roll (lean) can be exaggerated while using brakes. You should practice using brakes in situations other than straight-ahead driving so you will know what to expect. Handling deficiencies may be caused by weight imbalance, overloading, or poor shock absorbers. An RV whose handling is difficult to improve due to design deficiencies must be driven at slower speeds to allow reaction time in emergency situations.

LOADING AND LOAD RATINGS

RVs are subject to overloading and the problems that result from it. They include:

- Improper handling
- Lengthened stopping distance
- Increased wear on brakes
- Reduced acceleration capability
- Reduced service life of components such as wheel bearings and springs
- Component failures, primarily tires

Tire failures can lead directly to accidents, so it behooves every RV owner to become educated about weight and weight distribution and to take action by applying the knowledge to his or her specific situation.

Several items contribute to weight problems:

- Insufficient load capacity built into the vehicles by their manufacturers to reasonably cover the amount of weight owner will add
- Insufficient information distributed by manufacturers and dealers about the importance of weight and loading
- Lack of motivation by RV owners to acquire information (available in magazines and in books) they need to avoid overloading

All vehicles have load ratings, which determine how much weight (carrying capacity) the owner can add. The amount of information available to the consumer changed substantially in late 1996 when a weight labeling program introduced by the Recreational Vehicle Industry Association (RVIA) went into effect. At that time, the RVIA began requiring their members to affix labels featuring this information to all their units (Figure 5.9).

Prior to late 1996, labels included only load ratings, with no additional information offered on actual weight of the vehicle. Although manufacturers are inclined to list the weight of a typical RV in the specific model lineup rather than that of the actual unit to which the weight label is attached, it is far more detailed than the information previously offered, and it gives the owner specific limits on the weight of supplies and equipment that can be carried on trips.

Any RV can be overloaded, but travel trailers tend to be less susceptible because they don't have voluminous exterior storage capac-

ity; camping equipment, tools, and other supplies usually are hauled in the tow vehicle.

Fifth-wheel trailers have more storage
capacity, and their owners frequently travel
for longer periods, hence the tendency to
carry more supplies and equipment.
Motorhomes have the greatest potential for
overloading because of their "basement" storage compartments.

Unfortunately few RV owners bother to
weigh their vehicles, so they do not discover
overload situations that can lead to tire
blowouts, bearing failures, and, in severe
cases, wheel breakage. Also, overloading usually causes spring sag, poor handling, and
inadequate braking. Tires usually are the first
components to fail in overload situations; the
probability of failure is increased if tire inflation pressure is not maintained properly.

WEIGHING A VEHICLE

Owners of RVs built following the introduction of RVIA weight-labeling may not feel the
need to weigh their units; it's a wise move anyway because some manufacturers approximate. Owners of vehicles built prior to weight
labeling in 1996 usually were provided no reliable information on actual weight of their RVs
by the manufacturers and should acquire that
information. The following weighing procedures should be used:

1. Locate the manufacturer's identification
   sticker or plate for future reference. On
   cars and trucks it will be on the driver's
   door pillar; on motorhomes it usually is
   inside, near the driver's seat, or just
   inside the door; on trailers it's usually on
   the left front exterior.

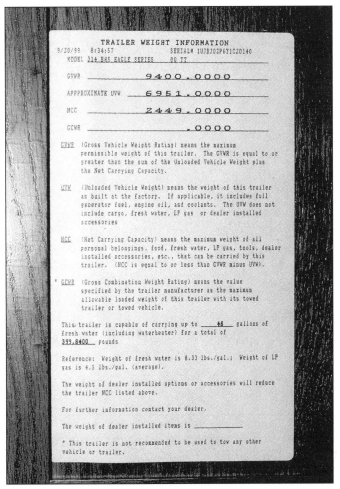

Figure 5.9
Labeling rules require
RV manufacturers to
post specific weight definitions to help owners
prevent overloading.

Weight Ratings and Descriptions

Gross Vehicle Weight Rating (GVWR) The maximum weight of the vehicle and all its contents, including passengers—i.e., the maximum to which the vehicle can be loaded.

Unloaded Vehicle Weight (UVW) Weight of the RV including factory-installed options, with full fuel, engine oil and coolant. The UVW does not include cargo, fresh water, LP gas or dealer-installed accessories or passengers.

Sleeping Capacity Weight Rating (SCWR) Motorhomes only. Effective September 1, 2000, designated sleeping positions should be multiplied by 154 pounds per passenger. Does not apply to trailers or pickup campers.

Cargo Carrying Capacity (CCC) The amount of weight the owner can add to an RV, minus fresh water (at 8.3 pounds per gallon), LP-gas (at 4.5 pounds per gallon). Calculated by subtracting the UVW and SCWR (motorhomes only) as well as the total weight of fresh water and LP-gas from the GVWR.

Gross Axle Weight Rating (GAWR) The maximum to which the specific axle can be loaded.

Gross Combination Weight Rating (GCWR) The maximum permissible weight of the vehicle and trailer (or motorhome and "dinghy" vehicle) with all passengers, fluids, and supplies.

Wet Weight (WW) Weight of an actual RV (as listed in *Trailer Life* or *MotorHome* magazines) with full fuel and water tanks but no supplies or passengers.

2. Weigh the vehicle while loaded for a trip. If the vehicle is a motorhome, camping van, or truck camper, weigh each wheel if an axle scale or a wheel scale can be found. In absence of such a scale, a platform scale will suffice, although it's not sufficiently accurate to measure individual wheel weights. If a platform scale must be used, weigh the vehicle five times: gross weight, front axle, rear axle, left side, right side. If the vehicle cannot be loaded for a trip, estimate the amount of weight you will add so you can determine if an overload condition might occur.

While weighing a trailer, get two figures: trailer wheels only (hitched to the tow vehicle, with tow vehicle off scale) and total trailer weight (trailer unhitched from tow vehicle).

3. Compare your weight figures with the manufacturer's load ratings and with the ratings stamped on the sidewalls of the tires. The weight of your loaded vehicle should not exceed the GVWR, either of the GAWRs, or the individual ratings on your tires. The reason multiple weight readings are necessary is that improper weight distribution may overload an individual tire or set of dual tires even though the GVWR has not been violated. One tire or a set of dual tires can be overloaded even while other tires are well within weight limits.

Finding and Using Scales

Platform or wheel scales can be found at equipment-rental yards, moving companies, grain elevators, and other such establishments. Check the Yellow Pages of your phone book under Scales, Weighers, Weight, or Weighing. Using a scale is a simple procedure, but one very important procedure must be observed: The vehicle being weighed must be level. All platform scales are flat, but the aprons surrounding them may not be. When the aprons are not level, the RV must be positioned so it is level even though one side or one end may be off the scale. Leveling blocks or boards may be needed.

Position the trailer wheels on the scale for a weight reading with the tow vehicle hitched to the trailer but off the scale (Figure 5.10). This is the figure you will use to determine if axle or tire load ratings are violated. Unhitch the trailer on the scale (vehicle off scale) to determine the trailer's gross weight.

Substantial lateral imbalance with trailers is unusual, which in most cases eliminates the need to weigh each side of the trailer. The exception would be a situation in which weighing the trailer's axle(s) indicates that weight is near or over the tire ratings. In that case, weighing each side of the trailer is advisable to make sure the heavy side is not above the tire maximum load ratings. If it is, reduction in weight is necessary.

In Table 5.1, the calculations determine if the weight carried by four 205/75R15ST load range C tires rated at 1,820 pounds each at 50 psi is in excess of the tire load ratings. The result: Tire capacity is in excess of the actual load—a safe situation.

Although it's not necessary when evaluating tire loading, you should also measure

Table 5.1
Weight ratings and actual weights of a 26-foot travel trailer
Manufacturer's weight ratings
GAWR, front axle ....3,500 lbs.
GAWR, rear axle............................3,500 lbs.
GVWR ....7,000 lbs.
Unloaded vehicle weight
Front axle* ....2,800 lbs.
Rear axle* ....2,800 lbs.
Total weight on trailer tires ....5,600 lbs.
*Weighing with trailer hitched to tow vehicle, utilizing a load-distributing hitch. Axle weights will differ when measured without the use of a load-distributing hitch.

hitch weight, which will help in evaluating the trailer's stability (see Chapter 6). Hitch weight is measured by positioning the trailer so the hitch support (tow vehicle or tongue jack) is off the scale. (Don't use load-distributing hitch spring bars, which will prevent an accurate hitch-weight measurement.) Weigh the trailer wheels only; subtract that figure from the trailer's gross weight to determine hitch weight.

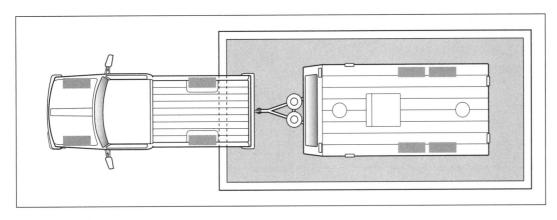

Figure 5.10
To determine a trailer's axle weight, position the trailer wheels on the scale and the tow vehicle rear wheels immediately off the scale.

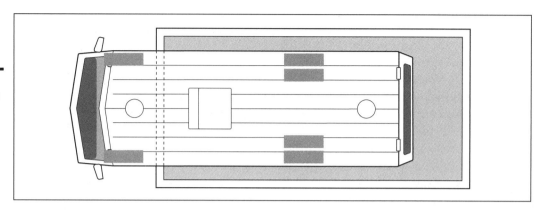

Figure 5.11
A motorhome may have an adequate carrying capacity on one axle while the other is overloaded, which can be detected by weighing each axle separately.

Weighing a Motorhome, Truck Camper, or Van Conversion

If a wheel or axle scale is available, weigh each wheel individually. If the weights must be taken on a platform scale, weigh the entire vehicle first. Then move it fore and aft for front and rear axle weights (Figure 5.11). Move it left and right to weigh each side (Figure 5.12). If the apron around the scale is not level, it is essential to position the vehicle so the off-scale tires are only an inch or so outside the perimeter of the scale on a surface that is level with the scale. Or, level the coach with boards or leveling blocks. Errors will occur if the coach is not level.

Table 5.2

Weight ratings and actual weights of a 32-foot Class A motorhome

Manufacturer's weight ratings

GAWR, front axle	6,000 lbs.
GAWR, rear axle	11,000 lbs.
GVWR	17,000 lbs.

Unloaded vehicle weight

Front axle	5,380 lbs.
Rear axle	9,740 lbs.
Left side	7,700 lbs.
Right side	7,420 lbs.
Total weight	**15,120 lbs**

Taking the weight of passengers and supplies into consideration, the motorhome in Table 5.2 has a realistic CCC and reasonably good balance so that the owner can make use of the coach without overloading either axle.

The tires are LT235/85R16E, rated to carry 3,042 pounds in single configuration or 2,778 pounds in dual configuration. This means 11,112 pounds of rear capacity—ample in this situation, even in view of the fact that both sets of tires rarely are loaded evenly and a margin of safety is needed to account for uneven loading.

Some motorhomes have tag axles—an add-on rear nondrive axles with single tires. These axles are designed to boost the rear GAWR and allow the coach builder to assign the motorhome a higher GVWR. Use of a tag axle, which raises the number of rear tires to six, does not change the rear-drive axle's load rating or the tire ratings. However, by supporting some of the motorhome's rear weight, rear-axle and rear-tire overloading can be avoided. To determine weight on the tag axle, weigh the coach with the tag axle off the scale and subtract that number from the motorhome's gross weight figure. Compare the readings to the manufacturer's GAWR rating and to the individual tire ratings.

Correcting an Overload

If weight figures indicate overloading, correction is necessary to assure safety. Correction is particularly important if tires are overloaded because they are subject to overheating and blowout, whereas the effect on other components may accrue more gradually. Tire load

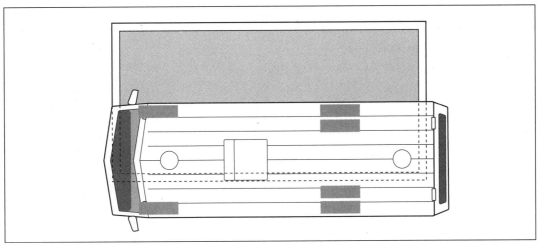

Figure 5.12
Weighing each side of a motorhome or camper can identify overloading that cannot be detected by a gross weight reading.

ratings usually are matched fairly closely with GAWRs, so overloading of an axle usually means tire overloading is imminent.

TOW VEHICLE/TRAILER MATCHING

When a prospective trailer buyer is attempting to select a tow vehicle, knowledge of trailer weight is necessary to make sure the tow vehicle is rated for the trailer weight. A very common error by prospective buyers who don't know the meaning of the load ratings is to assume that the GVWR is the trailer-weight figure they must deal with in selecting a vehicle with the correct towing rating. As the definitions listed earlier explain, the GVWR is not necessarily the actual trailer weight. In fact, the actual trailer weight may be considerably less than the GVWR, depending on how the owner loads the trailer.

When selecting a new trailer, refer to the UVW rating if the trailer was built after late 1996; otherwise, add the manufacturer's dry-weight listing to your personal estimated weight of water, propane, and all supplies for an estimated actual weight of the trailer, loaded for a trip.

The important factor in selecting a new self-propelled RV is to make sure there is enough load capacity. Again, this can be accurately assessed if the vehicle is a late model with the RVIA weight label; it can be estimated for an earlier model by adding the manufacturer's listed dry weight to the weight of fuels, water, supplies, and passengers.

Proper attention paid to weights and weight ratings will pay large dividends in handling and safety, particularly as insurance against tire failure. A bonus is fewer mechanical problems and extended tire longevity.

Chapter 6

SAFE TOWING

Although the basics of towing a trailer with a motor vehicle may seem rather simple—we've all towed rental trailers at one time or another—the dynamics of trailering can get rather complex. Indeed, the important criteria escape most trailerists, who may endure poor towing characteristics for many years without knowing the reason or realizing that something can be done about it.

Here, we'll go through a step-by-step procedure for evaluating tow-vehicle/trailer stability, followed by procedures for improving handling.

Trailers as well as tow vehicles have certain drawbacks: Trailers vary widely in weight distribution, while tow vehicles can vary widely in basic roadworthiness. Being confronted by one of these situations is unfortunate; suffering with both can be dangerous. However, improvements can be made; even in a worst-case situation, safety and the enjoyability of trailering can be greatly improved.

WEIGHT AND BALANCE

Trailers are available in two types: conventional travel trailers and fifth-wheel trailers (Figure 6.1). (Included in the travel-trailer category are folding camping trailers.) We will concentrate on the handling characteristics of conventional travel trailers here, since by design they are much more vulnerable to destabilizing forces than are fifth-wheels. That statement might suggest that fifth-wheel trailers are more preferred. (Owners of fifth-wheels undoubtedly would agree.) However, travel trailers have many positive attributes, one of which is that various types of tow vehicles can be used. Also, when the popular pickup truck is utilized, its bed is not occupied by a hitch and by the trailer's front overhang, which greatly improves travel flexibility. With proper balance and hitch equipment, conventional travel trailers will handle properly and are safe.

The problem that can occur with travel trailers is a phenomenon called sway, technically known as yaw, which does not occur with fifth-wheel trailers. Sway is a fishtailing (sideways see-saw) action of the trailer caused by external forces that set the trailer's mass into lateral motion with the trailer's wheels serving as the axis or pivot point (Figure 6.2). All conventionally hitched travel trailers will sway slightly in response to crosswinds or the bow wave of an 18-wheeler overtaking from the rear. The good ones will need little correction by the driver and will quickly restabilize. Only poorly designed trailers will continue to sway after the force that caused the instability has ceased. In fact, the sway motion of a poorly balanced trailer may increase until control is lost.

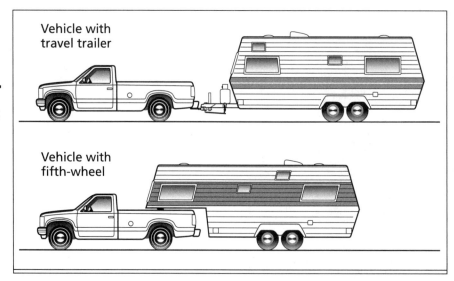

Figure 6.1
Travel trailers are subject to sway, which can be controlled, while fifth-wheel trailers are not.

Vehicle with travel trailer

Vehicle with fifth-wheel

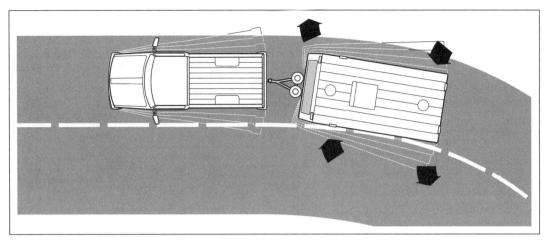

Figure 6.2
Lateral movement of a travel trailer exerts steering influence on the tow vehicle.

There are several ways to evaluate the potential of a travel trailer to sway and to correct the problem if it occurs.

STABILITY CHECKUP

A trailer's inherent stability is part of its design, based on the amount of weight in front of the axles versus the amount of weight behind. A weight-forward bias results in hitch weight (Figure 6.3) and is necessary for control. Trailers with insufficient hitch weight have two deficiencies:

1. The weight mass behind the axle(s) is too high; when set in motion it acts as a pendulum, and sway oscillations tend to increase until control is lost.

2. The distance between the hitch ball and the trailer axles is insufficient to give the tow vehicle steering leverage over the trailer.

Elementary physics helps explain why distance between the hitch ball and axles is important. We all know that we can use a board (lever) positioned on a rock (fulcrum) to move another rock that is too heavy for us to lift without assistance. The lever gives us a mechanical advantage (leverage) on the rock. Likewise, trailers that have considerably more length in front of their axle(s) than in the rear give tow vehicles a mechanical advantage: the tow vehicle has a long lever with which to steer the trailer. This balance question is dealt with in terms of pounds of hitch weight.

Simply stated, trailers with a high proportion of hitch weight to gross weight usually

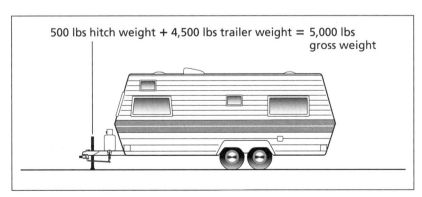

500 lbs hitch weight + 4,500 lbs trailer weight = 5,000 lbs gross weight

Figure 6.3
Proper travel trailer handling depends on balance, indicated by the proportion between hitch weight and gross weight.

Figure 6.4
The best emergency measure for control of sway is activation of the trailer brakes via the lever on the controller.

have more of their length ahead of the axles, and they handle better. The generally accepted industry standard is that hitch weight should be approximately 10 percent of gross weight. In fact, that is a bare minimum, and some trailers with 10 percent hitch weight don't handle well. Hitch weights of 12 percent or higher (up to the weight limit of the hitch being used) assure proper handling.

In marginal hitch-weight situations, the owner's ability to handle an unstable trailer will depend on the inherent stability of the tow vehicle, which is another variable. A truck or van with long wheelbase, relatively short rear overhang, and stiff springs will at least partially make up for a trailer's lack of inherent stability. But if the trailer is towed by a softly sprung truck or van or a passenger car, the trailer's shortcomings will be more obvious.

A brief driving test on a section of straight road with no other traffic in sight will give you an assessment of your trailer's inherent stability. The trial should be conducted with the tow vehicle and trailer loaded normally for travel. Make sure the refrigerator door is secured and that the contents of cabinets will not be dislodged. If you have a friction-type sway-control device, set the adjusting lever so the device is not operational. A sway-control device is a valuable asset and should be employed, but for the purposes of this test, it

should be disconnected so it does not camouflage inherent trailer instability.

For this trial, trailer brakes should be working effectively, and the manual control lever on the brake controller should be within easy reach of the driver (Figure 6.4). If your brake controller does not have a lever that allows you to actuate trailer brakes independently of tow-vehicle brakes, it's important that you change to a controller that does. *Independent use of trailer brakes is the single most effective countermeasure to reduce or eliminate trailer sway.*

Begin the test at about twenty miles per hour and crank the steering wheel sharply to the left, simulating an attempt to avoid an obstacle in the road. Note the reaction of the trailer. Repeat the experiment while increasing speed, but take care not to overdo it. Practice actuating the trailer brakes independently of the tow-vehicle brakes so you can do it almost instinctively. As speeds increase, the trailer will sway more dramatically. With each trial, note the severity of trailer sway and how many oscillations occur before the trailer restabilizes. Again, take care not to exceed the limits of your tow vehicle and trailer.

The most pronounced sway oscillations should be the ones produced by your sharp steering input; subsequent oscillations should diminish rapidly. If the second and third sway oscillations are equally as severe or worse than

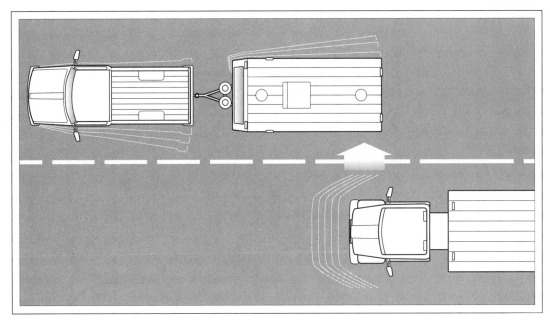

Figure 6.5
The bow wave of a truck overtaking from the rear may require defensive steering.

the first, the trailer is unstable (or marginally stable at best) and needs correction. Don't be lulled into complacency by the fact that the trailer handles much better when your sway-control device is in use. Sure it does! But an emergency maneuver may overcome the effect of the sway-control unit and result in an accident.

HOW A TRAILER SHOULD HANDLE

Many trailerists become accustomed to being uncomfortable or even frightened by sway when they encounter strong crosswinds, trucks overtaking them from the rear, or mountainous roads. They think it's normal—the way all trailers handle. Not so! Properly designed, well-matched tow vehicles and trailers have positive control and good road manners. Certainly, strong crosswinds may tend to push the tow vehicle/trailer combination laterally, and it may end up partially in the next lane if the driver isn't paying close attention. But the rig should be sufficiently controllable so that the driver can use corrective steering without being intimidated by sway. Likewise, it should be possible to drive a mountain road at brisk speeds while being able to keep the tow vehicle in the proper position on curves.

Speeding 18-wheelers present hazards to travel trailers that don't handle well, particularly while descending mountain grades. A tow vehicle/trailer rig is most susceptible to destabilizing forces while descending a grade at highway speeds, and such conditions are the true test of inherent stability.

It's natural for the bow wave (air pressure) of a speeding 18-wheeler to have an effect on a tow vehicle and trailer (Figure 6.5), requiring steering correction. But the effect should not be sufficient destabilization that driving is uncomfortable or scary. A properly balanced rig will not handle that way, although it will always be necessary to monitor one's rear-view mirror and anticipate the effects of an 18-wheeler overtaking from the rear. Drivers of all kinds of high-profile vehicles must do this; drivers of marginally stable vehicles who are caught napping usually are the ones who get into trouble because they tend to overreact to the effects of destabilizing wind forces. Even a marginally stable rig, steered deftly, can maintain stability if speed is not too high.

Table 6.1

Marginally acceptable hitch weight
Trailer (gross) 5,400
Hitch 620
Hitch (percentage) 620/5,400 = 11% (approximate)

Table 6.2

Unacceptable hitch weight
Trailer (gross) 6,200
Hitch 550
Hitch (percentage) 550/6,200 = 9% (approximate)

EVALUATING THE TRAILER AND HITCH

Even if your road trial produced good results, it's wise to check your trailer's weight and balance. The first step in evaluating a trailer for correction of stability is a trip to the scales (see Chapter 5 for the proper weighing procedure). If your hitch-weight percentage is down around 10 percent (or less), it can explain a trailer's unstable behavior. If hitch weight is 11 to 13 percent, towing stability still could be a problem if the tow vehicle is marginally stable. If hitch weight is 12 to 15 percent, the trailer should handle well and not be the cause of an instability problem. Exceptions are trailers that have high weight masses, such as the water tank in the rear, serving as a pendulum and partially overcoming the relatively lengthy steering lever (distance between axles and hitch ball) that otherwise would assure good stability. Trailers with 15 to 20 percent hitch weight are even better, but it's important that the weight does not exceed the rating of the hitch, which ranges between 800 and 1,700 pounds, depending on brand and model. Hitch ratings are stamped on hitch receivers.

In Table 6.1, hitch weight is marginal but acceptable. This trailer should handle well behind a truck or van with a long wheelbase but may not be ideal behind a short-wheelbase sport utility vehicle.

Table 6.2 illustrates a trailer that clearly has insufficient hitch weight and is undoubtedly prone to sway.

Figure 6.6
A friction-sway-control unit is essential for the best possible trailer handling.

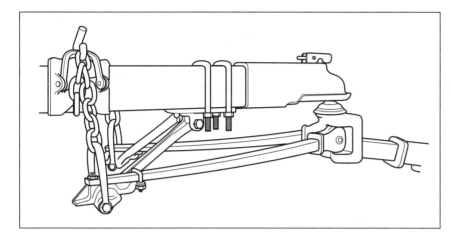

Figure 6.7
Reese Dual-Cam Sway Control utilizes friction between cams and brackets at the ends of spring bars.

The only solution is to move weight forward. This may be accomplished by relocating supplies or a rear-mounted spare tire. The worst place for a tire, or anything else that is relatively heavy, is on the back of the trailer. Carry it in the tow vehicle. Another possibility is the battery; if carried in the rear, it could be relocated to the trailer A-frame. The freshwater tank should not be located behind the trailer axles. This does occur, however, and when designers have properly compensated by assuring that hitch weight is adequate when the water tank is full, the trailer may handle reasonably well. If hitch weight is inadequate, a rear water tank may be replaced by one of a different shape that will fit under a sofa in the forward section of the trailer; the positive effect on stability will be dramatic. Ideally, the water tank should be located over the axles, so its varying content does not affect hitch weight. Of course, it's wise to empty holding tanks before traveling to minimize weight in the rear.

Assuming hitch weight is raised to at least 12 percent, the use of an effective sway control should give the trailer reasonably good road manners. Two types of sway controls are available: friction-type controls from Reese and Eaz-Lift (Figure 6.6) and the Reese Dual Cam Sway Control (Figure 6.7). Both are effective, but since the Reese Dual Cam depends on adequate hitch weight for its effectiveness, it's most suitable to trailers with moderate to high hitch weights. Proper adjustment of the friction cams of the Dual Cam system also is very

important for best stability. When it's not possible to achieve adequate hitch weight through relocation of supplies or appliances, two friction-type sway controls may be used as a stopgap measure.

PROPER HITCH ADJUSTMENT

Yet another important factor in tow vehicle/trailer stability is proper adjustment of a conventional load-distributing hitch. Proper adjustment means that the trailer is level and that the tow vehicle remains in the same attitude as before hitching. For example, if the tow vehicle was canted up at the rear before hitching (typical of pickup trucks), it should remain at that angle after hitching. The concept of a properly operating load-distributing hitch is that it should distribute hitch weight to all axles of the tow vehicle and trailer (Figure 6.8). To make certain this happens, follow these steps:

1. Measure the vehicle at reference points on front and rear bumpers with the vehicle loaded for travel but prior to hitching (Figure 6.9).

2. Hitch the trailer and adjust the spring-bar tension so weight appears to have been added to the front as well as the rear of the tow vehicle.

3. Remeasure the front and rear reference points. If, for example, the rear of the

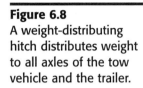

Figure 6.8
A weight-distributing
hitch distributes weight
to all axles of the tow
vehicle and the trailer.

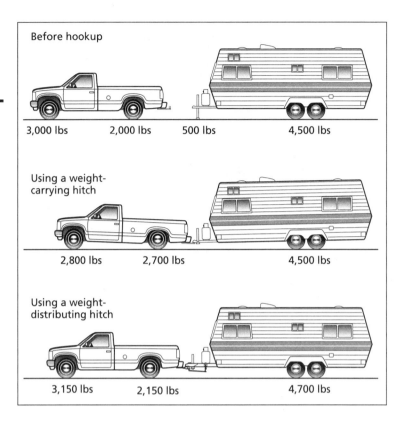

Before hookup

3,000 lbs   2,000 lbs   500 lbs   4,500 lbs

Using a weight-
carrying hitch

2,800 lbs   2,700 lbs   4,500 lbs

Using a weight-
distributing hitch

3,150 lbs   2,150 lbs   4,700 lbs

vehicle has dropped 1 inch and the front has only dropped ¼-inch, add more tension to the spring bars, which will raise the rear and lower the front. Continue adjusting until the measurements are approximately the same. If a discrepancy is unavoidable, the rear of the vehicle should drop slightly more than the front.

If the spring bars cannot be adjusted tight enough to achieve similar or identical vehicle-height reduction, stiffer spring bars may be needed. The spring bars should be rated for at least the amount of the hitch weight of the trailer, plus about 200 pounds if the tow vehicle is softly sprung. If, after proper adjustment of the tow-vehicle attitude is achieved the trailer is not level, the ball mount should be raised or lowered. Adjustable ball mounts per-

Figure 6.9
Proper adjustment of
spring-bar tension is
based on measurements at front and
rear of tow vehicle.

Figure 6.10
The unique PullRite hitch pivots under the vehicle, preventing trailer sway.

mit ball-height adjustment. If the ball mount is welded to the shank, replace it with an adjustable ball mount, available at most RV supply stores.

SWAY-CONTROL ADJUSTMENT

A sway control should be used, no matter how good trailer stability appears to be. The sway control dampens or slows the pivoting motion of the trailer coupler on the ball and is valuable during emergency maneuvers to counteract driver steering overreaction, not to mention its role in helping the tow vehicle and trailer to act in concert with each other.

With a friction-bar sway control, tighten the control until you notice that the tow vehicle doesn't quite straighten out after completing a sharp turn at slow speeds. Loosen the control a bit, to the point you feel comfortable. With the Reese Dual Cam Sway Control, the adjustment procedure involves driving straight forward very slowly while aiming the vehicle at a fixed object. Thus, with the tow vehicle and trailer in near-perfect longitudinal alignment, the sway-control brackets are centered over the friction cams. If the brackets aren't centered, loosen the hold-down bolts and move the cams forward or aft as necessary.

THE PULLRITE HITCH

Control of sway is available in several forms, and one of the most effective devices is a very unconventional hitch called the PullRite (Figure 6.10). The unique feature of this hitch is that it relocates the tow vehicle/trailer pivot point from its usual location behind the bumper to a point immediately behind the rear axle. The trailer no longer pivots on the hitch ball, so it's necessary to visualize the trailer A-frame having been extended about 5 feet underneath the tow vehicle to the pivot point. With the trailer, in effect, lengthened, a certain amount of maneuverability is sacrificed. The PullRite also functions as a load-distributing (equalizing) hitch.

The PullRite has a dramatic effect on towing stability. Even a basically unstable trailer is cured of its bad road manners. The principle is similar to that of fifth-wheel hitching, although the applications differ widely. The fifth-wheel hitch pin normally is positioned a couple of inches ahead of the rear-axle center line, topside in the bed of the truck, while the PullRite pivot point is underneath the vehicle, a few inches to the rear of the axle housing. Results are similar; on the road, directional control of the tow vehicle is not significantly affected by the steering forces of a marginally stable trailer.

The PullRite also differs from conventional load-distributing hitches in the amount of hardware installed under the tow vehicle. The PullRite utilizes a long draw bar and a radius bar, adding about 60 pounds beyond the weight of a conventional hitch receiver. The draw bar extends 11 inches behind the vehicle's bumper when the bar is straight to the rear. It can be swung out of the way when the hitch is not in use and locked in a stored position at the right rear corner of the unit.

While making turns, the PullRite causes the trailer to follow the tow vehicle farther toward the inside of the turn, similar to the way a fifth-wheel trailer behaves. This requires some relearning by the driver to keep from towing the trailer over curbs and into obstacles.

THE HENSLEY ARROW

Another very effective stabilizing trailer hitch is the Hensley Arrow (Figure 6.11). It's a fairly complex system, part of which replaces the conventional hitch-ball mount; the remainder of the system is attached to the trailer coupler and A-frame.

The system uses linkages to, in effect, make a virtually solid linkup between tow vehicle and trailer while traveling in a straight course. The hitch functions as if all of the normal pivoting action of the coupler on the ball is gone—making the tow vehicle and trailer function as though they are linked solidly. Thus, any tendency of the trailer to sway is not applied as steering force on the tow vehicle. But amazingly, when the driver wants to turn, the linkages permit a normal turn. The result is a system that eliminates trailer sway.

The Hensley system consists of many components but is suitable for installation by the owner. Once the system is installed, hitching is simplified. All the components stay with the trailer when the tow vehicle is unhitched. Rehitching involves backing the tow vehicle's hitch receiver onto the hitch bar shank, which requires practice before it becomes routine.

EVALUATING THE TOW VEHICLE

Tow vehicles come in all shapes and sizes and with varying inherent stability for trailer towing. Factors that affect stability include wheelbase length, rear overhang, steering characteristics, and center of gravity. The most significant factor is the proportion between the wheelbase and rear overhang (Figure 6.12). A longer wheelbase makes a vehicle respond more slowly to steering input. A short rear overhang gives the trailer less mechanical advantage over the tow vehicle. The combination of the two—long wheelbase and short rear overhang—provides the greatest stability. These two proportions are usually best in vans.

Figure 6.11
The Hensley Arrow locks the tow vehicle and trailer in a straight-ahead position; any tendency of the trailer to sway is not applied as steering force on the tow vehicle.

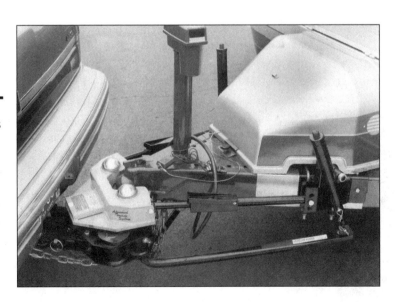

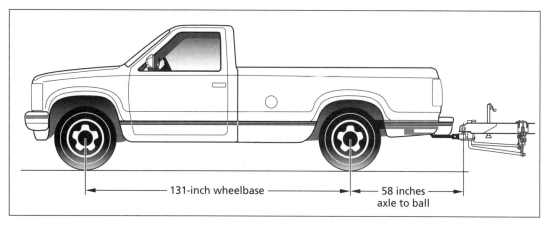

131-inch wheelbase ———————— 58 inches
axle to ball

Figure 6.12
The long wheelbase and short rear overhang provide excellent resistance to trailer instability.

Typically, older short-wheelbase sport utility vehicles are not as stable as are vans, trucks, and Suburbans built by the same manufacturers. Late-model versions such as the Ford Expedition and GM Tahoe/Yukon with longer wheelbases and much more sophisticated suspensions, are excellent tow vehicles. In particular, the Ford Expedition has a very good proportion between wheelbase and rear overhang.

If sway tends to be a problem even though the trailer has a good proportion of hitch weight versus gross weight and hitching is proper, it may be necessary to raise the trailer's hitch-weight proportion still higher. The sway-control device being utilized should be very effective. If a Reese Strait-Line is used with a trailer that has less than 12 to 15 percent hitch weight, it may be necessary to add a friction-type sway control and use both sway-control devices.

For the tow vehicle itself, use the air pressure (molded on tire sidewalls) in rear tires to stiffen their sidewalls; use the vehicle manufacturer's recommended pressure in front. Use good-quality gas-pressure shock absorbers, which tend to keep the vehicle in better control on unlevel road surfaces. If the vehicle responds too quickly to steering input, have an alignment shop set the front end to the manufacturer's maximum positive caster setting. Additional caster tends to reduce steering response. A friction-type sway control adjusted to a stiff setting is especially important for

comfortable towing with four-wheel-drive sport utility vehicles.

CORRECTIVE DRIVING TECHNIQUES

The best defense against sway is a good offense-correction of weight distribution, proper hitching, and use of a good sway control. If stability still occasionally becomes marginal under exceptionally bad driving conditions, the driver must compensate by reducing speed, which will slow the reaction of the vehicle to external forces and allow you more time to react.

When sway occurs, by far the best technique for counteracting it is independent actuation of trailer brakes, even though it requires removing one hand from the steering wheel. In an emergency situation, this may require good self-control. But the driver who is vigilant about monitoring driving conditions and the scene in his rear-view mirror will anticipate a destabilizing situation and be prepared to use defensive techniques so the situation does not get out of control.

Although few hitch shops give it much thought, the location of the brake controller is a critical safety consideration. If it's positioned far under the dash and is hard to reach, relocate it to a better position, accessible to the hand you can most comfortably remove from the steering wheel—usually the left hand.

With a properly balanced rig, you probably won't need to use the manual brake-control lever. But being capable of using it is your insurance policy against loss of control in an emergency situation involving trailer sway.

If severe sway occurs, don't step on the tow-vehicle brake pedal unless you're in danger of hitting something. Just lift your foot from the accelerator pedal and apply trailer brakes sharply via the hand control. During adverse driving conditions such as severe crosswinds, reduce speed and anticipate terrain that can produce sharp wind blasts. Be prepared to use trailer brakes if necessary.

This discussion of defensive tactics may sound severe and discouraging to travel-trailer ownership. In fact, proper towing setup involving a travel trailer can be just as enjoyable as towing a fifth-wheel with few, if any, anxious moments. But it does require proper attention paid to tow vehicle suitability, trailer balance, and correct hitching combined with a knowledge of defensive measures.

FIFTH-WHEEL TOWING

Directional stability with fifth-wheel trailers is usually so good that it's hardly worth discussing. Only in cases where the fifth-wheel hitch pin is located behind the center line of the truck's rear axle does stability become a factor, and even then it's rarely a problem.

Safety factors that definitely are worth discussing include secure attachment of the hitch, proper attention while hitching, assuring the pin is securely locked in the coupler, proper tire pressures, and proper tire/wheel compatibility.

Fifth-wheel hitches should be bolted through the truck bed to the truck frame for rigidity. If there is any doubt about your installation, contact the manufacturer of your hitch and ask for installation instructions.

Maintenance of proper tire pressures is important with any vehicle, but especially for large trailers. Low tire pressures, even for just a few hours, can cause insidious damage that can lead to a blowout later, when the low-pressure incident is long forgotten and there appears to be no explanation for the tire failure. Also, especially with the larger fifth-wheel trailers, wheel suitability may be questionable. This is particularly the case with styled wheels, many of which are rated for 2,000 to 2,200 pounds each and 40 psi maximum pressure, whereas the tire may be rated for considerably more weight as well as pressure.

FREEWAY HOP

A bouncing, jerking motion commonly known as freeway hop occurs in some trailer rigs enough to become uncomfortable. The problem is very difficult to solve, even though it has existed for many years. It's caused by poor highway design—unfortunate spacing of the seams in the concrete (typically, 15-foot sections) so they set up a rhythmic bounce that reverberates throughout the tow vehicle and trailer (Figure 6.13). Whether or not it happens—and to what severity—depends on the spacing of tow vehicle and trailer axles and how they strike the pavement seams.

Theoretically, changing the distance between tow vehicle and trailer axles should have an effect. However, the amount of that effect is impossible to predict. The simple way to change this distance is to extend the ball 3 to 4 inches farther behind the bumper. This can be done by changing to a longer hitch bar. The downside of this is that extension of the hitch can adversely affect towing stability.

Short of the hitch length change, good shocks and 1,000-pound hitch spring bars are recommended. Another change that improves some rigs and not others is the addition of shock absorbers to the trailer (assuming it does not already have them). Check with the manufacturer of your trailer chassis to see if a shock-absorber-parts kit is available.

Changing to better shock absorbers for the tow vehicle, although of benefit for overall vehicle handling, does not appear to solve the bounce problem.

EQUIPMENT MAINTENANCE

Maintenance procedures for tow-vehicle chassis usually are very clearly defined in owners'

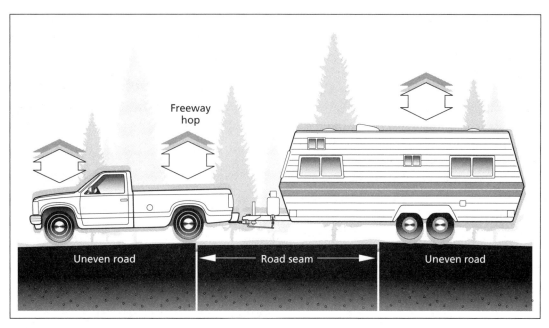

Figure 6.13
Improper freeway design can cause rhythmic bouncing of the tow vehicle and trailer.

manuals. In contrast, few trailer manufacturers offer advice on chassis maintenance.

In fact, very little is necessary, except for trailer brakes and bearings, which should be checked once a year, prior to the travel season, or more often if the trailer is towed long distances in mountainous terrain. Electric-brake components may wear rapidly under such conditions, and hubs should be removed to check the condition of the magnets, armature, and brake shoes. Wheel bearings should be repacked and grease seals should be changed when such inspections are performed.

However, regular inspection is necessary because trailer springs and particularly shackles—the brackets that attach the springs to the trailer axles and frame—are subject to wear. Make it a point to regularly inspect the shackles as well as the bolts used to secure them. Since shackles often become elongated, check them at the bolt holes and replace any that have elongated holes. Also check for spring wear and breakage. If a trip over exceptionally rough roads is planned, buy a couple of spring leaves for use in emergencies. When replacing spring shackles, use a replacement kit made by Dexter Axle Company that includes grease fittings, which extend repair intervals.

By evaluating trailer stability and taking the proper steps to assure better handling, towing travel trailers can be much more enjoyable.

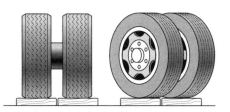

Chapter 7

TAKING CARE OF TIRES

Tires may be the weakest link in the RV owner's ultimate quest, which is to travel trouble-free. It's not that tires, per se, are unreliable. The problem is that their owners don't pay enough attention to two important items: inflation pressure and load. And, often, they're handicapped at the outset by the RV manufacturer, who may not have built in enough weight capacity for supplies and passengers.

Underinflation and overloading are far more common than neglect of other important vehicle items such as engine oil, transmission oil, and coolant. Even owners who usually are very thorough in their maintenance procedures, covering all items including inflation pressure, may not know how much weight their tires are carrying.

Thus, tire maintenance deserves every RV owner's specific attention. Important tire and tire-related chassis points include:

- Regular monitoring of inflation pressure

- Evaluation of tire loading

- Regular tire rotation

- Periodic wheel alignment

- Good shock absorbers

Beyond actual hazards, proper maintenance can dramatically affect tire life. The combination of improper inflation and infrequent tire rotation greatly reduces tire life. This chapter will deal with these factors as well as tire design, radials versus bias-ply, wheel suitability, mixing of tires, and matching of dual rear tires.

LOAD VERSUS INFLATION PRESSURE

A tire can be inflated properly only if it is not overloaded, so it is impossible to discuss one topic without the other. Simplified maintenance of inflation pressure merely requires that the tire owner read the numbers on the tire sidewall (Figure 7.1) and make sure the tires are continually maintained at the prescribed level. Beyond the basics, tire loading should be considered in order to assure best possible wear rates and traction.

One of the first steps is to recognize that passenger-car tires and light-truck tires are dif-

Figure 7.1
The essential information for proper tire loading and maintenance is molded on the sidewall.

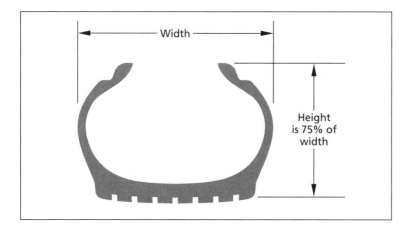

Figure 7.2
Height is 75 percent of width in a tire that has an aspect ratio of 75.

ferent. When passenger-car tires are used on light trucks (only on the lesser-rated models), they are still regarded as passenger-car tires. Trailer tires are labeled ST (special trailer) and may be in either the car or light-truck category for load and inflation, according to specifications published by the Tire and Rim Association. These specifications are used by all tire manufacturers (with minor exceptions) for the purpose of creating commonality of load ratings and inflation pressures among various brands. In the case of ST tires, the size designation identifies the category—automobile or light truck—to which the tire belongs.

Passenger-Car Tires

Most present-day car tires are designated with the letter P in front of a set of numbers (for example, P225/75R15), known as the P-metric system. The alphanumeric system preceded the P-metric system, and few tires are still manufactured under the alphanumeric system.

How to Read a P-Metric Tire

Using the following example, the elements of a P-metric tire become clear:

Example: **P225/75R15**
  P = passenger-car tire
  225 = cross-section width in millimeters
  75 = aspect ratio
  R = radial
  15 = rim diameter in inches

The aspect ratio is the proportion of a tire's cross-section height (from the tread to the bead seat) compared to the cross-section width (side to side). The height is 75 percent of the width of a tire that has an aspect ratio of 75 (Figure 7.2).

How to Read an Alphanumeric Tire

Example: **GR78-15**
  G = load capacity
  R = radial
  78 = aspect ratio
  15 = rim diameter in inches

Inflation pressures molded on the sidewalls of all passenger-car tires are the ***maximum pressures for the maximum loads listed on the tire, and should not be exceeded.*** For example, the P225/75R15 is rated for 1,874 pounds maximum load at 35 psi, cold. Pressure should not exceed 35 psi, cold, under any circumstances because the tire was not designed for higher pressures. Inflation maximums for passenger-car tires are:

- Standard Load (SL), 35 psi

- Extra Load (XL), 41 psi

The pressure ratings are intended for use when the tires are cold; the ratings assume that higher pressures will occur while traveling due to heat buildup, and the pressure increase should not be bled off.

When a car or light truck equipped with passenger-car tires is used to tow a trailer, it's best to inflate all tires to the maximums shown on their sidewalls, which will produce the best possible towing stability.

When passenger-car tires are used on light trucks and trailers, the Tire and Rim Association recommends that load ratings be downrated to 91 percent. For example, if the tire must carry a 1,600-pound load, a tire rated for a maximum of 1,760 pounds (or thereabouts) is needed. Maximum inflation pressures shown on the tire sidewalls still apply.

Special-trailer (ST) tires that have passenger-car size designations are of the same design, except that special rubber compounds are used to reduce deterioration caused by sunlight and ozone.

Light-Truck Tires

Light-truck (LT) tires may have either the traditional numeric (for example, 7.50-16LT) or metric (LT235/75R15) identification. A typical motorhome tire would carry truck designation (LT225/70R19.5).

How to Read a Metric Light-Truck Tire

Use the following two examples to read a metric light-truck tire and a standard light-truck tire.

Example: **LT235/75R16**
LT = light-truck tire
235 = cross-section width in millimeters
75 = aspect ratio
R = radial
16 = rim diameter in inches

How to Read a Standard Light-Truck Tire

Example: **7.50R16LT**
7.50 = cross-section width in inches
R = radial
16 = rim diameter in inches
LT = light truck

Flotation Tires

Flotation-type tires have their own special category under the light-truck classification, and they're distinguished by a set of numbers beginning with the tire's overall diameter in inches.

How to Read a Flotation-Type Tire

Example: **31x11.50R15LT**
31 = overall diameter in inches
11.50 = cross-section width in inches
R = radial
15 = rim diameter in inches
LT = light-truck tire

It seems logical that a partially loaded tire should be inflated only partially. The tire manufacturers publish load and inflation tables that indicate the correct inflation pressure for a given tire load (see Appendix A). This is important on light trucks and motorhomes where tire loading can differ considerably from one vehicle to another.

Different Tire Ratings

Unlike passenger car tires where the maximum inflation pressure shown on the sidewall should never be exceeded, the pressure marked on the sidewall of a light truck or motorhome tire is the *minimum pressure for the maximum load* and can be increased by 10 psi providing that the maximum inflation rating of the rim is not exceeded. The 10-psi "bonus" pressure does not increase the load-carrying capacity of the tire.

The 10 psi recommendation also applies to bias-ply tires, but additional pressure beyond the minimum for the specific load may lead to accelerated wear in the center of the tread.

The additional 10 psi above minimum-rated pressures for specific loads for light-truck tires stiffens the tire sidewall slightly, which may improve vehicle handling without a tendency to wear out the center of the tread of a radial tire. More important, it's insurance against underinflation that can occur from the slight pressure loss that gradually occurs with all tires—loss that should be detected and corrected with frequent pressure checking but often is not.

Manufacturers of light trucks typically recommend specific pressures for the maximum load the truck is designed to carry. The ratings usually are listed in identification plates attached to the driver's side-door frame. However, light trucks usually are driven empty much of the time, and the actual load being carried by the truck is dramatically lower than the maximum load rating of the tire. Using maximum inflation when the tire is loaded far below its maximum degrades ride quality, lowers impact resistance, and reduces the size of the tire footprint. It usually will also cause accelerated wear in the center of the tread, although radial tires are minimally affected compared with bias-ply tires. Using the graduated load-inflation tables will allow you to inflate specifically to your load.

For example, an LT245/75R16 tire in D-load range is rated for 2,623 pounds load (single) at a minimum of 65 psi. In a typical situation with a pickup truck used occasionally to tow a trailer, the tire may actually be carrying about 1,200 pounds at the rear while the truck is empty. The minimum inflation pressure listed for this tire is 35 psi, rating the tire for 1,500 pounds of load.

Front tires of this same truck may be loaded to about 1,500 pounds. Adding the recommended 10 psi as a safety margin brings the appropriate inflation pressure to 45 psi for front and rear.

If a load of firewood is added to this truck while it also tows a trailer, the load on the rear tires might increase to 2,000 pounds per tire. Minimum inflation pressure for 2,000 pounds per tire is 45 psi; adding 10 psi brings the recommended pressure to 55 psi. If the tires were loaded to their maximums, correct pressure would be 75 psi, established by adding 10 psi to the 65 psi cold-inflation pressure rating appearing on the tire's sidewall.

Motorhome weights do not fluctuate widely and are usually high enough that the recommended tire pressure shown on the sidewall can be presumed appropriate if accurate weight figures are not available for the loaded motorhome. The exception may be front tires, especially on mini motorhomes. Thus, it's necessary to weigh the vehicle to determine correct tire pressures for the actual load.

Michelin's Numbers

The load and inflation ratings of most Michelin tires differ from Tire and Rim Association standards. If the load is near the maximum molded onto the tire sidewall, it's best to inflate to the pressure shown there as well. If the load is less than the maximum, consult a Michelin dealer for the correct inflation pressure for the specific load and add 10 psi. Michelin will supply a copy of the company's "Recreational Vehicle Tire Guide" on request by calling (800) 847-3435.

Overloading

If a trip to the scales seems too much trouble, and the owner is prone to simply assume that inflating to the pressure listed on the tire sidewall is okay, hazards still exist because the tires may be overloaded (a common occurrence). Weighing a motorhome is a very important safety consideration (see Chapter 5). Individual wheel scales often are unavailable, but it's possible to weigh a motorhome's axles individually on a platform scale.

Again, if the motorhome's tires are loaded to their maximums, 10 psi can be added to the inflation pressure shown on the tire sidewall. The extra pressure does not increase the load-carrying capacity of the tire.

A common situation in which the additional 10 psi may be desirable is when the vehicle tends to wander. Some vehicles wander more with tires that are inflated to the minimum pressure for the actual load than when higher pressures are used. Correction of a wander problem should start by weighing the vehicle. Begin with minimum inflation pressures for the actual load and adjust pressures upward in stages (not exceeding the cold-inflation pressure molded on the tire sidewall, plus 10 psi for light-truck tires) to determine the ideal pressure for minimum vehicle wander.

Tire inflation should be checked prior to each trip, at least once a week during trips, and a visual check should be made each morning. Always check pressures when tires are cold. A visual check of tires should be included in a routine walkaround inspection that occurs every time you take a break from driving. Tires build pressure while the vehicle is moving, and the pressure increase is taken into account in the manufacturer's (cold)

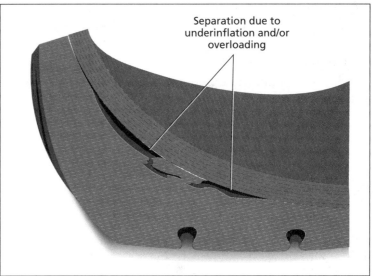

Separation due to
underinflation and/or
overloading

Figure 7.3
The result of heat
caused by underinflation
and/or overloading is
tire delamination and
failure.

inflation-pressure recommendation. Thus, if you begin the day with tires at 45 psi and find them at 50 psi later, don't reduce the pressure. When the temperature drops, the tires will return to the original 45 psi.

Finally, make sure your pressure gauge is accurate! Ask your tire dealer to verify it.

TIRE DAMAGE YOU CAN'T SEE

The significance of proper inflation and loading is not appreciated by most drivers because the results of underinflation and/or overloading often don't show up immediately. A temporarily underinflated/overloaded tire may fail long after the inadequacy has been corrected, depending on driving conditions.

Heat is a tire's worst enemy, and excessive heat is the result of underinflation/overloading, as well as the cause of tread separation (Figure 7.3). When the temperature of the tire's core compound exceeds approximately 250°F, cords lose strength; the bond is loosened between the cords and the surrounding rubber compound, making the tire more susceptible to failure. If the owner escapes a failure and is not even aware of the underinflation until later, the underinflation incident then appears to have had no consequence. To the contrary, an overheated tire does not cool to its original strength; it is permanently weak-

ened, and a blowout or tread separation probably will occur later, after the underinflation incident is long forgotten. When the tire eventually fails, the owner may blame it on manufacturing defects or poor quality when in fact the tire was damaged by negligence.

When is a tire overheated? It's not practical to measure tire temperature with a thermometer, so the primary defenses against excessive heat are proper loading and adequate inflation. The worst condition is traveling superheated highways, so it's best to avoid the heat of the day in summer, if possible.

Damage from tire overloading and/or underinflation can be readily detected by tire service personnel. Such tires often rupture in the upper sidewall area after cords break. The evidence may be ripples, bulges, soft spots, wrinkles, creases, or other signs of weakness in the sidewall.

HOW TO MAKE TIRES LAST LONGER

In addition to proper inflation and loading, routine tire rotation is important to tire longevity. Even though we attempt to maintain ideal inflation pressures to maximize a tire's footprint, it may be impossible to avoid at least limited overinflation when loads vary. Accelerated tire wear may be inevitable with bias-ply, but proper tire rotation can hold it to a minimum. Radial tires are minimally affected by overinflation.

Again, tire companies differ. At least one major truck-tire manufacturer says it's not necessary to rotate unless abnormal wear is noticed but suggests consulting the vehicle owner's manual for a rotation recommendation. Others assert tires should be rotated before improper wear characteristics are visible. The Chevrolet light truck owners manual recommends rotation every 7,000 miles, emphasizing that the first rotation is the most important. If you notice abnormal

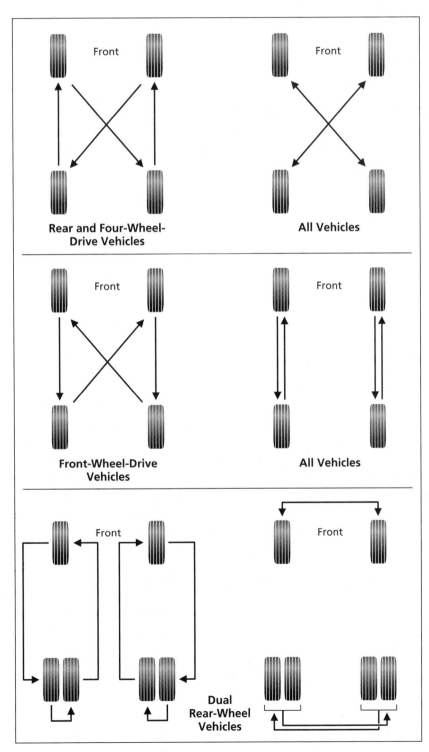

Rear and Four-Wheel-Drive Vehicles

All Vehicles

Front-Wheel-Drive Vehicles

All Vehicles

Dual Rear-Wheel Vehicles

Figure 7.4
Best possible wear depends substantially on regular tire rotation, particularly when abnormal wear patterns are evident. Tires need not remain in their original direction of rotation.

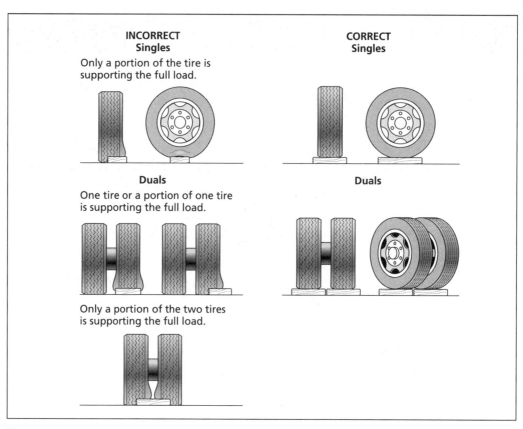

INCORRECT
Singles
Only a portion of the tire is
supporting the full load.

CORRECT
Singles

Duals
One tire or a portion of one tire
is supporting the full load.

Duals

Only a portion of the two tires
is supporting the full load.

Figure 7.5
Damage to tire cords may occur from improper blocking while leveling an RV. The entire
tire contact surface must be supported.

wear, have the alignment checked and rotate tires immediately.

If abnormal tread wear becomes noticeable, some manufacturers say it's too late for maximum tire life because a pattern of uneven wear, once established, may be impossible to reverse.

The cost of rotating tires varies with the type of vehicle and can be somewhat expensive for motorhomes. Owners who are reluctant to rotate tires regularly should inspect them closely, and measure tread depths with a gauge (available in auto-supply stores).

When rotation is deemed necessary, use the pattern recommended by the manufacturer of your vehicle, or use one of the patterns featured in Figure 7.4. The original rolling direction of tires does not need to be maintained unless tread design dictates a specific direction! The rolling direction can be reversed by moving the tire to the opposite side of the vehicle (as indicated), except when using mud/snow tires that are clearly designed for best traction in a specific rolling direction.

Use of Blocks

Also important to tire life is proper use of blocks while leveling. The entire footprint of the tire should be supported by blocks, with no tread hanging over the sides, which exerts excessive stress on the tire cords (Figure 7.5).

Summarizing, the keys to extended tire life are:

- Proper inflation for the specific load

- Proper loading

- Proper tire rotation

- Proper wheel alignment and use of effective shock absorbers.

Some Causes of Improper Tire Wear

Some causes of improper tire wear may be apparent, while others are more difficult to diagnose.

- ■ Irregular wear (also called heel/toe wear): Tread blocks wear more on one end (longitudinally) than the other. This wear pattern may indicate worn suspension parts, but in many flotation and mud/snow treads it's a characteristic of the tire design. Rotate frequently to keep adverse wear patterns from becoming severe.

- ■ Improper camber: One shoulder of front tire will wear more quickly than the other.

- ■ Excessive toe-in/toe-out: Rapid, uneven wear on front tires, often feathering the edges of tread serrations.

- ■ Overinflation: Center of tread will wear more quickly than shoulders (primarily with bias-ply tires).

- ■ Underinflation: Shoulders will wear faster than center of tread, and tread may tend to ripple.

Tire Composition

Tires vary widely in design as well as materials. We usually think of tires as made of rubber, but in fact natural rubber is a relatively minor ingredient. The basic building blocks of the rubber compound are polymers, combinations of natural rubber and two types of synthetic rubber. These combinations vary with the intended use. Another important building block is carbon black, a reinforcing material that provides strength in the rubber compounds. Actually glorified soot, its use in conjunction with rubber provides the matrix structure that gives strength. Then there are oils, used as softeners to provide traction within the compound. A high-performance tire will have more oils, helping the tire conform to the road.

Next, sulfur is used as a cross-linking agent or network to keep the carbon black and rubber together for strength and flexibility.

Accelerators control the rate of cure of the rubber compound. Finally, antioxidants and antiozonants are used for protection.

Radial-ply tires dominate the market today with a few bias-ply tires still available for trailers. The radials are available with steel belts or a combination of fabric and steel. Tires with all-steel belts are preferred in the trucking industry for their performance as well as retreadability.

CHOOSING REPLACEMENT TIRES

When choosing replacement tires for a vehicle, the replacements can usually duplicate the original tire size and type if the original tires have provided good service. Exceptions include overload situations.

If a tire has worn abnormally fast, with accelerated wear on the shoulders of the tread, the tire probably has been overloaded and/or underinflated. The vehicle should be weighed (loaded) before purchasing new tires to make sure the tire-load capacity is adequate. Don't rely on the vehicle's load ratings for tire selection because an overloaded vehicle may exceed the load ratings of either or both axles. Weighing the vehicle by axle or preferably by each wheel is very important when abnormal tire wear suggests overloading has occurred.

If failures have occurred and a trip to the scales indicates an overload, selection of tires with higher load ratings may be appropriate. However, be aware that tire overloading usually is a reliable indicator that other chassis components are overloaded as well and that weight is beyond the unit's GVWR. Use of higher-rated tires will not prevent accelerated wear and/or failure of other components, including wheels. The load and inflation pressure ratings of larger tires may exceed the load and inflation pressure ratings of the wheels. Check with a tire dealer regarding tire/wheel load and inflation pressure matching.

Unfortunately there are few reliable ways to compare truck, light truck, and trailer tire quality other than by the manufacturer's reputation, although speed and wear parameters are available for passenger-car tires. Tires that look the same are not necessarily the same because the quality of the materials—particularly the rubber compound—can vary widely. Poor-quality tires shed tread material rapidly, while those of good quality have high resistance to tread wear. All-purpose and mud/snow tires generally wear faster than tires with highway tread. Tire compounding is a compromise aimed at providing the optimum mixture of performance characteristics for the intended use.

Passenger Tire Designations

Passenger tires display government-mandated grades for quality and speed. The speed-rating system uses letters, commonly S (112 mph) and V (above 130 mph) in combination with load index numbers that indicate the capacity of the tire. Example: Reference numbers 97S following the size designation mean the tire's

maximum load is 1,609 pounds and its speed rating is 112 mph. The tire also will carry specific maximum load and inflation ratings.

Treadwear ratings vary from 60 to 500, with higher numbers indicating higher tread durability. Traction grades range from A to C, with A being the highest grade available. Temperature grades range from A to C, again with A being highest, indicating a tire's ability to dissipate heat.

Trailer Tires

When choosing trailer tires, any of three types (car, light truck, or special trailer) can be used, providing the load range is adequate for the weight, and the wheels are suitable. Special Trailer (ST) tires are compounded for extra resistance to deterioration (cracking) from the effects of the sun and ozone in the air and are preferred because most RV owners take several years to wear out a set of tires. In addition, trailer tires usually fit into the Extra Load category, which is identified on the tire sidewall.

When using passenger tires on trailers, the Tire and Rim Association recommends reducing their load ratings by 9 percent. The reason is not that trailers inherently are harder on tires, but that they are capable of being overloaded more dramatically than are passenger cars.

Radials on Trailers

Most trailers are fitted with radial tires at the factory. When replacing them, choose the same size and load rating unless abnormal tire wear or failures have occurred.

When choosing replacement tires, select load capacity high enough to ensure that the tires are not loaded to their maximums. If your trailer load requires tires with considerably higher ratings than were originally fitted, and those tires require higher inflation pressures, new wheels with higher load and inflation-pressure ratings may be necessary. Check existing wheels for inflation-pressure maximum ratings and for load maximums.

Dual-Tire Spacing

When choosing tires that are a different size from the originals for a motorhome or truck

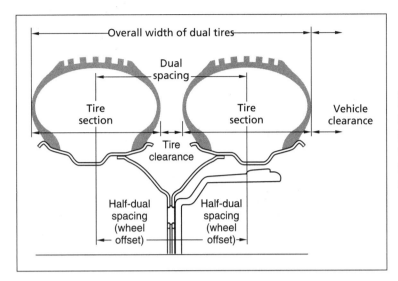

Figure 7.6
Proper spacing of dual tires is important to prevent sidewall contact, which can result in damage.

with dual rear tires, pay close attention to wheel size and to spacing of the rear tires. Dual-wheel spacing is measured from the center line of one tire to the center line of the other (Figure 7.6). Insufficient dual spacing causes the insides of the tire sidewalls to touch, which results in excessive heat and sidewall wear. In addition, rocks or debris can be trapped more easily between the tires, causing punctures. Tire chains should not be used when dual spacing is inadequate.

Tire and Wheel Matching

Tires used as sets on a dual-wheel axle must be properly matched. The tires should have the same size designation, be of the same type, and have the same or nearly the same outside diameters. Mismatched dual sets cause friction and heat because one tire is larger than the other, which causes slippage, excessive heat, and wear in both tires. Tire diameter should not vary more than ¼-inch (tires inflated equally). Diameter can be calculated by measuring circumference with a steel tape measure that conforms properly to the tire or by marking the tire and ground with chalk, driving forward, and measuring the distance between chalk marks. Divide the circumference measurement by 3.1416 to get diameter. If tires are new, wait at least twenty-four hours after initial inflation to check diameters.

When replacement tires exceed the load rating of the original tires, wheel suitability becomes an important factor. For example, original motorhome 8R19.5 load-range D tires may be due for replacement, and the owner may assume that moving up to the E-load range would offer an extra margin of safety. Unfortunately, the reverse may be true with many chassis, such as Chevrolet. The original wheels supplied with the gasoline-powered chassis having the highest GVWR were rated for 2,780 pounds maximum load and 95 psi maximum inflation pressure, suitable for 8R19.5 tires rated for 2,800 pounds at 80 psi in load-range D. When moving up to load-range E, the tire is rated for 3,170 pounds at 95 psi; in load-range F the tire is rated for 3,500 pounds at 110 psi.

The load as well as inflation limits of the 8R19.5 load-range E or F tires are beyond the load-carrying capacity of the wheel. Load-range E or F tires should not be used on wheels designed for maximum load/inflation of load-range D tires because their sidewall markings will encourage wheel overloading and overinflation.

Tire Mixing

If radial and bias-ply tires must be mixed, the radials should be used on the rear to prevent oversteer. When changing tire sizes, more than one rim width usually is specified as suitable. For example, rim widths of 5½ to 7

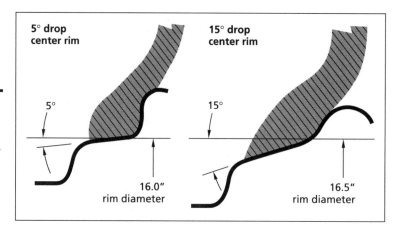

Figure 7.7
Rim contours differ for varying tire designs. Incorrect tire/rim combinations create danger.

inches may be specified for a 15-inch tire. The wider rims offer better road stability, but are more easily damaged when striking curbs or other obstacles.

Make sure replacement tires are of the correct size and contour for the rims.

Warning: It's possible to fit a 16-inch tire on a 16½-inch rim, but the tire cannot be safely inflated or used. In addition to the size error, rim contours are not correct. The 16-inch tire requires a 5-degree drop-center rim while the 16½-inch tire requires a 15-degree drop-center rim (Figure 7.7).

Calculating Effect on Performance

When purchasing replacement tires of a different size from the originals, it's wise to estimate the effect on performance. Tires that are larger in diameter than the originals will have the effect of lowering the numerical axle ratio. The opposite is true of smaller-than-original tires. A formula can be used to calculate the difference (rpm is revolutions per mile):

$$\frac{\text{Original Tire rpm}}{\text{New Tire rpm}} \times \frac{\text{Indicated}}{\text{Speed}} = \frac{\text{Actual}}{\text{Speed}}$$

The actual axle ratio does not change, but the relationship between engine rpm and road speed is altered as if the axle ratio had been changed. The reason is that the larger replacement tires will travel farther in one revolution than will the original tires. The reverse is true

for smaller tires. Speedometer error caused by a change in tire size also can be calculated:

$$\frac{\text{New Tire rpm}}{\text{Original Tire rpm}} \times \frac{\text{Original}}{\text{Axle Ratio}} = \frac{\text{Effective}}{\text{Axle Ratio}}$$

Tire rpm can be calculated from measurement of circumference. Measure the tire's circumference with a steel tape measure. Divide the circumference (inches) into 63,360 (the number of inches in a mile), and the result is approximate revolutions per mile.

A speedometer shop can recalibrate if the error created by a tire change is excessive—more than 3 or 4 mph.

Aging and Ozone Cracking

RVs normally are not driven as far each year as family or business vehicles. Thus tires last longer and are more subject to deterioration from ozone in the air and the effects of sunlight. Protectants blended into the tire compound gradually bleed to the surface of the tire to provide some protection when the vehicle is used regularly. When it is parked for long periods, as is typical of RVs, the protectants do not bleed to the surface as rapidly, and the tire is more susceptible to damage.

Surface cracks usually are not a problem. But when the cracks extend into the tire compound, durability is affected. According to Michelin North America, cracks that are ¹⁄₃₂-inch deep should not cause concern. Between ½₂ inch and ¹⁄₁₆ inch, the tire is suspect and should be examined by a tire dealer. If cracks are deeper than ¹⁄₁₆ inch the tire should be replaced.

Cracking can be retarded by exercising proper care:

- Cover the tires when the vehicle is in storage, even for a few days

- Keep tires clean

- Keep tires properly inflated

- Do not park the vehicle near electric generators or transformers, where welding is in progress, or inside a building equipped with mercury vapor lamps

- Do not use tire dressings and other products that contain petroleum distillates or alcohol

Time for Replacement

The Rubber Manufacturers Association recommends that tires on vehicles of more than 10,000 pounds gross weight be replaced when less than ⅛ inch of tread depth remains (not including tread-wear indicators). On vehicles less than 10,000 pounds gross weight, front tires should be replaced when worn to tread-wear indicators, or when ¹⁄₁₆ inch or less of tread remains. At least one major tire company recommends that tires be replaced if they are more than seven years old, regardless of the amount of tread remaining.

A tire's age can be determined by a series of letters and numbers molded on the sidewall. The series begins with "DOT." On tires made prior to the year 2000, the last digit on the right represents the last digit of the year of production, and the 1990s decade is indicated by a triangle to the right of the last digit—i.e., the numeral 9 followed by a triangle would indicate 1999. For 2000 and beyond, the triangle will not appear and four digits will appear on the right, the last two of which will indicate year of manufcture—i.e., 00 means 2000. Although it's tempting to continue using tires that have good tread depth, despite age nearing 10 years, replacement is good insurance against failure than could result in an accident.

ABOUT WHEELS

A wheel is composed of a rim and a disc. The tire is mounted on the rim and the disc is used to attach the wheel to the vehicle. The assembly will vary widely in design, depending on tire size, type, and vehicle application. Wheels are tested by their manufacturers to withstand specific maximum weights and air pressures. All wheels are rated for maximum load and inflation pressures, although the ratings are not always marked on the wheels. It may be necessary to check with the wheel manufacturer.

Errors are common in wheel selection when replacement tires are purchased, and errors are common even at the RV-factory level, especially when styled wheels are used. Many styled wheels are rated for less than 2,000 pounds. Few tire dealers pay much attention to the fact that the wheel has limits and that the tires and wheels must be compatible. It is dangerous to mount a tire rated, for example, at 3,000 pounds on a wheel rated at 2,000, although it happens often. Few wheels break, but when they do, it is with explosive force, possibly resulting in an accident.

Determining Suitability for Radials

A decision to replace bias-ply tires with radials on an older vehicle, especially a motorhome, should be preceded by an inspection of the wheels for the word radial or by a circled R stamped on the rims that will indicate suitability for use of radial tires. If the wheel does not have these markings, it may not be designed for radials, and the wheel manufacturer should be consulted regarding the wheel's rating. Few trailer wheels have these markings, although many are suitable for radials.

Wheels used on trailers may be passenger-car type, light-truck type, or they may be specifically designed for use on trailers. Late-model wheels usually are suitable for use with radial tires. Wheels on earlier trailers probably weren't specifically designed for radials, but are not typically prone to break unless tires are loaded to their maximums. When in doubt about wheel suitability, contact the wheel manufacturer for information on radial-tire use and for load and inflation-pressure ratings.

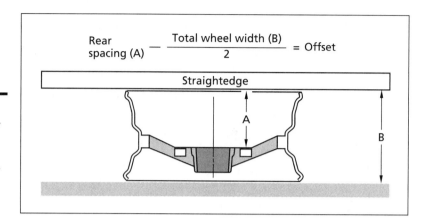

Figure 7.8
When changing wheels, measurement of offset will indicate if the new wheel has proper clearance from suspension and body components.

Wheel Dimensions

Styled replacement wheels have become very popular during the last decade, and it's helpful to know how to check dimensions before choosing replacement wheels.

When buying new wheels, make sure they are approved for the tires that will be used. Your tire dealer has additional listings. It's wise to measure wheel offset when comparing new wheels with the originals.

Offset is the difference in distance between the center line of the rim and the mounting surface (surface of the bolt pad that contacts the hub). A wheel with negative offset positions the tire farther from the vehicle's frame, widening the vehicle's track. Positive offset moves the tire inward, reducing the vehicle's track. When offset is zero, the disc is positioned in the center of the rim.

To calculate offset it's necessary to measure wheel spacing. Divide the total wheel width

(B) by 2 and subtract the result from rear spacing (A) to get offset in positive or negative (Figure 7.8). Use the same formula to calculate offset with a tire mounted on the wheel (Figure 7.9). Divide section width (D) by 2 and subtract that figure from rear spacing (C) to get offset. Figures for the wheel alone and for the wheel with a tire mounted on it are valid for comparison.

TIRE STORAGE

When the vehicle is out of service, position the vehicle's tires on a vapor barrier such as a heavy piece of plastic. Cover all tires and maintain correct inflation pressure. It is not necessary to elevate the vehicle.

Tires are a critically valuable component of any vehicle. When proper care is taken, they should provide the performance and safety of which they're capable.

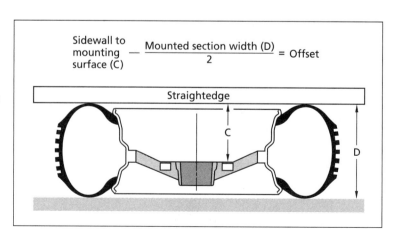

Figure 7.9
Offset can be calculated even if the tire is mounted on the wheel.

Chapter 8

THE BASICS OF RVING

Whether your RV is a small folding camping trailer or a 40-foot motorhome, it should be fun to drive and fun to use for exploring the great camping sites of North America (Figure 8.1). While the smaller rigs are fairly simple, the larger ones tend to be a little more complex—especially motorhomes—because they combine a chassis and living quarters in one vehicle. Although getting acquainted with an RV may seem intimidating at first, the systems are user friendly.

RVs vary widely in size and in complexity. The more sophisticated ones succeed in providing virtually all of the comforts of home (packed into a considerably smaller space), while the more simple RVs provide only some of those comforts. The various types of self-contained RVs have many similarities, and this chapter, aimed at the novice, will define the basic component systems, describe how they are used, and prepare the new owner for the road and for the campground.

Ideally, this chapter should serve as an addendum to a thorough owner's manual provided with the RV. If such a manual wasn't provided with yours, check to see if one is available and was inadvertently omitted. However, many manufacturers do not provide total-systems owner's manuals; they simply include the basic literature on individual appliances and accessories provided by the respective RV manufacturers.

PLUMBING

One nice aspect of most RVs is that they provide one of the more important comforts of a

Figure 8.1
RVs are suitable for use in a wide variety of camping locations, including primitive spots such as this one. Regardless of the site, good basic knowledge of the RV's systems is essential.

Figure 8.2
A regulator is necessary to prevent excess water pressure from damaging the RV water system.

home: a plumbing system. Without it, RVing wouldn't be nearly as popular as it is. Freshwater and waste systems are included, and they are relatively simple.

The freshwater system operates much like that in a house: water flows automatically when a faucet is turned on. The water may come from a tank inside the RV (filled with a hose from an outside source) or via a hose from an outside faucet in a campground. When it comes from the on-board tank, pressure is created by an automatic 12-volt DC pump. When the switch (usually located in the kitchen) is turned on, the pump automatically cycles on and off as needed to pressurize the system to 20 to 40 psi. The on-board tank is filled through an inlet on the side of the RV that is clearly marked.

Also on the side of the RV is a fitting, usually labeled "city water," that can be used to pressurize the system so the on-board pump is not needed. When outside pressure is turned off, the on-board pump automatically takes over. When the RV is not in use, be sure to turn the water pump switch to the "off" position; if the tank is dry, the pump may run continuously. When connecting a hose to the city-water hookup, turn the

faucet on briefly to fill the hose before connecting it to the RV. This will reduce the amount of air entering the system.

When the water tank is being filled, the hose is inserted in a filler spout and the faucet is turned on; care should be taken to shut off the water as soon as the tank is full. Excessive water pressure can damage the tank. Freshwater tanks in some RVs are filled via the city-water hookup. If this is the case, special valves will be used to route the water into the tank. Make sure you keep these valves in the intended position.

If the RV is new, air should be released from water lines after the tank is filled. To do this, turn on the pump and open all faucets one at a time, hot and cold, allowing water to flow until air is purged. Purge air from the cold-water line each time you reconnect to a campground faucet.

When a hose is connected to the city-water inlet to pressurize the system, a pressure regulator should be used to prevent damage to the plumbing inside the RV (Figure 8.2). Faucet pressure may be over 100 psi, while the RV system is designed for not more than 40 psi. Pressure regulators are built into the city-water inlets in many RVs. If yours has one, the hose

Figure 8.3
Most campgrounds offer 30-amp receptacles, which are preferred over the common household 15-amp receptacles.

receptacle will be recessed in a dished fixture, and the brand name (for example SHUR-flo) will be identified. If such a regulator is not present, buy a regulator designed for use between the end of your hose and the campground faucet (available at RV supply stores).

Waste Systems

The waste water (gray water) from sinks and the shower drain into one holding tank while waste from the toilet drains into another. The toilet usually drains into the smaller of the two tanks. A monitor panel typically is included with the RV to indicate content level of the water and holding tanks. In typical use situations, it takes considerably longer to fill the waste tank than the gray-water tank due to the volume of water from dishwashing and showering.

Dumping the holding tanks requires a special 4-inch hose, typically provided with the RV or available in any RV supply store (details on procedure appear later in this chapter), and should occur only at an approved dumping station or at a campsite equipped with sewer hookups. Dump stations are located at campgrounds, some service stations, and some roadside rest stops. Listings of locations for campgrounds, RV supply stores, and other services are included in the *Trailer Life Directory* published by TL

Enterprises and sold at bookstores, or available by calling (800) 766-1674.

THE ELECTRICAL SYSTEM

Almost all RVs have two basic separate systems, one for 12-volt DC power (same as motor vehicles) and another for 120-volt AC, which is used in homes. (Our reference to the home-style electrical system as 120-volt AC describes the so-called "110-volt" system; the actual voltage hasn't been 110 for decades, although the reference to 110 has continued.)

The 12-volt DC system is self-sufficient, allowing the RV to function without outside power. In cases where 120-volt AC power is available, a power cord is used to make the connection between the RV and an outside power source (Figure 8.3).

Basic Components of Electrical Systems

Differences in electrical systems among types of RVs usually focus on the number of sophisticated appliances used in the more elaborate RVs, particularly motorhomes, and the electrical systems used to support these appliances. Basic components of the systems include:

Figure 8.4
When 30-amp service is not available, an adapter may be used to connect to a 15-amp receptacle, although this restricts usage of appliances inside the RV.

The 12-Volt DC System

- One or more batteries reserved for RV appliances; the engine starting battery is automatically separated from power draw by RV appliances, although it is charged by the vehicle alternator.

- Wiring system, including fuse panel

- Lights, 12-volt DC water pump, monitoring system

The 120-Volt AC System

- Wiring, including outside hookup cord rated for 30 or 50 amps and several circuits for individual appliances, wall outlets

- Power distribution box that includes circuit breakers

- Charger/converter. When the RV is connected to an outside power source, this device provides 120-volt AC power for the charger/converter, which transforms it to 12-volt DC power for appliances, lights, and battery charging

- Air conditioner(s), which must use 120-volt AC power either from an outside source or an onboard AC generator

- AC generator (on some RVs), with power connected to the 120-volt AC system via automatic or manual switching devices

Separate 120-volt AC circuits supply the air conditioner, microwave oven, possibly a television (although 12-volt DC televisions also are available), and wall outlets that provide power to a wide variety of home-style appliances ranging from food mixers to hair curlers.

It's Automatic

When the RV power cord is plugged into a 120-volt AC external power source (campground receptacle), power is automatically supplied for the AC system, and the electrical converter automatically provides power for 12-volt DC appliances and battery charging. When an external source of 120-volt AC power is not available, the RV automatically operates on the batteries (excluding appliances that require 120-volt AC power) or a motor-driven AC generator (if the vehicle is so equipped).

Battery recharging occurs automatically while driving by means of the engine alternator. While parked without hookups, battery recharging may be accomplished by running an on-board AC generator, which is common to motorhomes and to the larger fifth-wheel trailers.

Other chapters describe function, maintenance, and safety procedures for electrical systems. Suffice it to say here that the RVer

Figure 8.5
Home-style appliances such as microwave ovens give RV camping much of its appeal over more primitive ways of enjoying the outdoors.

should be equipped with an adapter to convert a large three-prong 30-amp plug to the smaller home-style 15-amp plug when a 30-amp receptacle is not available, which is rare (Figure 8.4). Those RVs equipped with 50-amp service may need adapters to step down to 30-amp service. A roof air conditioner usually can be operated via the 15-amp adapter (available in RV supply stores), but the power supply will be marginal, and other 120-volt AC appliances should not be operated at the same time.

If an extension cord is used to lengthen the RV's original power cord, it should be the same size as the original power cord, or sufficient power for the air conditioner will not be provided. For light-duty electrical usage—not including an air conditioner or appliances rated at more than 1,000 watts—a 14-gauge three-wire extension cord of 25 feet or less may be used.

A systems monitor panel is included in most RVs, and it takes much of the guesswork out of monitoring levels of freshwater and wastewater tanks, battery condition, and (on some models) propane. Readings given by most of these panels are approximate.

RV Appliances

RVs wouldn't be comfortable or convenient without appliances, and the latest ones, including microwave/convection ovens, are not only more efficient but easier to use than their predecessors (Figure 8.5).

Furnaces

For living-area comfort, all RVs are provided with forced-air furnaces. The newer furnaces contain numerous safety features and use electronic igniters instead of pilot lights. To operate such a furnace, make sure the propane valve is turned on. Then simply set the thermostat to the desired temperature level. In an older RV, the furnace may have a pilot light. Instructions for lighting pilots on all such furnaces are listed inside the furnace grilles.

Water Heaters

The water heater is also operated on propane and has many of the same safety features as gas water heaters in homes. It's important to make sure that the water system is fully operational (water heater filled) before it's turned on. To make sure, turn on any hot-water faucet until a continuous stream of water flows (no air). Many late-model water heaters are automatically spark-ignited and controlled by on/off switches inside the RV, while others must be lighted manually. Procedures are described on the water heater controls. Don't expect the manually lighted water heaters to stay lit while traveling; they must be reignited when you arrive at your destination.

Gas Ranges

Gas ranges in RVs are quite similar to standard household units, with the exception of models that do not have pilot lights and must be manually lighted. A spark igniter or gas-flame igniter, available at RV supply stores, makes this chore easier. Ranges don't require any maintenance other than routine cleaning. To light a pilot, follow directions supplied with the range, which usually requires turning on a small valve under the stove top. The valve controls stove-top as well as oven pilots. If pilots blow out, the gas flow is not sufficient to present a danger of fire or explosion. Combustion byproduct gases, including carbon monoxide, are produced by ranges because they are not vented outside, as are furnaces. Ranges should not be used to heat the interiors of RVs. While the range produces relatively little carbon monoxide during normal cooking, amounts can increase if the range oven is improperly used to heat the interior of the vehicle over several hours.

Refrigerators

One of the most important appliances in an RV is the refrigerator. Virtually all refrigerators can be operated on propane or 120-volt AC power, and many also can be operated on 12-volt DC. While camping in a self-contained mode, propane is the only power source to use. If the vehicle is connected to outside power, the 120-volt AC electric mode should be used. Using the refrigerator's 12-volt DC system can rapidly deplete batteries and is recommended for use only while driving. The refrigerator should be cold before switching to

12-volt DC power, since this position is only a holding mode.

It's illegal in a few areas of some states (such as tunnels) to have flames burning while traveling. The reasoning is that, in the event of an accident, the flame in the refrigerator may provide a ready source of ignition. Use of the 12-volt DC mode avoids this hazard. If the refrigerator is not equipped for operation on 12-volt DC power, a small inverter, which transforms 12-volt DC power into 120-volt AC power, can be used. Such inverters are available at RV supply stores. Otherwise, traveling with the refrigerator on propane is a calculated risk—one that most RV owners regularly take.

Air Conditioners

Roof air conditioners usually are optional but are very common on RVs. Basically they are similar in concept to 120-volt AC window-mounted room air conditioners designed for homes. Operation is controlled by wall-mounted thermostat controls in many RVs or by using two knobs that control on/off, fan-only, and air conditioner operation on high and low fan speeds (on units that are not ducted). Few problems occur with air conditioners, but occasionally the RV owner may encounter low voltage at a campsite hookup. The air conditioner should not be used when voltage drops below 105, which may be indicated by low fan speeds and the compressor cycling on and off. Always make sure the air conditioner is turned off before connecting the RV power cord to an outside source of power or when starting an AC generator. This prevents an electrical surge as the plug is inserted into the receptacle, or the AC generator is started.

THE LP-GAS SYSTEM

At this point it should be obvious that an RV wouldn't be very enjoyable without fuel for the refrigerator, stove, water heater, and furnace. A good working knowledge of the safe use of that fuel—LP-gas, which is better known as propane—is necessary. Details are included in Chapter 9; a few basic items are covered here.

The LP-gas system includes cylinders or tanks that contain the fuel under pressure, plus a distribution system that controls pressure and feeds gas vapor to the appliances. It's a wonderfully efficient system that is the key to RV comfort and convenience if used properly—or a very hazardous system if used improperly.

The most important precaution when using propane is awareness of the peculiar smell of the fuel—a very pungent sulfur-like odor. When the odor is detected, extinguish all open flames, pilot lights, and smoking materials, and exit the RV immediately. Shut off the gas valve at the tank. Allow the vehicle to ventilate for a few minutes or until the odor dissipates. Don't resume use of propane systems until the source of the odor has been located and corrected.

It is important to personally monitor filling of cylinders on trailers or campers to make sure they are not overfilled, a real danger. The tanks used on motorhomes are equipped with automatic stop-fill devices that prevent overfilling (stop-fill devices are also being used on some cylinders). Follow other precautions described in Chapter 9. Most RVs are fitted with monitoring panels displaying the content of water and holding tanks and battery condition. Motorhome panels may also display propane-tank levels.

OUTFITTING YOUR RV

After acquiring a working knowledge of the systems in your RV, it's time to outfit the rig with necessary gear, utensils, and gadgets. However, before you start to load, bear in mind that all RVs have specific load limits that are all too often ignored, at the owners' peril. The limits are indicated on stickers that, prior to 1996, define gross vehicle weight rating (GVWR), which is the maximum weight of the vehicle and all its contents, as well as gross axle weight ratings (GAWR), which indicate maximum loading for each axle. Stickers on RVs built after late 1996 feature more information, including unloaded vehicle weight (UVW) and net carrying capacity (NCC), which are very helpful in avoiding overloading.

If your RV was built prior to use of the expanded weight sticker, it's important to weigh your rig before loading to see how much weight you can add—or, if that's not possible, to weigh the rig after loading to make sure you haven't violated the specific GVWR and GAWR ratings. Chapter 5 includes more information on weight and loading.

On a trailer, the sticker usually is affixed to the outside left front; on a motorhome it usually is on an inside wall near the driver's seat. GVWR listings on cars and trucks usually are found on door frames on the driver's side.

Weight must be distributed properly so overloading can be avoided and the vehicle will handle properly. The total weight of water, fuel, passengers, and all of your gear may be surprisingly high.

Basic Equipment

Before the maiden voyage, it's important to have specific equipment for utilities hookups, leveling, and for inhabiting the coach. Every new tow vehicle and most motorhomes will have been sold with a jack and tools for tire changing; if the coach was purchased used, make sure the equipment is on board. Some manufacturers of larger motorhomes have concluded that the owner is not capable of changing a tire, and have omitted tire-changing equipment. If your coach is among these, consult a truck-tire service shop on the physical aspects of changing a motorhome tire and the equipment necessary to do the job; then, decide if you want to tackle it. If you decide not to, be sure you are signed on with a reliable emergency road service provider that specifically covers large motorhomes.

Basic RV equipment should include:

- Barbecue supplies
- Battery jumper cables
- Campground directory
- Emergency road kit with approved reflectors
- Fire extinguisher
- First-aid kit
- Flashlight

- Good set of tools, including a 12-volt DC test light
- Hydraulic and/or scissors jack suitable for weight of your vehicle's heaviest tire(s)
- Folding chairs
- Leveling blocks or boards (if the vehicle is not equipped with leveling jacks)
- Matches or lighter
- Sewer hose with appropriate hookup fitting(s)
- Shovel
- Spare fuses
- Tire-pressure gauge
- Water hose (designed for drinking water)
- Wheel chocks

These are important basic items, and you might start a list to keep in the rig. Each time you find that you're without a needed item (keep weight limits in mind), add it to the list.

Supplies for Cleaning and Personal Use

It's impractical to carry an upright vacuum cleaner on trips. In most cases, a small portable unit such as the Red Devil vacuum cleaner or a rechargeable DustBuster will suffice. Most rigs can be cleaned with an all-purpose cleaner and paper towels. Availability of glass, bathroom, and all-purpose cleaning towelettes has virtually eliminated the need for heavy bottles and cans of cleaner, accompanying a bucket and mop. Dish soap and detergent for clothing should be included, along with personal toiletries.

The following items should be stocked in the bathroom cabinet:

- Aspirin
- Baking soda
- Deodorant
- Hand lotion
- Hand soap
- Holding-tank chemical
- Insect repellent

- Insect spray or pest strips
- Lip balm
- Peroxide or antiseptic
- Personal items
- Shampoo
- Sunscreen or sunblock
- Toothpaste

In the event of unforeseen problems it's nice to have a few rubber bands, paper clips, wire, tape, and maybe an eyeglass repair kit. It's best—but not a necessity—to use toilet tissue that is recommended for use with septic tanks or RV holding tanks. If you can't locate it, use single-ply toilet tissue.

GETTING READY TO TOW

If your RV of choice is a trailer, it and your tow vehicle must be mated with a hitch that is rated for the weight of your trailer and installed properly (Figure 8.6). Make sure the trailer is fitted with two safety chains, even though two may not be required in your state. If you have a motorhome and are towing a "dinghy" vehicle, use safety chains even though some states do not require them.

A trailer must be fitted with a breakaway switch and cable (standard equipment) designed to actuate electric trailer brakes if the trailer should separate from the tow vehicle. The switch typically is mounted on the trailer A-frame, and a small wire cable must be attached to any nonremovable hitch component on the tow vehicle.

All travel trailers should be fitted with sway-control devices, which dampen the trailer's lateral movements while also reducing the tendency of a tow vehicle to respond too rapidly to steering input.

All trailers weighing more than 1,500 pounds should be fitted with brakes. Small trailers may be fitted with surge-type hydraulic brakes, but most travel trailers have electric brakes that require a controller in the tow vehicle. The tow vehicle provides the power to operate the brakes, utilizing the controller, which senses tow-vehicle brake action and actuates trailer brakes in varying degrees to simulate tow-vehicle braking.

It's important to properly adjust the trailer-brake controller. It's set correctly when the driver can feel the action of the trailer brakes, but the action does not seem substantially lower or higher than the braking action of the tow vehicle. Too little trailer-braking action can be dangerous (extended braking distances), and too much trailer-braking action can result in premature trailer-wheel lockup.

The trailer-brake controller should be positioned so the driver can easily reach the unit's manual actuation lever, which is designed to permit independent use of the trailer brakes. The use of this lever is a very effective defensive maneuver if unusually severe driving conditions should cause trailer sway (fishtailing). Controller adjustments and functions are covered in the controller operating manual.

Travel-Trailer Hitching

While it may seem difficult at first, hitching will become routine. Before hitching, perform a complete safety inspection of the components:

- Pin in place to secure ball mount in coupler

- Ball tightened on ball mount

- Chains, frame brackets, and other parts intact

Make sure the hitch ball is the proper size! Trailer couplers designed for 2$\frac{5}{16}$-inch balls can be towed unknowingly with 2-inch balls (Figure 8.7), presenting the possibility that the trailer could come unhitched while traveling.

The proper procedure for adjusting an equalizing hitch is described in Chapter 6. The hitching procedure is relatively simple although at times exasperating if the owner has trouble backing the tow vehicle into proper position. It requires practice. Simple aids can help, such as a mirror mounted on the jack post of the trailer that allows the driver to see the hitch-ball-and-trailer coupler. Other hitch aids are available in RV supply stores.

Backing instructions from an assistant can help, if the driver is able to relate to the assistant's instructions. Some couples use CB radios (standard CB in the tow vehicle; hand-held radio used by the assistant) to relay backing instructions.

Figure 8.6
Use of the right load-distributing hitch, adjusted properly, is essential to safe towing.

The Hitching Procedure

Follow these steps to hitch a trailer to a towing vehicle:

1. Raise the trailer tongue a couple of inches higher than the ball.

2. Back the tow vehicle into position so the coupler is directly above the ball. Make sure that the locking lever on the coupler is open. Slowly lower the coupler so it fits securely on the ball.

3. Close the coupler latch. If the latch lever does not seat properly, it may signal that the coupler was prevented from fully seating on the ball—a dangerous situation. Look underneath the coupler at the position of the latch. Try again. When the coupler latch is properly seated, lock it with a bolt or a pin. Never use a locking device (requiring a key) while on the road. In the event of an emergency, you don't want to be fumbling for a key if you have to quickly disengage the coupler.

4. With the coupler latched on the ball, raise the tongue jack high enough to permit easy installation and tensioning of the spring bars. Follow the instructions provided with the hitch and described in Chapter 6 for proper tensioning of spring bars. Retract the tongue jack until the wheel or pad can be removed, and raise the jack to its highest position.

5. Connect the safety chains by running each through a loop or over a structural member of the hitch receiver, and hooking the chains back on themselves using connector links (available in RV supply stores) or the largest bolt you can fit through the chain links, capped with a locking nut. The chains should be crossed and be long enough to permit the tightest of turns without becoming taut, yet they should be short enough to keep the tongue from dropping to the pavement in the event the trailer becomes disconnected (highly unlikely).

6. Attach the breakaway switch cable to the tow vehicle and make sure you can turn full left and right without activating the cable. Do not attach the breakaway cable to the ball or any other part that detaches from the vehicle.

7. Connect the wiring harness from the trailer to the tow vehicle and check to make sure turn signals, lights, and trailer brakes are functional.

Figure 8.7
Erroneously using a 2-inch hitch ball when a 2⁵⁄₁₆-inch ball is needed can be dangerous. The proper ball size is stamped on all trailer couplers.

Your tow vehicle may not be fitted at the factory with adequate mirrors, in which case they must be purchased at an RV supply store. Mirrors should offer unobstructed rear views on both sides. Also, it's best to have a convex (wide-angle) mirror on the right for expanded field of vision.

Fifth-Wheel Hitching

Hitching a fifth-wheel trailer requires fewer procedures, but does take a bit of practice in backing the truck so the coupler moves correctly to the pin.

Make sure the hitch lever is in its "cocked" position (open) unless it's designed to open automatically. Back the truck so the hitch encircles the fifth-wheel pin. Gentle contact of the hitch saddle against the pin will cause the mechanism to close. Secure the hitch lever as specified by the manufacturer.

After hitching, attach the electrical connector and the breakaway cable, and be sure to raise the tailgate. Before unhitching, place a reminder on the dash or steering wheel so you won't forget to lower the truck's tailgate.

THE SHAKEDOWN CRUISE

A checkout procedure is wise prior to the shakedown cruise to reduce or eliminate the chance of unpleasant surprises (a system or appliances not functioning properly).

1. Check all fluid levels (fuel, engine oil, transmission oil, coolant, water, propane).

2. Check tire pressures. Inflate to the pressure number stamped on the tire sidewall, or refer to Chapter 7 for more specific information.

3. Turn on the water pump and open each faucet to purge air from the lines; make sure the pump cycles off and stays off when all the faucets are closed. If it cycles periodically, a water leak is indicated. Turn the pump switch off.

4. Check to make sure both valves on the holding tank system are closed.

5. Pour the prescribed amount (instructions on the container) of holding-tank chemical into the tank through the toilet.

6. Operate each appliance prior to departure. Make sure the refrigerator will cool down to at least 40 degrees (the RV should be approximately level before turning the refrigerator on), that the furnace produces heat, and that the water heater will go through a complete cycle and shut off. Check television and radio reception.

7. Check under the vehicle to make sure the leveling jacks or stabilizers are retracted. Also, make sure entry steps and television antennas/dishes are retracted.

8. Put personal supplies aboard.

DRIVING—IMPORTANT POINTS TO REMEMBER

The get-acquainted procedure varies among different types of RVs, with trailers requiring a bit more acquired skills than motorhomes because of the need to back a trailer, which is an articulated vehicle. Motorhome backing may require some practice and adjustment too, if the driver is only accustomed to passenger cars. Most important, get accustomed to using mirrors rather than looking rearward while backing. All RVs must have oversize outside mirrors, which must be adjusted properly for the driver's view before departure.

With any RV it's also necessary to monitor tailswing. The rear of any vehicle with considerable overhang past the rear axle will swing in the opposite direction of the turn. Get into the habit of checking the rear-view mirrors to see where the rear is going when you pull away from a site with any kind of fixed object that might put a dent in your new RV.

The first step of a shakedown cruise for a novice is to locate a large, empty parking lot and practice turning and backing. Make several sharp turns while watching in your mirrors to see how a trailer tracks behind the tow vehicle or how wide a turn must be made with a motorhome to avoid hitting a curb. Turning corners takes practice to make sure you don't run over curbs and into obstacles. Find a quiet place to practice and make several right turns while glancing back and forth from the roadway to the appropriate mirror. It will help you correlate the information from these two viewpoints.

If possible, have a helper safely positioned outside to watch the rear while backing and help you get the hang of it. You might try backing into a marked parking space from different angles.

While backing, keep your side clearances in mind. Backing a trailer might be difficult at first because the trailer moves in the opposite direction of the vehicle. But practice is all that's required. A helpful technique is to steer with one hand on the bottom of the wheel, and move the hand in the direction you want the trailer to go. Take it slow and focus, getting used to the reverse images in the mirrors.

Fifth-wheel trailers respond differently to backing maneuvers. As with conventional trailers, they move in the opposite direction of the tow vehicle's turn; again, it's necessary to find a vacant lot and practice.

With the motorhome loaded and the fluids topped off, first get the feel of the rig, which will be different from a pickup truck or van used to tow a trailer. First, acclimate yourself to all of the controls so you don't have to search for the right switch while driving. Adjust the seat to your preference. Take it easy until you get a feel for the motorhome's turning radius and handling characteristics. Find an empty parking lot and practice backing into an imaginary camping site. Note how the motorhome's rear overhang swings wide when you're turning sharply, which can cause accidents when maneuvering at slow speeds if you don't take tailswing into account.

You should be able to drive the vehicle at normal highway speeds without excessive body roll (lean to one side) or a tendency to respond too quickly to steering input. Always keep in mind the fact that your fully loaded rig isn't going to stop like a sports car. When clear of other traffic, simulate an emergency stop. Adjust your driving techniques so you have

time to stop based on what you know about your motorhome's stopping ability.

For the initial trip, it's best to stay close to home and to pay special attention to handling and stability. Evaluate handling on curves and in crosswinds. In an area clear of traffic, reduce speed and carefully test your ability to make lane changes, as if avoiding an obstacle in the road. Keep an eye on the tow vehicle's gauges while climbing hills, so you'll notice any tendency of engine coolant temperature to increase beyond normal. Listen for any unusual sounds that might indicate trouble. If the vehicle makes unusual sounds, pull safely off the road and investigate before proceeding.

Think "Clearance"

Regardless of the type of RV, it's imperative to develop a mindset that your rig is relatively large. Learn to automatically check top and side clearances. One of the most common and costly errors by novice RV owners is crashing into overhanging tree limbs or hitting low canopies (Figure 8.8). When in doubt, exit the vehicle and look. Measure the height of your rig at the highest point (roof air conditioner, satellite dishes, or antennas) and post the number in plain view on the instrument panel. These numbers will come in handy while pulling into service stations, most of which display the amount of clearance under their canopies.

Road Safety

Now that your rig is properly loaded and safely fueled, it's time to hit the road and see what the RV lifestyle is all about. It's important to be alert at all times. Use your mirrors and keep a mental reference of the traffic on all sides. Drive defensively and try to give the other driver ample space and time to do something unexpected without involving your vehicle. While passing other vehicles or changing lanes, take into consideration the overall length of your RV. Allow ample time because most RVs don't have the passing power of the typical passenger car. Varying terrain, road surfaces, traffic flow, and weather conditions such as gusting winds, rain, or fog may dictate slower speeds.

Figure 8.8
Low service station canopies and tree limbs are a hazard for novice RV owners, who must keep overhead clearance in mind.

Courtesy is an important aspect of safety. RVs often are traveling slower than passenger cars, and they block the view of following drivers, which can be exasperating. Always monitor drivers in your rear-view mirrors, and drive slightly to the right when safe, so drivers intending to pass can check oncoming traffic. When it's safe, use turnouts to let other drivers pass, even if you have only one vehicle behind you.

SETTING UP CAMP

You've arrived at your destination, and there are a few chores before the fun and relaxation can begin. If you were lucky enough to find a level campsite, you're already doing well. In the past, leveling was critical for proper operation of RV refrigerators, but late-model units

are not as sensitive. Thus the main reason for leveling today is personal comfort. RV supply stores offer bubble level indicators that can be attached inside or outside an RV (or in both places) for quick reference while leveling, but they're not necessary. If the rig appears comfortably level, it's level enough for proper refrigerator operation.

To level a trailer, place one or more blocks of 2 x 6-inch boards ahead of the tires on the low side and drive the trailer on the boards. This levels the trailer side to side. Chock the wheels so the trailer can't roll. Then unhitch. Using the tongue jack, level the trailer from front to back. If you have stabilizing jacks, lower them onto a piece of 2 x 6 lumber (if you are parked on a soft surface) until they are snug. They aren't intended to lift the trailer, just stabilize it.

Figure 8.9
A block cut so that it resembles a ramp is the simplest device for leveling an RV.

Ideally, a motorhome will be equipped with power leveling jacks. In the event it is not, blocks or boards will suffice. Place boards or blocks under the wheels on the low side and drive onto them until the vehicle is level (Figure 8.9). Set the parking brake and put the transmission in the park position each time you leave the driver's seat after maneuvering on boards or blocks. Gaining the judgment to know how many boards or blocks are required under which wheels takes practice. Walk into the rig and make a visual check. When level,

Figure 8.10
The gray-water tank is serviced by a small pipe (right), while the sewage tank is connected to a 4-inch pipe.

How to Dump a Holding Tank

Many new RV owners might be apprehensive about this procedure, having heard stories about messy accidents. But it's simple, and accidents are easy to avoid. The procedure is as follows:

1. Check to make sure all valves are closed and that the drain hose is securely attached.

2. Pull the handle to open the sewage gate valve first, emptying that tank. The sewage tank is the one directly below the toilet, and it is serviced by a 4-inch pipe. The gray-water tank is serviced by a smaller pipe.

3. After the tank is drained, close the valve and fill the tank to at least the halfway point with a hose you have fed into the bathroom through a window or door, or by pouring water down the toilet (an empty wastebasket works well for this chore). There are also a number of commercial flushing devices available. If your RV has one of these convenience items, follow the manufacturer's instructions.

4. Open the valve again and allow the flushing water to drain. Close the valve. When the RV is in long-term use, don't leave the blackwater valve open when the system is attached to a campground sewer; the tank should be at least half full to get proper flushing action. After the waste tank is flushed and drained, make sure the valve is closed and locked.

5. Open the gray-water valve. The gray-water tank may not require flushing because it doesn't contain solids, but some built-in devices provide this option. When it's empty, close the valve, lock it, disconnect the hose and replace the cap. Flush the hose with fresh water, remove it from the dump station, and replace it in its holder.

6. Replace the sewer cap and tidy up any mess you might have made. Once you are finished, add holding-tank chemical to the waste tank and flush the toilet a couple of times, adding enough water to distribute the chemical.

---

make sure the brake is set and chock the wheels. Of course, if you have leveling jacks, this step is not necessary.

Hookups

If the campsite has power and sewer hookups, connect the necessary hoses. Connect the sewer hose first, and open the gray-water holding-tank valve (Figure 8.10). Again, make sure you know which valve this is. It's the one connected to the smaller (2-inch) of the two pipes that feed into the hose connector. Leave the sewage tank valve closed; that's the valve on the 4-inch pipe. Connect the water hose to the campground faucet using a pressure regulator, and connect it to the water inlet on the RV. Plug in the electrical cord and check to make sure that the circuit breaker is switched to the "on" position.

Inside, set the refrigerator on the desired power source—electricity, if you have it; light the water heater pilot if it has one (many late-model RVs have automatic-ignition water heaters controlled by an on-off switch).

Extend your awning (having already read the instructions), set out the folding chairs,

Return-Trip Checklist

Prior to departure, it's best to follow a checklist, at least initially, to make sure you haven't forgotten something that will cause problems or cost money. Here's a basic list, to which you can add items from your owner's manual:

✔ Dump holding tanks if dump station is available.

✔ Roll up and store awning, power cords, and hoses.

✔ Close all windows, vents, doors, drawers, and hatches.

✔ Check roof rack or storage pod.

✔ Lower TV antenna/satellite dish.

✔ Retract entry step.

✔ Secure interior: items on counter tops, refrigerator/freezer doors, and television.

✔ Turn off water pump and furnace (unless you require them for winter travel).

✔ Turn off water heater (or close pilot).

✔ Lock refrigerator door.

✔ Retract stabilizers or jacks; store wheel chocks.

✔ Check lights/turn signals, tires, and engine oil.

✔ Drive away from the site a few yards, stop, and walk back to make sure you didn't leave anything—and that you left the site cleaner than you found it.

---

and you're ready for a relaxing stay. If you have questions or problems, it's usually easy to find a helping hand—or two or three. RVers usually are very friendly and helpful.

HEADING HOME

Now that you've spent some time enjoying yourself and recharging your mental batteries, it's time to face civilization again—but not before a routine of predeparture chores.

- Follow the procedures listed in the checklist on page 102 to dump your holding tanks.

- Make sure all electrical devices are turned off, so the house batteries will not be depleted. If you're unsure, disconnect the negative line to the house batteries. Reinstall prior to the next trip. If your rig is fitted with disconnect switches, make sure they are off before storing.

For long-term or cold-weather storage, it's necessary to drain the freshwater system or protect it with nontoxic antifreeze, available at RV supply stores, to prevent damage from freezing. Instructions on the use of the antifreeze are included with the product. Pour antifreeze in all drains to prevent P-traps from freezing.

Short-Term Storage Checklist

After returning home, a little thought should be given to storage of the RV until the next trip.

✔ Flush the sewage holding tanks if this was not done when the tanks were dumped at the campsite.

✔ Shut off propane.

✔ Make sure all systems and appliances are turned off.

✔ Check roof rack or storage pod.

✔ Check the freshwater tank. There is no need to drain the freshwater tank and lines if the RV is to be stored less than a month or unless equipped with a filtering system that permits chlorination, in which case the water can be stored for several months without deterioration.

✔ Clean refrigerator and leave door(s) ajar to dry out the interior (helps prevent odor and mildew). An open box of baking soda works well here.

✔ Clean and vacuum interior.

✔ Close windows, drapes, and shades.

✔ Fill gasoline tank (prevents water contamination due to condensation).

✔ Fill propane tank if necessary (contamination is not a problem).

✔ Check tire pressure.

Because RVs are essentially homes on wheels, they require regular maintenance. Not only must regular attention be paid to automotive systems (tow vehicle or motorhome chassis), it must be focused on the "house" systems and the RV structure itself. However, if properly maintained with a program that covers the entire rig and its appliances, years of trouble-free service are not uncommon.

Chapter 9

PROPANE USE AND SAFETY

It's safe to say that RVs would not be anywhere near as comfortable, as well developed or as popular as they are today without liquefied petroleum gas (LP-gas or LPG). The most commonly available form of this gas in the United States, propane, has been used in RVs for several decades as a source of energy for cooking, heating, and refrigeration. This versatile, relatively inexpensive fuel allows us to keep ourselves warm, clean, well fed, and comfortable.

Of course, propane can be dangerous if handled carelessly or used improperly—very dangerous. So can gasoline. RV owners' attitudes about propane range from lackadaisical to paranoid. Both attitudes usually are based on lack of knowledge of the fuel's characteristics.

Gasoline and propane are cousins. The same people who may view propane as a mysterious unexploded bomb awaiting accidental ignition may pay little attention to safety when handling gasoline. Of course, there are people who pay scant attention to safety with either fuel. To help you understand propane better, possibly saving you from a very serious accident, this chapter will cover:

- The way propane works, its benefits, its characteristics, and its hazards

- Inspection, maintenance, and storage of propane containers; proper marking and filling, plus information about service valves

- The pressure regulator: its function, protection, and inspection

- Testing you can do on your gas system

- When to seek a competent professional

THE FUEL

Liquefied petroleum gas consists of a number of hydrocarbon gases that will turn to liquid under pressure. The gas used in RVs is called commercial propane. It consists of 95 percent propane and/or propylene and 5 percent other gases, mainly of the butane family. All of these gases are petroleum products separated out of the natural-gas or crude-oil streams. Butane is a close cousin to gasoline; propane is closer to the natural-gas side of the family. The chemical formulas may help us understand the relationship of this hydrocarbon family. Natural gas is a mixture of gases resulting in a C_2H_4 range of hydrocarbons. Propane is C_3H_8. Butane is C_4H_{10}, and gasoline blends are about C_6H_{14}.

Propane is a colorless, odorless liquid that looks somewhat like water. One big difference is its boiling point. Water boils at 212°F, and propane boils at about -50°F. The vapor that comes from propane will burn. So, when temperature is above -50°F we have a flammable gas under pressure.

The pressure varies with temperature and volume, as you learned in your high-school physics class. Remember Charles's and Boyle's laws on gases?* A closed container of propane at -50°F will have zero pressure. At 0°F, pressure will be about 24 pounds, and at 100°F it will be over 200 pounds. The higher the temperature, the more pressure we have. Tanks are even painted in light, reflective colors to keep pressures lower in summer.

An odorant is added as a warning agent so you can detect leaks. Make sure you recognize the smell (it's similar to rotten eggs), and be aware that your nose doesn't always work well. Every RV should be equipped with a gas detector, and if your sense of smell is poor, a detector is even more critical.

Since propane boils at -50°F, the liquid absorbs heat when the pressure is released. You have seen the stream of liquid at your outage valve (also called the 20 percent valve) when the tank is being filled. It looks like steam, but instead of being hot, it is very cold. Remember, it's flammable, it's under pressure, and it can freeze your skin.

*Charles's Law states that the volume of a given mass of gas is directly proportional to the absolute temperature if the pressure is constant; or: VT + constant; V + volume of gas; T + absolute pressure. Boyle's Law states that the volume occupied by a given mass of gas varies inversely with the absolute pressure if the pressure remains constant; or: PV + constant; P + absolute pressure; V + volume of gas.

Expanding Liquid = Gas

The propane liquid expands 270 times to form the gas. One gallon of liquid propane makes 36.6 cubic feet of gas with 2,500 Btus. Natural gas has 1,000 Btus per cubic foot, so propane has twice the heat.

The one characteristic everyone seems to know about propane is that it's heavier than air—about 1½ times as heavy, while natural gas is about half as heavy as air. This feature is usually exaggerated with both gases. We are sometimes taught that propane fumes collect on the floor. If the fumes are what make it dangerous, then beware of gasoline fumes, which are 3.6 times as heavy as air and more than twice as heavy as gaseous propane. The truth is that all these gases continue to expand as the temperature increases, as described in Charles's and Boyle's laws, and they do not usually collect near the floor because of constantly moving air currents caused by convection. Regardless of where the gas concentrates, don't turn on light switches, don't light matches, don't provide any source of ignition—high or low—when you detect escaping gas.

If you think you have a leak, get out, turn off the gas, and leave doors open to ventilate the RV. Don't use fans or anything that might cause a spark.

Liquid propane weighs 4.24 pounds per gallon, about half the weight of water. Propane liquid expands dramatically when it warms, growing 1½ times bigger for each 10°F it is warmed. This is why we only fill propane cylinders and tanks 80 percent full (Figure 9.1); that level is indicated by the fixed liquid-level gauge, also called the outage valve or 20 percent valve. Do not allow your tanks to be overfilled beyond the fixed liquid-level gauge.

Another propane characteristic that needs some understanding is the rate of vaporization in a container. Many propane tanks are built to the ASME code for unfired pressure vessels; in other words they are boilers. As with RV water heaters, these "gas boilers" are limited in size and output. The heat that causes the gas boiler (propane tank) to operate is the ambient heat that causes the container to be above minus 50°F. In zero-degree weather, the tank

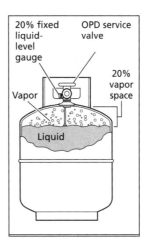

Figure 9.1
Propane cylinders are filled to only 80 percent of capacity to allow for expansion of the liquid fuel.

sometimes cannot absorb enough heat to provide all the pressure (fuel vaporization) needed to operate the appliances. When the propane tank runs low, this problem worsens due to the reduction of surface area of propane exposed to absorb heat. One step that will help in cold climates is to fill your tanks or cylinders when the gas level drops below 30 percent.

You may have noticed frost on your tanks during use in cool, moist weather. When the liquid propane cannot absorb the heat needed to create the amount of gas your appliances are demanding, it becomes refrigerated. This is the same action as moisture collecting on a glass of iced tea. There is no cause for alarm, and in fact this refrigeration can be useful in showing you the level of liquid propane in the tank if you don't have a gauge.

Many years ago, the codes required the use of two-stage regulators to provide appliances with their required gas pressure even when this vaporization rate dropped. If you have a single-stage regulator, have it replaced with a two-stage regulator for proper appliance operation and greater safety.

When It Won't Burn

One other important characteristic is propane's rather narrow limits of flammability, saving many a careless act from becoming an accident. Sadly it has made many believe their careless acts were acceptable behavior, leading to the classic post-accident statement: "But I've done it this way for thirty years!"

The limits of flammability are from 2.2 percent to 9.6 percent gas in air. Mixtures that are too rich or too lean won't burn. On some burners, the air adjustments can be opened so far that they dilute the mixture, causing the burner to go out. Too little air to the burner causes sooting. When there is more than 10 percent gas in a combustion chamber, the fire goes out or the flame travels, trying to find air to burn.

You should always shut off pilots and electronic reigniters before entering gasoline or propane refueling facilities. Devices designed to do this automatically, by switching off refrigerator and water heater electrical circuits, are available in RV supply stores.

PROPANE VESSELS

All propane vessels are manufactured in accordance with strict quality codes. The first of these two codes is the DOT (Department of Transportation) specification. DOT (formerly ICC) vessels are called cylinders (Figure 9.2). They can only have openings in their hemispherical portions or heads. ASME (American Society of Mechanical Engineers) vessels are correctly called tanks and can have openings in their shells as well as their heads (Figure 9.3).

Container thickness is related to the diameter and the code. DOT cylinders used on travel trailers, campers, and other RVs are usually about 12 inches in diameter. The minimum allowable thickness for a steel DOT cylinder is .078 inch, or about the same thickness as the

Figure 9.2
Propane cylinders, often mistakenly called bottles or tanks, are used on trailers and campers.

Figure 9.3
Propane tanks are framed-mounted on motorhomes.

guard or foot ring on the cylinder. Aluminum cylinders are .140 inch thick.

Rust pits, gouges, scrapes, or sharp dents can seriously compromise the safety and integrity of this vessel. Do yourself a favor and keep it rust free and painted a heat-reflective color. Especially check the tank bottom where condensation collects and where it is harder to paint under the foot ring.

The DOT requires visually checking each tank for these obvious defects and for leaks before filling. Furthermore, filling personnel are not allowed to fill a DOT cylinder that is more than ten years older than its date of manufacture. If your cylinder exceeds the ten-year rule, seek out a certified cylinder requalifier. Unfortunately, many refillers fail to observe the requalifying requirement, and the conscientious refiller may have to take a lot of abuse from the customer when he refuses to fill an illegal container.

It's best to periodically check your cylinders for leaks and damage. If you are concerned they are unsafe, take them to a qualified propane dealer for checking and, if necessary, disposal.

Both DOT cylinders and ASME tanks must have valve guards intact. Do not cut away portions of a guard or alter it in a way that weakens its strength. Screw caps are used on some cylinders, and these caps must be in place when transporting.

ASME horizontal tanks are most commonly found on motorhomes. These tanks need to be inspected and maintained free of rust and leaks; however, the ASME rules do not require the twelve-year recertification. The metal in ASME tanks is almost half again as thick as the metal in DOT cylinders of the same diameter. Even so, ASME rules for dents and corrosion are very strict. Give your motorhome tank an annual inspection; clean and repaint in a light color. Be sure to check the mounting brackets and bolts. Loose brackets not only can cause a tank to fall off, they can also lead to stress cracks in the vessel.

Welding a propane container can only be handled by a certified shop. The container must be heat-treated after being welded to relieve the welding stresses. Both types of vessels must be retested according to their manufacturing codes.

The racks that hold cylinders on a trailer A-frame are designed to hold eight times the filled containers' weight. (Old racks were designed for four times full weight.) Make sure your hold-down bars are properly positioned and the wing nut is securely tightened before travel. Make this check a routine part of your trailer-hookup procedure. Hold-down bars that fit into the square holes in the tank guard are somewhat forgiving, but the more common saw-blade-shaped hold-downs must be secure.

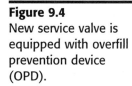

Figure 9.4
New service valve is equipped with overfill prevention device (OPD).

Mount your cylinders with the openings of the relief valves pointing away from the trailer. The guard opening will be toward the trailer, allowing better protection for the valve from flying debris; the regulator will also be better protected between the cylinders and the trailer wall.

A fairly common service-valve complaint is a leak around the valve stem. When the O-ring seal becomes cold, dirty, old, or worn, it may leak at the stem threads. Happily this leak can be controlled by opening or closing the valve all the way. Gently backseat the valve stem when opening to prevent stem leakage; you can then operate safely until proper repair or replacement can be made. Sometimes opening and closing the valve a few times will remove dirt from the internal O-ring.

The service valve should close off gas flow when hand tight; avoid the use of tools. If tools are required, the valve should be replaced.

OPD SERVICE VALVES

All cylinders designed to contain 4 to 40 pounds of fuel, which covers all RV cylinders, were fitted with a new service valve design beginning in 1998 (Figure 9.4). A new triangular-shaped knob makes the new valves easy to identify. All such valves are equipped with overfill prevention devices (OPDs), although attendants also should monitor fill level via the traditional fixed liquid-level gauge.

These gauges are called a variety of names; spit, bleed, outage, 10 percent, 20 percent, 80 percent, and release are just a few. This valve was operated by a small finger-operated knurled knob for many years. The valve now operates using a screwdriver, avoiding liquid burns and smelly fingers (Figure 9.5).

This valve opens a small passageway to an internal tube extending into the tank to its 80 percent level or the maximum safe filling level. When filling a cylinder by volume (as opposed to filling by weight), the filling must by stopped by an OPD or by the service attendant when a steady stream of white liquid appears. Many accidents involving propane were caused by overfilling, and OPDs have made the use of propane cylinders safer.

POL Service Valves

This type of service valve was standard on cylinders manufactured until 1998. The threaded high-pressure connector of this service valve is a special bullet-nosed part called a POL (Figure 9.6). The name originated with the Prest-O-Lite Company, but it's helpful to remember it as "put-on-left" to designate its left-handed-thread feature.

If the male end of the pigtail gets nicked by dropping or from a blow, and it will not seal, replace it. If that's not possible, there is an appropriate O-ring that can be inserted in the valve to fix the leak. Check your POL connection after each hookup. Sniff, listen, and coat the connection with leak detection solution (soapy water) to determine if there is any any leakage.

Cylinders of 45 pounds propane capacity or

less must have the POL valve plugged or capped when not hooked up for use, empty or full. A plastic POL plug is an inexpensive way for RVers to protect their families from accidents in which the valve is opened by a child. This plug also keeps air and moisture from entering the cylinder when empty, thus eliminating the opportunity for internal rust, false container pressure, or odorant oxidation.

If overfilling occurs with a cylinder that has the old-style valve (no OPD), the overfill should be discharged through the outage valve in a well-ventilated area until the white liquid stops and the stream is only vapor. Open the outage valve from one-half to one turn. If opened too far it will come out and possibly become lost. On most cylinders, this valve is in the left side of the service valve body; however, on some vertical and most horizontally

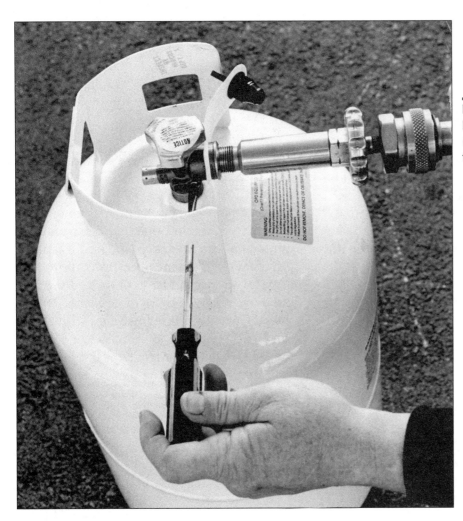

Figure 9.5
Liquid-level indicator (bleeder) is a screw in the side of the valve.

Figure 9.6
A bullet-nosed left-hand-threaded connector is called a POL valve.

used cylinders, the valve is a separate part screwed into a ¼-inch National Pipe Thread (NPT) opening.

Dimensions

The proper length of this valve's dip tube (in inches) is stamped in the guard of the cylinder. DT 3.5, indicating a 3.5-inch dip tube, would be the likely stamping for a 20-pound cylinder, commonly referred to as 5-gallon.

Another stamping in the guard shows water capacity in pounds; a common figure is, for example, WC 47.7 pounds. By moving the decimal one place to the left, we get the propane capacity in gallons. There are about 4.7 gallons in a 20-pound cylinder, about 7.2 gallons in a 30-pound cylinder, and 9.2 gallons in a 40-pound cylinder.

Another component of the cylinder valve, the pressure-relief valve, is the small opening facing opposite the threaded opening for the OPD or POL nut (Figure 9.7). This automatic spring-loaded valve is installed to keep the pressure from bursting the cylinder in case it is overfilled or subject to excessive heat. Never plug, tamper with, or attempt to adjust this valve. If it is leaking, cool the tank with a water stream.

Caution: Take care and stand back as you do this. If practical, seek the assistance of trained gas- or fire-fighting personnel. If not, check the fixed-level gauge for overfilling, move the cylinder to an open area, and bleed it as discussed later in this chapter.

Pressure Relief and Overfilling

The activation of a relief valve signifies a potentially serious problem. This valve can open suddenly and discharge large amounts of liquid. Keep in mind that liquid expands 270 times and can freeze your skin. Keep the cylinder upright. Remember: Don't allow overfilling of any of your tanks or cylinders! This is the most common cause of accidents. Due to the previously discussed natural expansion of the fuel in response to temperature changes, the relief valve of an overfilled cylinder or tank that is subjected to a large temperature change may open and release a potentially large amount of gas. This situation can be created by very simple, understandable circumstances, but it's the reason why some users believe the fuel is unpredictable.

For example, a service attendant carelessly overfills an RV owner's cylinder early one morning in a location where overnight temperatures have dropped to near zero. The next day, the RVer may have covered hundreds of miles and reached an area where daytime highs are near 100°F. If little or no propane is used, the volume of fuel in the overfilled cylinder will increase 15 percent—forcing the relief valve open and releasing enough gas to fill a small house. When that happens, all that's needed to complete the scenario for a disastrous fire is a source of ignition. Take personal responsibility for making sure the service attendant does not overfill your cylinder!

Proper filling should not be determined by a gauge. Some cylinders and most motorhome tanks have gauges that are operated by floats inside the tanks. The accuracy of these gauges is similar to a car's gasoline gauge: They are not precision instruments and are not to be used for filling. However, the dramatic expansion rate of the liquid can make a gauge change as much as 10 percent from a cool night to a warm day. Use the gauge to check when you are running low and need to refill. Only three methods are used to determine when a tank is full: when white liquid appears at the outage (20 percent) valve; when a stop-fill valve automatically shuts off the gas flow, or when the filling station is equipped with an accurate scale to weigh a cylinder. When the

appearance of white liquid at a outage valve indicates a full tank, the filling service should be shut off immediately. Any delay will require that the excess fuel be bled off.

ASME tanks on motorhomes utilize a service valve somewhat similar to a DOT cylinder; however, they are not interchangeable. The relief on a DOT cylinder is set at 375 psi and RV-size (45 pounds or smaller) cylinders have small-capacity relief-valve openings. ASME tanks have larger-opening relief valves set for 312 psi, and the valve is larger and heavier.

Motorhome tanks built after 1993 utilize a separate relief valve; it is no longer an integral part of the service valve. This relief valve is protected from contamination by a plastic cover, which should be replaced if it becomes damaged or worn.

The relief valve resembles a plug and is frequently located in the lower section of the tank, in a special recessed coupling. Also, the new tanks have an internal excess-flow valve in the tank on the service valve. Open the valve slowly to avoid activating the excess-flow unit. If restricted flow is apparent, close the service valve, wait a few seconds for it to click, resetting itself, and reopen the valve.

Outage (20-percent) valves on ASME tanks are separate from the service valve. They are still the knurled-knob type, since some are not

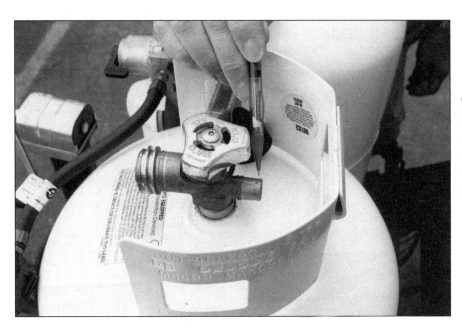

Figure 9.7
If excessive pressure occurs from overfilling or excessive heat, it is vented through a pressure relief valve.

easily operated with a screwdriver because of their location.

Permanently mounted ASME tanks have fill fittings separate from their outlet valves, and since 1983, the fill fittings are required to include automatic stop-fill devices—a code change necessitated by overfilling, fires, and explosions. Like many safety devices, these are frequently misunderstood and abused. Also, as with many other new items on the market, early stop-fill devices were troublesome. Even so, do not remove or obstruct these devices. To do so is to cause a perilous situation. Read and follow the operating instructions, especially with the Auto-Stop valve. You already learned to open an outage valve only a little, and now here is a device that won't allow any gas to enter the tank unless the outage valve is open all the way (about three turns). Don't worry, this one won't come all the way out.

All fill valves are sensitive to dirt, but automatic stop-fills must have their dust caps on when not being filled (Figure 9.8). Also, the hose nozzle can catch rain or dirt and inject it in the next fill if the nozzle is not properly plugged or protected.

The Auto-Stop can be easily serviced and parts can be replaced without emptying the tank. Only trained service people should work on these devices, but if the serviceman knows the valve and has the parts, it can be completely rebuilt in thirty minutes.

The other float-type stop-fills cannot be repaired; they must be replaced. The gas must be used or flared to zero pressure before removal. Don't blow gas into the atmosphere unless you want to get rid of your RV quickly. Static electricity may automatically ignite a large release of gas. The rule is to bleed through an opening not larger than a Number 54 drill bit (the size of your outage valve). A torch can be used by a professional technician to flare this gas when necessary.

PRESSURE REGULATORS

The proper control of your propane-system pressure is the work of the regulator that is connected to the service valve of the cylinder or tank. The correct operation of your appliances, as well as your safety, depend on this device. For this reason it's often called the heart of the propane system. Its job is to reduce tank pressure to the appliance-operating pressure of 11 inches water-column (WC) pressure or about one-third of a pound.

Figure 9.8
Contaminants must be kept out of the fill valve of propane tank by a plastic cover.

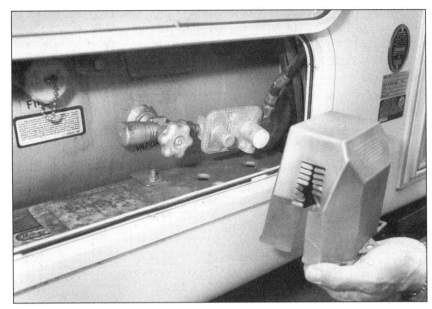

Figure 9.9
A two-stage regulator accurately maintains constant pressure at 11 inches of water column, or about ⅓-PSI. Regulators "breathe," and plastic covers are used to protect their vents from debris and ice.

When RVing became a popular winter activity about fifteen years ago, the regulator had great difficulty maintaining a constant outlet pressure with low inlet pressures caused by cold weather; these regulators were designed for inlet pressures of 60 psi or more.

In 1977 the design code was changed to require the use of two-stage regulators (Figure 9.9). These are really two regulators in one:

The first stage reduces the varying tank pressures to about 10 to 15 pounds, and the second stage reduces pressure to the desired 11 inches WC pressure.

The first stage can take the form of an automatic cylinder changeover device on trailers or a rectangular section attached to the second stage on units that don't have automatic changers. RV regulator life is most likely less

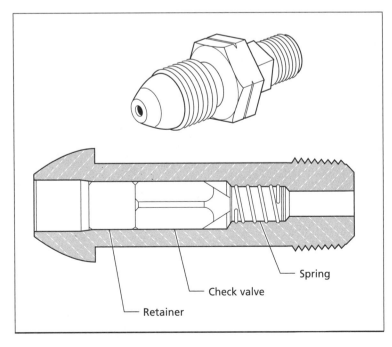

Figure 9.10
Excess-flow device built into POL fitting automatically reduces gas flow in event of a line break.

Spring

Check valve

Retainer

than fifteen years due to intermittent use, exposure to road spray (salt), and contaminants that come loose from the vibration and shaking. Regulator failure not only can cause inconvenience but is dangerous. Don't wait until you have trouble. Each time you turn on the container, open the valve slowly for the first turn. Quick opening causes excessive pressure and may cause regulator diaphragm leaks.

Prior to 1998, the industry used UL/CGA-approved pigtails with excess-flow devices in the old-style POL spud (Figure 9.10). The UL label is a silver band about ½ inch long around the pigtail. The required excess-flow device is a spring-loaded metal component in the POL nose that will close automatically when a sudden surge of gas occurs. This device is designed to close automatically if the cylinder(s) gets knocked off in a collision, and it will work to protect your regulator if you open your service valve too quickly.

Since 1998, QCC pigtails are required (Figure 9.11), and they incorporate a thermoplastic nut that is designed to soften and back out of the service valve if subjected to too much heat.

An excess-flow device in the POL spud will not close and protect you from leaks in the pipeline. It can't tell a leak from a furnace burner coming on, for example. Should you hit your excess-flow device with sudden pressure by turning your valve on too quickly, you may find only a small amount of gas flowing to your appliances. The excess-flow device doesn't shut off all gas flow. Turn the service flow off, listen for a click, then slowly reopen to reset the check valve. Sometimes you can also hear the click of the excess flow when it closes.

When you turn on the service valve, always listen to the regulator for the sound of gas flowing. While this is only a rough leak indicator, you can usually hear flow if a burner is open or a line is disconnected. If you hear a leak, turn the gas off. Check your range valves and inspect your lines for damage. Don't plug in electrical power, and don't light matches.

Checking for Leaks

You can check the regulator connections, diaphragm seals, and vents for leaks by using soap and water or special leak-detecting solution. A bottle of Mr. Bubble does not contain harsh chemicals, such as ammonia, that may corrode lines and brass fittings, and it mixes into a reliable bubble-mix consistency. Leaks at the diaphragm seal or vents indicate the regulator should be replaced.

Regulators that are not enclosed in compartments, such as those in campers and some fifth-wheel and travel trailers using cylinder covers, are required to have regulator covers. Several types of inexpensive plastic covers are available.

Figure 9.11
Thermoplastic connectors are designed to shut off gas flow when subjected to excessive heat.

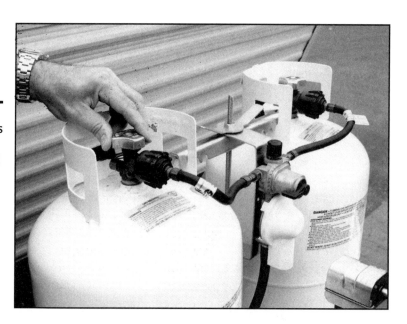

An RV serviceman or parts dealer can help you select the proper one for your application.

Regulator vents must point downward within 45 degrees of vertical to drain any moisture from the diaphragm. The drip-lip design on the vent prevents ice from forming over the vent screen. You must select the correct design for your application. A motorhome regulator will have vents on the side, and an automatic regulator will have a vent on the bottom, next to the gas outlet. Water from wheel spray can otherwise collect in the diaphragm area, causing rust on the metal parts and rotting the diaphragm rubber, thus reducing useful life. Regulator manufacturers do not make any replacement parts available and specifically advise against attempting any repairs. If you have reason to suspect your regulator, have it checked or replaced by a qualified service technician.

Regulators should be checked with an instrument called a manometer (Figure 9.12). The pressure output should be 10½ to 11½ inches of water-column (WC) pressure when about half your appliances are operating (measured by Btu rating). When everything is turned off, the "lock-up" pressure can be measured. This must not exceed 14 inches WC or one-half pound.

These tests could be performed properly at a gas-range orifice on most RVs until about 1987. Then gas regulators were added to all ranges, making orifice readings inaccurate, so a test must be performed elsewhere. A manometer leak test is required when a gas line is temporarily disconnected; be sure this test is performed by a competent serviceman when work has been done on your system.

Low operating pressure can be the result of improperly sized, damaged, or crimped pipelines. Check them if your operating pressure drops when you turn on more equipment. Do not attempt any of these regulator tests or adjustments. We have not tried to cover the many additional steps required to perform these tests safely and properly; this should be left to qualified service people.

There is a generic term called "freeze-up" that applies to regulators. True freeze-up alludes to moisture in the tank that freezes in the regulator inlet orifice where expansion of

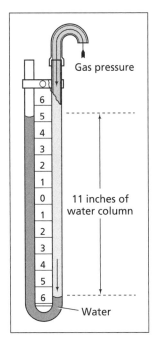

Figure 9.12
A manometer measures gas pressure in inches of water column—the differential between one column of water and the other.

the gas causes refrigeration. This phenomenon occurs most commonly when the air temperature ranges from 30°F to 40°F. If you can restore gas pressure by pouring a pint of warm water on the regulator, you have moisture in your gas. Have some gas-line dryer (methyl alcohol) injected by a propane refiller. Only one pint per 100 gallons is needed, so the serviceman must measure with a shot glass, not a milk bucket. Be sure it comes from a sealed container, since alcohol stored in a barrel will already be saturated with water.

Other gas interruptions also are referred to as freeze-up. They may be the result of a regulator vent being plugged so the diaphragm cannot breathe. Look for signs of bug nests in vents. Also, mud or salt corrosion in the vent screen will restrict breathing.

Finally, liquid propane being fed to the regulator may create interruption of flow. Liquid can enter the regulator if the tank or cylinder is used in an improper position. Observe the arrows and warning decals. Horizontal DOT cylinders are constructed with internal tubes so they can be used either vertically or horizontally. However, when used horizontally, they must be used in a specific, well-identified position (stickers state which position of the cylinder is "up"). Liquid propane reaching the regulator may indicate overfill. Check the liq-

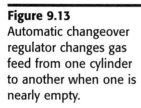

Figure 9.13
Automatic changeover regulator changes gas feed from one cylinder to another when one is nearly empty.

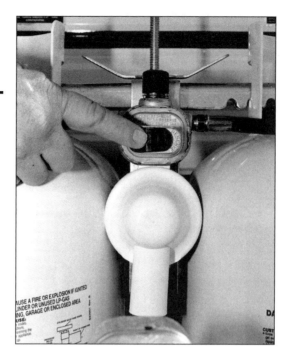

uid level by using the outage valve, and bleed if necessary.

Small amounts of liquid can splash into the drop tube, the tube within the tank that goes up into the vapor space of ASME tanks or horizontal cylinders. This normally does not affect a two-stage regulator but can cause a possible gas interruption if you use an old-style single-stage regulator. Vibrations can cause a drop tube to crack or even break off. If this condition is suspected, have your tank checked by a qualified technician. Continuing regulator problems would indicate that this is a possibility. Your regulator may also show frost or feel cold even when the air temperature is above 40°F.

TESTING AND INSPECTING PROPANE SYSTEMS

There are several testing and inspection procedures for propane tanks that are necessary for both safe and efficient operation.

Checking Gas Quantity

A test to determine the quantity of gas in a DOT container requires a scale. Merely weigh the cylinder and subtract the tare weight as stamped on the guard, for example, T.W. 18; the difference is the weight of the fuel. (Propane weighs 4.24 pounds per gallon, as previously mentioned.)

Moisture on your cylinder or tank may be visible on cool, but not freezing, mornings, after overnight use of your furnace. The visible demarcation line between the moisture and the dry upper surface of the cylinder/tank will indicate the liquid level. A frost line may be visible in cold weather.

In warm weather, you can pour a glass of water over your cylinder tank after use and there will usually be a visible area of difference in the way the water shows bubbles, indicating the liquid level.

The Automatic Regulator

The automatic regulator is designed for use with two cylinders connected by high-pressure lines called pigtails (Figure 9.13). With both valves turned on, the regulator will use the cylinder (called the service cylinder) indicated by the arrow or marker on the regulator. As long as there is fuel in the service cylinder, the full-empty indicator on top of the regulator will show white (silver). When the service cylinder goes empty, the indicator will show red, and the regulator will change the gas supply to the reserve cylinder without interruption.

When you observe the red indicator, you may close the service-cylinder valve. Rotate the selector knob so the arrow/marker points to the reserve. This transforms the reserve cylinder to the service cylinder. Now disconnect the POL pigtail on the empty tank. Refill, reconnect, open the valve, test the connection, and you have a full tank in reserve again.

If you experience a gas leak when disconnecting the pigtail, you have forgotten to turn the arrow or close your empty tank valve. The full-empty indicator on the changeover regulator is simply a pressure gauge calibrated at about 10 pounds. It can also be used as a leak-detecting device. Check that all burners and pilot lights are turned off. Then turn on your cylinder valve slowly. Listen to the regulator for the sound of gas flow. If you hear no flow, turn off both tanks. Wait thirty minutes and check the full-empty indicator. If it has turned red, you have a leak.

Try this test with a range pilot turned on; either the top-burner pilot or oven pilot will do. The gas that escapes through one of these pilots will take about ten minutes to turn the indicator red. The larger the leak, the earlier the red will show. Doing the test with a gas leak of known size (pilot) will help you better understand the process. If your pipe system loses pressure after several hours, remember that gas controls have minute leaks. Don't test for leaks with a match; leave power disconnected while testing.

Motorhomes do not have automatic regulators. However, other devices can be used as leak detectors on motorhome systems and are available at many RV supply stores.

The propane system provides a dependable, safe fuel that adds comfort and convenience to our RV experience, no matter where we choose to camp. A little knowledge and care will add to its reliability and our peace of mind.

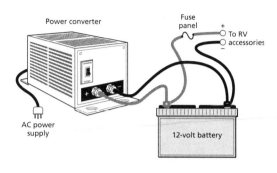

Power converter

Fuse panel

+ To RV accessories
−

AC power supply

12-volt battery

Chapter 10

RV ELECTRICAL SYSTEMS

Although electricity can be a complex topic, the RV owner doesn't have to be an engineer to grasp the fundamentals of electrical systems and to perform basic troubleshooting. A problem could be something simple that appears complex, but even if it's a major problem, knowing what's wrong and how the system works will help when dealing with a repair facility.

HOW ELECTRICITY IS SUPPLIED

The electrical requirements of an RV are supplied from one of three sources: an outside source of 120-volt AC (campground hookup), power from an on-board AC generator, or an automotive alternator (another type of generator). When we want to save some of this power for later consumption, we use storage batteries. RV storage batteries are of the lead-acid type, with lead plates and sulfuric acid as a component of the electrolyte. These batteries convert electrical energy to chemical energy. Then, on demand, they reconvert the chemical energy back to electrical energy.

Alternating and Direct Current

Electrical power (or current) can be produced and transmitted in two different forms: alternating current (AC) and direct current (DC). Direct current is constant; the electrons flow steadily in one direction. With alternating current, the electrons rapidly and constantly reverse direction. The frequency with which they reverse direction is measured in cycles per second, or Hertz (Hz). The standard frequency for alternating current in the United States, 60-Hz standard house current, sometimes known as "110 volts," actually is 117- to 120-volt 60-Hz AC.

Batteries can only store and supply direct current. Mechanical generating devices can produce either direct or alternating current. DC generators were commonly used on cars and trucks through the 1960s to charge the batteries and provide for the electrical needs of the vehicles.

With the advent of solid-state electronics, compact, efficient AC generators (commonly called alternators) were introduced in vehicles because they were more efficient than DC models. Automotive alternators produce alternating current and employ diodes to convert (rectify) it to direct current for automotive 12-volt DC systems. RV generators such as those used in motorhomes to supply "house" power mainly produce 120-volts AC.

Units of Measurement

When you work with electricity, an understanding of the following terms will be helpful:

Voltage can be defined as electrical pressure—the amount of electrical force pushing the electrons through the circuit. In principle, it's the same as pounds per square inch in a water system.

Amperes (amps) are units of electrical flow, or volume. This is analogous to gallons per minute of water. Often, small currents such as those which run clocks are rated in milliamps. One milliamp is $\frac{1}{1,000}$ of an amp.

Ohms are a measure of resistance to flow, or restriction. Think of it relative to the size of the pipe or how far the faucet has been opened.

Watts are a measure of electrical power, or work. One watt equals one volt times one amp, or said another way, volts multiplied by amps equal watts. Larger amounts of power are measured in kilowatts (1,000 watts).

All of these terms are interrelated. Amperage varies directly based on how much voltage is applied and is inversely proportional to resistance (ohms). The relationship can be stated in several ways:

- When voltage goes up or down, current goes up or down with it, assuming resistance doesn't change.

- When resistance goes up or down, current flow goes up or down, assuming voltage stays the same.

- When voltage goes up or down, wattage goes up or down, assuming resistance stays the same.

When dealing with these concepts, Ohm's Law can be helpful. The formula, conceived by German physicist George Ohm in 1826, can be used in several ways, with these values:

R = resistance, measured in ohms
E = voltage
I = current, measured in amps

$$\frac{E}{IR}$$

The formula can be altered for various purposes by using any of the three values as the unknown element:

$$E = I \times R \: ; \: I = E \div R \: ; \: R = E \div I \: .$$

Example: You want to know the voltage required to drive a 6-amp current through a resistance of 2 ohms. Use E as the unknown; 6 (amps) × 2 (ohms) = 12; the voltage needed is 12.

Example: How much resistance occurs when 12 volts push 2 amps of current through a wire? Use R as the unknown; 12 (volts) divided by 2 (amps) = 6; the answer is 6 ohms.

AC AND DC SYSTEMS

RVs utilize three separate electrical systems: two 12-volt DC (12VDC) systems and one 120-volt AC (120VAC) system.

The 12-Volt DC Chassis System

The 12-volt DC system is used to provide power for chassis components such as the ignition system, electronic fuel injection, running lights, air conditioning, etc. (Figure 10.1). It includes an alternator, a battery for engine starting, and all the necessary wiring, fuses, circuit breakers, and other components common to an automotive system.

Trailers utilize the tow-vehicle's electrical system to operate their electric brakes, turn signals, stop lights, and running lamps.

The other 12-volt DC system has its own batteries and is often referred to as the "house" system (Figure 10.2). This system operates such accessories as the furnace, the water pump, interior lights, and fans. It's usually iso-

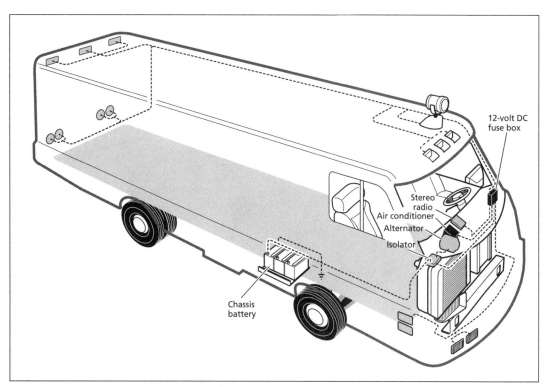

Figure 10.1
Power for chassis 12-volt DC electrical needs is provided by the vehicle alternator, which also powers "house" appliances.

lated from the chassis electrical system so the coach appliances cannot accidentally drain the engine-starting battery. The house batteries are charged by the same engine-mounted alternator that charges the vehicle battery, by means of an isolator that prevents the coach batteries from draining the engine battery. The house-battery bank also can be charged by an RV electrical converter, which changes 120-volt AC to 12-volt DC when the RV is connected to a 120-volt AC power source. This source can be either campground power or the AC generator.

The wiring layout for this system is similar in principle to that of the chassis system but less complex since it doesn't involve an engine. Typically, one or more deep-cycle RV batteries provide the power, which is then channeled to one or more fuse panels via positive (+) wires of appropriate size. The negative (-) or ground side is usually also connected to the coach frame.

From the fuse panel(s), power is routed to various 12-volt appliances (the furnace, interior lights, the water pump, fans, and outlets for 12-

volt DC portable appliances, such as a television or a radio). The AM/FM stereo, tape, or CD unit built into the dash of a typical motorhome usually is connected to the chassis 12-volt system rather than to the coach system.

The 120-Volt AC System

The 120-volt AC system (Figure 10.3) allows the use of household-type AC appliances and motors and is very similar in concept to the electrical system in a home, except that the source of power for the system is not a utility pole in the backyard but an umbilical cord designed to be plugged into a campground receptacle or an AC-generator electrical system. The AC system usually has circuits for such permanent appliances as air conditioners and microwave ovens, and wall outlets for powering other appliances. Most RVs include an electrical converter that converts 120-volt AC into 12-volt DC. When a source of 120-volt AC is present, the AC system provides power for appliances such as those found in a home, while the converter supplies power for the 12-volt DC system. The converter also may serve

Figure 10.2
"House" 12-volt DC systems, appliances, and batteries are supplied by the vehicle alternator. An AC generator may also provide 12-volt DC power via an electrical convertor.

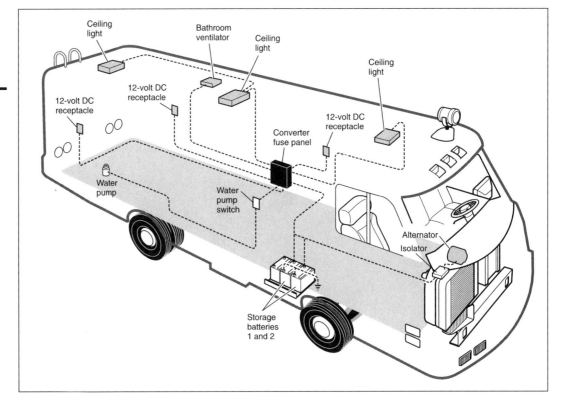

as a charger for the house batteries. The more sophisticated RVs may also include inverters, which change 12-volt DC (taken from batteries) into 120-volt AC when an outside hookup is not available.

The heart of the 120-volt AC system in an RV is the main distribution panel (Figure 10.4), into which the input wires from the RV hookup cord and the AC generator (if so equipped) feed. With 30-amp service, there are three incoming wires from either source, two for power transmission and a third (ground) for safety. With 50-amp service, a third power transmission wire is added. All appliances and wall outlets in the RV should have three connections—a Line (or "Hot"), Neutral (or "Common") and Ground connection. The power is fed to several circuit breakers that serve as the source for all the individual circuits that feed appliances and the wall outlets.

It's important to be aware of potential overloads. For example, if the receptacle in a campground and the campground hookup cord on your RV are rated at 30 amps, it's possible to turn on enough appliances to exceed that rating. If an RV has two roof air conditioners, most manufacturers wire the coaches so only one can be operated from the campground hookup; the other must be operated from an on-board AC generator. The arrangement is designed to keep people from operating both air conditioners and then turning on yet another appliance, such as a toaster, coffeemaker, or the microwave oven.

A list of appliances frequently used in RVs and their typical power requirements can be found in Table 10.1 (p.127). Appliances differ, and power ratings will vary. For exact ratings, refer to the identification plate on the appliance.

ELECTRICAL SAFETY

Electrical hazards are silent and invisible. The two prevalent dangers are fire and shock. Fires may be caused by short circuits and overloads if the system is not set up and used correctly. Shock is caused when electricity finds an easy path through a person to ground.

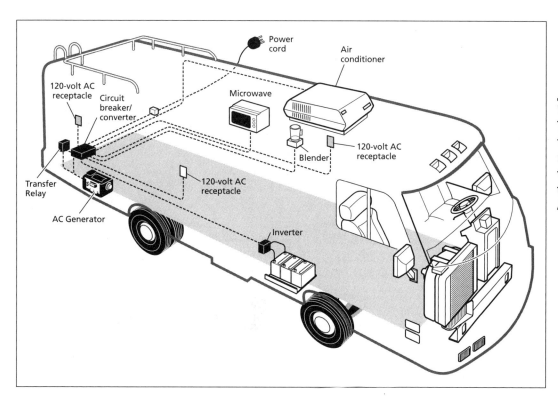

Figure 10.3
The 120-volt AC system is similar for motorhomes and trailers, except that trailers may not have AC generators.

Figure 10.4
The main power-distribution panel provides circuit protection for all 120-volt-AC appliances.

Short Circuits and Shock Hazards

A short circuit occurs when a "hot" wire comes in contact with a ground (return) connection. This can happen when wires come loose and touch something or insulation is rubbed through. When a short circuit occurs, the safety device (circuit breaker or fuse) should prevent any problems.

Shock and electrocution aren't a danger with 12-volt DC systems, but 120-volt AC systems can knock you for a loop. To protect yourself from shock, disconnect the power source before working on any electrical device.

Before you plug your rig in, be sure all major loads are shut off. Check the electrical outlet, plug, and wire for damage and fraying. The insulation on all wires should be intact and unbroken. Cover the exposed spots with electrical tape, and replace any wiring if the conductors are damaged.

Beyond personal danger, the result of a short circuit can be very high current flow, melted insulation, and fire at the place of contact if the circuit is not properly protected by a circuit breaker or if the circuit breaker is rated for more current than the circuit can handle.

Problems can be caused by improper wiring in the receptacle at a campground, and it's wise to check the receptacle with a wiring-checking device before plugging into it. Although you should not attempt to correct a fault in a campground receptacle, you should know that 120-volt AC wiring is conventionally color coded with black as "hot" or positive and white as "return" or "neutral." These are the two flat prongs on a common three-prong plug; the round pin is the ground connection, which is usually connected to a green insulated wire or a bare wire (Figure 10.5).

Polarity-checking devices (Figure 10.6) are available at most RV supply stores. If the circuit does not check out properly, don't connect to it. Find another that tests okay, and ask the park management to repair the problem receptacle.

To protect against short circuits, inspect the electrical system for loose connections and damaged or chafed insulation. Be sure all circuit breakers and/or fuses are the correct capacity.

Figure 10.5
Correct polarity of the 120-volt AC system can be checked at any wall outlet wth a test light, multimeter, or polarity check device.

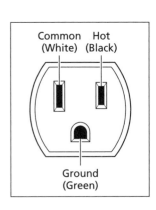

Table 10.1

Common RV Appliances and Their Power Requirements

Appliance	Watts	Appliance	Watts
Air conditioner	1,400	Ice maker	600
Blender	1,000	Microwave oven	800 to 1,500
Coffeemaker	1,400	Popcorn popper	1,400
Computer	200	Refrigerator	600
Drill motor	350	Television (13 inch)	700
Electric blanket	120	Trash compactor	800 to 1,000
Freezer	500	Videocassette recorder	25
Hair dryer	1,500	Satellite dish	200 to 300

Figure 10.6
Polarity-checking devices can be purchased at RV supply stores.

Overloads

Overloads occur when circuits are forced to handle more current than they are designed for. The more amperage, the more heat is produced. If the fuse or circuit breaker doesn't shut down an overloaded circuit, the insulation on the wiring may melt, and the wires could touch, causing a fire. Although we commonly think that only 120-volt AC systems have the capacity to cause fires, a 12-volt DC system can easily create enough heat to do so.

Overloading can happen when an RV owner adds lights or appliances and installs higher amperage fuses or circuit breakers to handle the additional load. Fuses and circuit breakers are supposed to be the weakest link in a circuit. Before adding any electrical devices to a circuit, be sure the added load will not exceed the rating of the wiring and circuit breaker or fuse. Never replace a circuit-protection device with one of a higher amperage rating. Instead, install a separate fuse holder or circuit breaker and use wire rated for higher amperage than the circuit protection when adding accessories. See Table 10.2 for wiring loads.

120-Volt AC Cords

Sometimes an extension is needed as an add-on to the RV power cord so it will reach a power outlet. The extension cord must be large enough to carry the expected loads. To feed an RV with 30-amp service, the cord should be 10-gauge wire. The cord should also be as short as possible; the use of long or undersize cords results in additional voltage drop, which reduces the voltage available to appliances, possibly causing motor damage through overheating.

Adapters

Low voltage may also be caused by the risky practice of using an adapter for connecting a 30-amp power cord to an outlet rated lower—usually 15 amps. Most of us do it because 30-amp outlets are not always available. The use of an adapter probably will cause problems if we use the rig as if it was still plugged into 30-amp power. An air conditioner alone may require more than a 15-amp circuit can handle, and the 15-amp plug will become warm. It's not wise to run a 13,500-Btu air conditioner from a 15-amp receptacle; smaller air conditioners are okay on 15-amp circuits unless other appliances that consume substantial power are used simultaneously.

If you have to use adapters, be aware of their ratings, and match your loads to the ratings. This goes for 50-amp to 30-amp adapters, too. Make sure the adapter is in good condition. Loose connections create high resistance and heat. Be wary of the odor of hot electrical equipment, and investigate any popping sounds emitted by such equipment.

Load-Shedding Devices

Load-shedding devices are available to automatically turn off the air conditioner if current flow exceeds a preset amount. There are also devices that run one air conditioner and then the other. If your RV is not equipped with such devices, this task is left to you. To determine the load, add the total amp draw of every appliance you plan to operate simultaneously. Keep that total at or below the rated limit of the power supply and wiring. If you only have the watt rating of a 120-volt AC appliance, divide that rating by the voltage (120) to determine the amperage draw. If a 12-volt DC device draws 10 amps from the converter, it will only add a little more than 1 amp draw to the 120-volt AC circuit.

Ground Fault Circuit Interrupters

All RVs of recent manufacture are equipped with 120-volt AC Ground Fault Circuit Interrupter (GFCI) outlets where receptacles are located in the bathroom and kitchen (Figure 10.7) with outdoor plugs included in the circuit. They can be identified by the small buttons marked "T" for test and "R" for reset on the face plates. The GFCI monitors the variance in current between the "hot" and "ground" wires in the outlet. If a short circuit is drawing current to ground (such as through a human body), the levels of current in the two wires will differ. Sensing this, the GFCI will shut down the outlet. To be sure the GFCI is working properly, press the "T," or test, button. When you do this, the "R," or reset, button should pop out and the outlet will go dead. Pressing the "R" button again should lock it in and restore power. If the GFCI doesn't work properly, check for faulty wiring and connections. If they check out, the GFCI receptacle may need replacement.

Surge Protectors

Both lightning and man-made electrical noise can induce extremely short-duration high-voltage "spikes" on the AC power line, which

Table 10.2
Amperage Load in Circuit

Gauge	1	1.5	2	3	4	5	6	7	8	10	12	15	20	24	30	36	50	100	150	200
					Allowable Conductor Length—(Feet) in Circuit Before 1-Volt Loss															
20	106	70	53	35	26	21	17	15	13	10	8	7	5	4	3	3	2	1	0	0
18	150	100	75	50	37	30	25	21	18	15	12	10	7	6	5	4	3	1	1	0
16	224	144	112	74	56	44	37	32	28	22	18	14	11	9	7	6	4	2	1	1
14	362	241	181	120	90	72	60	51	45	36	30	24	18	15	12	10	7	3	2	1
12	572	381	286	190	143	114	95	81	71	57	47	38	28	23	19	15	11	5	3	2
10	908	605	454	302	227	181	151	129	113	90	75	60	45	37	30	25	18	9	6	4
8	1452	967	726	483	363	290	241	207	181	145	120	96	72	60	48	40	29	14	9	7
6	2342	1560	1171	780	585	468	390	334	292	234	194	155	117	97	78	65	46	23	15	11
4	3702	2467	1851	1232	925	740	616	529	462	370	307	246	185	154	123	102	74	37	24	18
2	6060	4038	3030	2018	1515	1212	1009	866	757	606	503	403	303	252	201	168	121	60	40	30
1	7692	5126	3846	2561	1923	1538	1280	1100	961	769	638	511	384	320	256	213	153	76	51	38
0	9708	6470	4854	3232	2427	1941	1616	1388	1213	970	805	645	485	404	323	269	194	97	64	48

Table is computed for a 68°F (20°C) ambient temperature.

may then enter an RV via the shore power cord. The damage caused by low-level spikes is often cumulative in nature, so affected appliances fail for no apparent reason. Larger spikes (such as those caused by a nearby lightning strike) may cause immediate failure.

A variety of surge suppressors is available for protection against spikes. These devices typically include a circuit that momentarily conducts current whenever the voltage rises to an abnormal level, thereby short-circuiting (or "clamping") the spike. A suppressor's effectiveness is determined in part by its energy-dissipating capacity (often expressed in joules), its response time (often expressed in microseconds or picoseconds), and its location within the circuit. Generally, a suppressor that is located "upwind" of the device to be protected will be more effective than when it is located "downwind." Also, suppressors that provide clamping across all three wires in a 30-amp circuit (or all four wires in a 50-amp circuit) are more effective than models that simply clamp spikes between the "hot" and "neutral" wires.

Handling an Emergency

If an electrical fire occurs, first disconnect the power source by switching off the circuit breakers, unplugging the power cord, shutting off the AC generator, or disconnecting/switching off the batteries. Be careful because the wiring may become very hot. Then aim a dry-chemical, carbon-dioxide, or Halon fire extinguisher at the base of the flames. Read the instructions on your fire extinguishers now; don't wait until there's a fire! Never use water on an electrical fire while the electricity is on. After the electricity is unplugged, the fire is no longer electrical in nature and water may be used, unless there is a Class B fuel source like flammable liquids involved.

To assist someone who has received a severe electrical shock, shut off the power source first if the person is still near or connected to the electrical source; then check for breathing and pulse. Call for help and begin artificial respiration and cardiopulmonary resuscitation if needed and if you know how. (The Red Cross offers classes on these subjects.)

ELECTRICAL-PROBLEM DIAGNOSIS

The goal of electrical diagnosis is to find the faulty component that keeps the current from flowing through the circuit as originally designed. As manufacturers load up modern RVs with electrical devices, the potential for problems increases. Given the complexity of these systems and the high cost of many replacement parts, a "hit-or-miss" approach to troubleshooting must be avoided. An organ-

Figure 10.7
Ground fault circuit interrupters, which help prevent electrical shock, should be tested periodically.

ized and logical approach to diagnosis is essential to repair these electrical circuits quickly and cost effectively. Since electricity is invisible, special testers are needed to check circuits and components.

Using Test Equipment

Before you begin chasing electrical gremlins, you must know how to use test equipment. Most testers come with instructions. If they differ from the general procedures described here, follow the specific instructions provided by the manufacturer of the tester.

Caution: Never connect circuits to a higher voltage than they were designed for, and never test them with any device other than a good high-impedance tester, such as a digital multimeter.

Test Lights

Test lights are used to check for voltage in AC and DC circuits while power is connected (Figure 10.8). Test lights for 12-volt DC and 120-volt AC should be included in every toolbox unless a multimeter is included. In that case, the 120-volt AC test light can be omitted. Although accurate voltage measurements aren't possible with a test light, large differences may be detected by the relative brightness of the lighted bulb. Before using a test light for diagnosis, check it by connecting it to a known source of power to insure that the bulb is functional.

Using a 12-Volt Test Light

Twelve-volt test lights have a multitude of uses, such as this common example:

1. Connect the ground wire of a test light to a clean, bare metal ground.

2. With the circuit switched on, insert the probe into the 12-volt terminal or socket to be checked. If necessary, the probe may be pushed through the insulation to make contact with a wire (some testers have a special insulation-piercing probe).

3. The bulb should light if there is sufficient voltage present.

4. After testing is complete, tape over any wires exposed by the probe. Test lights are not sensitive to polarity and can be connected either way.

Uses for a 120-volt test light are more limited. Such a light can be used, for example, to test for power to all circuit breakers in a power-distribution panel.

Continuity Testers

Continuity testers, also known as self-powered test lights, are used to check for open or short circuits on 12-volt DC systems. Continuity testers must not be used on powered circuits, since any external voltage may burn out the low-voltage bulb in the tester. Never use a self-powered continuity tester on circuits that contain solid-state components, since damage to these components may occur.

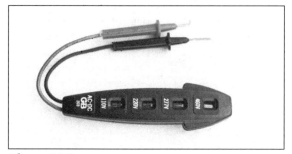
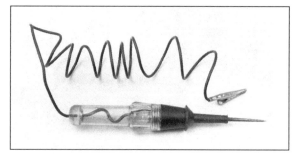

Figure 10.8
Test lights can be used to check for presence of voltage in 12- and 120-volt systems.
Be sure to use the correct light for the 120-volt system.

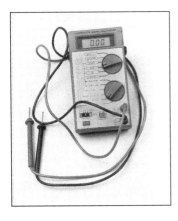

Figure 10.9
A multimeter performs a variety of functions and is essential for electrical troubleshooting.

Continuity (an unbroken circuit) may be checked with a number of devices. If the circuit has power in it, a voltmeter or test light may be used as previously described. If the circuit is not powered, an ohmmeter or self-powered continuity tester should be used.

To use a continuity tester, first isolate the circuit by disconnecting the battery or removing the fuse or circuit breaker. Select two points along the circuit through which power should pass. Connect one lead of the tester to each point. If there is continuity, the test lamp will light, meaning there is a path for current flow.

Multimeters

Analog multimeters (needle on dial) are suitable for most 12-volt DC and 120-volt AC RV test functions requiring the measurement of volts, ohms, and amperes. If you own an analog unit, use it for the tests described in this chapter. However, if you buy a new multimeter, choose a digital model, which will perform all the tests of which an analog unit is capable, is more accurate, and is compatible with solid-state devices (Figure 10.9)

All multimeters are sold with instructions explaining how to perform a variety of tests. An example of multimeter use is measurement of voltage. The leads are pressed against the contact surfaces to be measured. If the power source is 120 volts AC, be sure your hands are not in contact with the meter probes. Most multimeters will measure a broad range of DC- and AC-voltage levels, including battery and charging voltage in the DC system of an RV. For example, a reading lower than 13 volts at

either the chassis or house batteries while the engine is running at about 1,500 rpm or higher can indicate loss of alternator output. While AC voltage of 110 to 120 volts may be adequate without a load on the system, it may drop to 105 volts or lower when an air conditioner is switched on, which is too low.

ELECTRICAL TESTING

Testing for Open DC Ground Connections

To test for an open DC ground connection:

Connect a jumper wire (Figure 10.10) between the component case or ground terminal and a clean, bare metal spot on the vehicle chassis. If a circuit works properly with the jumper wire in place but doesn't work when the jumper wire is removed, the ground circuit has an open section (high resistance) that needs correction.

Testing a Battery-Voltage-Operated Component

To test a component designed to operate on battery voltage:

Ground the device with a jumper as described above and also connect a fused jumper wire from the positive battery terminal to the positive terminal on the component being tested. If it now works normally, remove the ground jumper wire, and if the device stops working, repair the ground connection. If the device still doesn't work, look for a break in the positive side of the circuit.

Checking Resistance

Resistance is checked with the ohm-measuring function of a multimeter. Turn the scale-selector switch to the proper ohms range for the device you will be measuring. Insure that the wires are connected to the proper plugs in the meter and turn the meter on. Check that the meter reads "infinity" before testing is begun, and then touch the test probes together to make certain that the meter goes to zero, which means no resistance. Note: Resistance tests must not be used on powered circuits, since any external voltage will cause a false reading, and may also damage the meter.

Checking Voltage Drop

Perform this test for voltage that is lost when current travels through a wire, connection, or switch:

1. Connect the positive lead of a multimeter to the end of the wire (or to one side of the connection or switch) that is closer to the battery.

2. Connect the negative lead of the multimeter to the other end of the wire (or the other side of the connection or switch).

3. Select the multimeter range just above battery voltage.

4. Switch on the circuit.

5. The multimeter will show the difference in voltage between the two points. A difference (or drop) of more than about one volt typically indicates a problem, depending on the load. When heavy current passes through a wire, more voltage drop occurs.

6. Clean and repair the connections as needed or replace any faulty components.

When no current is flowing, there can be no voltage drop.

Warning: On 120- or 240-volt AC systems, do not touch test leads while they are connected to power.

Checking Direct-Current Flow

Ammeters are always connected in series with the circuit being tested (except shunts and units with inductive pickups). Make sure the meter is rated to handle more current than you plan to measure. Select the highest scale and work down if that scale is too high for what you are measuring.

1. To place an ammeter in a circuit, unplug one of the connectors in the circuit and attach the test leads to the two connectors.

2. Switch on an appliance connected to the circuit and read the amperage (or current draw) shown on the meter. If it shows a negative reading, reverse the test lead connections. No reading indicates an open (incomplete) circuit.

3. Compare the reading to the specified current rating (when available) to deter-

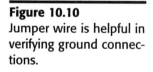

Figure 10.10
Jumper wire is helpful in verifying ground connections.

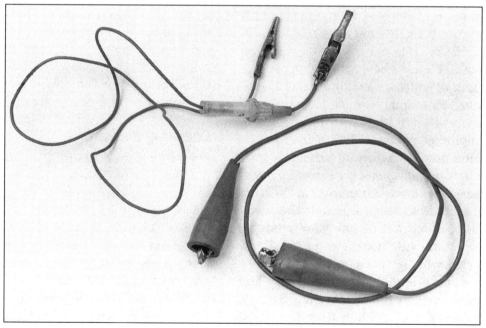

mine if the component is defective. Many electrical components have voltage and amperage ratings stamped on their cases.

ELECTRICAL TROUBLESHOOTING STRATEGIES

Before you begin troubleshooting a circuit, formulate a plan of action. Let's take a look at some of the methods professionals use when tracking down problems.

Intermittent Electrical Problems

The toughest type of electrical problem to diagnose is an intermittent one. Intermittent opens or shorts are usually caused by something rubbing or a component that changes resistance when it heats up. Corroded and loose connections are also frequently the cause of such problems.

Observe when the problem occurs, and try to discover how to duplicate the problem. For example, does it only happen when going around a corner or over a rough railroad crossing? Sometimes wiggling the wiring harness or tapping your hand on the fixture will locate the problem. Once you can duplicate the problem, follow the test procedures that follow. (Any items that are corroded or have recently been disturbed or worked on are prime suspects.)

Identify the Problem

Operate the problem circuit in all modes. What doesn't work properly? Is it a complete or partial failure? Which systems does it affect? When does it occur?

Determine which components in the circuit, if any, still work. For example, if you find that only one device in the circuit is out, you have eliminated the fuse, switch, and main wiring harness as potential sources of the problem.

Obtain the wiring diagrams for the specific vehicle you are working on, when possible. Familiarize yourself with the current flow in the circuit by tracing the path in the wiring diagram. Determine where the circuit receives current, what the circuit protection is, which switches and/or relays control current flow, and how the components operate.

Check the fuses and/or circuit breakers. If the circuit-protection devices are blown, look for a short circuit; if they are intact, look for an open circuit.

Test the Cause

Most electrical failures are caused by these four items:

1. The wire or component is not receiving current. Test for voltage at the component.

2. The component is not grounded properly. Test for voltage drop between the component side of its ground connection and a good ground with power on, or check for resistance between the component and ground with the power off.

3. The wiring is faulty. With the power on, check for voltage drop across each connection. With the power off, check for continuity or resistance.

4. The component itself is faulty. With the power off, check for resistance through the appliance. If there is voltage at the positive wire going to the appliance and a good ground connection, the appliance is probably faulty.

As a general rule, if the fault affects a single component of a circuit, begin testing at that component. If the fault affects several components of a circuit, begin testing at the point where the circuit draws its power. Check for obvious problems first, such as corroded connections, broken wires, or burned-out bulbs.

Elusive Problems

If access to a circuit is a problem, it may be easier to disconnect an old, damaged circuit at both ends and create a new circuit—in effect, wiring around the problem. Check the wiring diagram (if available) to determine how circuits are connected. In the absence of a diagram, check all the connections at both ends to make sure no other circuits will be affected and that no feedback problems will occur.

Always use wire of at least the same size as the original. If you're not sure, use the next-size-heavier wire. Wire-gauge numbers get lower for heavier wire. For example, a 12-gauge wire is heavier than a 14-gauge wire.

Consult Table 10.2, page 126, to determine the proper gauge based on the round-trip length of the circuit and the fuse rating. For example, if the circuit and fuse must handle 15 amps and the circuit length is 24 feet, use 14-gauge wire. The amp rating of the fuse must always be the same or lower than the wire.

12-Volt DC Lighting Circuits

Interior lighting on RVs is fairly trouble free, but exterior lighting requires more attention because of weather and physical damage. The most common types of problems are bad ground connection, burned-out fuses or bulbs, damaged fixtures, corroded terminals, and pulled-out or broken wires. Check the obvious items first. If the fuse is good, check for voltage at the socket with a test light. If voltage is present, try a new bulb. If no voltage is present at the fixture, check for power at both sides of the switch (switch on). Also look for a bad ground-return path, which is very common in taillights, marker lights, and turn signals.

When a tow vehicle and trailer are involved, make sure the ground connection between tow vehicle and trailer is valid. Checking for proper ground is easily done with a jumper wire connected to a known good ground and to the external surface of a light socket.

If power is not present in a light socket or other terminal, work your way backward in the circuit toward the fuse panel, paying special attention to connections.

Charging Systems

The alternator supplies electricity for charging batteries and operating accessories when the engine is running. Alternators are usually mounted on the front of the engine and driven by a belt off the crankshaft pulley.

A voltage regulator is used to limit the cur-rent output of the alternator. The voltage regulator automatically limits alternator output voltage to a preset level, varying from about 14.0 to 14.8 volts depending on brand, type, operating temperature, and charge level of one or more batteries.

If the vehicle is equipped with a charging light on the dash, it should be illuminated when the ignition key is turned on, then go out after the engine starts. If the light fails to go out after the engine starts, the alternator, voltage regulator, or connecting wiring is faulty. If the light is illuminated when the ignition is turned off, one or more diodes is defective.

Begin your charging-system inspection by checking cleanliness and security of the battery terminals at the battery, as well as the connections on the back of the alternator. Then check the drive belt for tension, glazing, and cracks. Adjust or replace as necessary. Never disconnect a battery cable when the engine is running.

If the vehicle's lights are excessively bright and bulbs burn out frequently, the voltage regulator may be faulty. Connect a voltmeter to the battery terminals with the engine off and note the reading. Start the engine and again take a reading. On a normally functioning 12-volt DC system, starting battery voltage at rest should be about 12.6, unless the battery is depleted. When the engine is started, voltage should rise quickly to the aforementioned 14.0- to 14.8-volt level. The higher levels usually are reached only in cold weather by a voltage-compensating alternator. Those same temperature-compensating alternators may cut voltage below 14.0 volts during hot-weather driving. However, a voltage reading of at least 14.0 when the engine has not heated the alternator to high levels indicates that the alternator is working properly. Low alternator voltage output causes inadequate battery charging.

Excessively high voltage with the engine running indicates a need for regulator replacement. If the voltage is too low, the alternator, regulator, wiring, or connections could be defective. Specialized help should be sought for checking voltage regulation.

Battery Isolators

Because RVs have battery-powered appliances that must be operated while the vehicle is parked, a battery isolator is necessary to make sure only the house batteries are used for RV appliances (see Chapter 8). An isolator allows one battery to be kept fully charged for engine starting. Through the magic of electronics, the one-way electrical valves (diodes) of a solid-state battery isolator allow power to flow from the engine-mounted alternator to charge all the batteries while preventing electricity from flowing out of one battery into another. This function also may be provided by an electrical relay. When triggered by the ignition switch, the relay contacts close and bring all batteries into parallel for charging by the alternator. When the ignition switch is turned off, contacts open and the house batteries are separated from the engine-starting battery.

Trailer-Wiring Connectors

The trailer-wiring connector must be capable of carrying power from the tow vehicle to the trailer lights, brakes, and batteries. A thorough inspection is in order every time you connect it. Make sure that the plug is clean and tight, and the prongs are undamaged.

Most travel trailers use 7- or 9-flat-pin Bargman or Pollak plugs and receptacles. The 9-pin plugs are used only when a trailer is equipped with a refrigerator that is operated on 12-volt DC power while traveling. To simplify matters, color codes have been standardized by the RV industry (Figure 10.11).

Some late-model vehicles have separate brake lights and turn signals. An electrical converter sold at RV supply stores must be wired into the harness to make this system compatible with most trailers.

To troubleshoot trailer-connector electrical problems, have an assistant operate each circuit, one at a time, from the tow vehicle. With the trailer plug disconnected, use a test light to probe the tow-vehicle side of the connector for power in the appropriate terminal. If the terminal doesn't have power, the problem is in the tow-vehicle wiring. If the terminal has power, check the trailer connector and

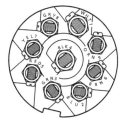

7-Pin Connector
(Socket Interior)
1. White, ground
2. Blue, elect. brake
3. Green, tail
4. Black, batt. charge
5. Red, stop/left-turn
6. Brown, stop/right-turn
7. Yellow, aux. circuit

9-Pin Connector
(Socket Interior)
1. White, ground
2. Blue, elect. brake
3. Green, tail
4. Black, batt. charge
5. Red, stop/left-turn
6. Brown, stop/right-turn
7. Yellow, aux. circuit
8. Gray, aux. circuit
9. Orange, refrigerator

Figure 10.11
Diagrams for trailer connectors are essential in verifying correct wiring hookup.

wiring harness for continuity. The most common problem is a faulty (usually corroded) ground connection.

Electric Trailer Brakes

Electric trailer brakes utilize a revolving armature located in the brake drum. An electromagnet pivots on an arm with a cam that is attached between the brake shoes. When the magnet is energized, current flows through it, causing a magnetic attraction between it and the armature. The magnet attempts to follow the rotation of the armature. This causes the cam to rotate, actuating the primary brake shoe into the drum and energizing the secondary shoe, resisting the rotation of the drum.

Most problems with electric brakes are electrical, occurring in the connecting wiring or

Table 10.3

Trailer Brakes—Maximum Current in Amps

Brake Size (inches)	Two Brakes	Four Brakes	Six Brakes
7	3.8-4.4	7.6-8.8	11.4-13.2
10, 12	6.0-6.5	12-13	18-19.5

the brake controller (Figure 10.12). To test electric brakes, connect an ammeter in series between the controller and the electric brakes. Actuate the controller with the manual lever and note the reading. Current should vary depending on how hard the brakes are applied. The maximum depends on the size and number of brakes (Table 10.3).

If a high or low current is registered, check for faulty wiring, bad grounds, and corroded trailer plugs. If an electrical problem is isolated to the trailer, check all exposed wiring for electrical short circuits caused by chafing of wires against metal. Use a multimeter to check for resistance of

wiring inside axle tubes where they sometimes chafe and make contact with the metal tube. Inspect the electromagnets for wear or shorting.

Brake Controls

There are two major categories of brake controls, hydraulic/electric and electronic. Hydraulic controls tee into the brake lines near the master cylinder and use line pressure to modulate the electrical current sent to the trailer brakes. The use of a variable resistor may be necessary in order to prevent excessive brake actuation when a hydraulic/electric control is used. This type of control is rarely used

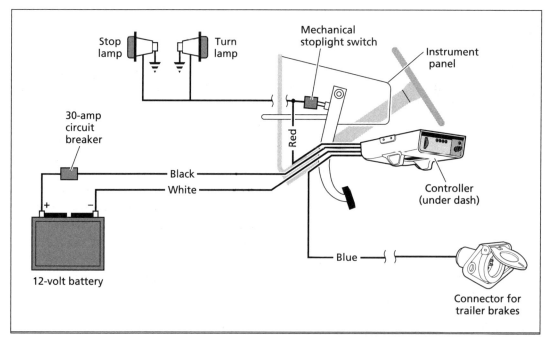

Figure 10.12
Electronic brake-control units for electric trailer brakes are effective, easy to install, and have made tie-ins with the vehicle brake master cylinder unnecessary.

because vehicle manufacturers advise against tapping into vehicle hydraulic systems.

Electronic brake controls utilize either a timer circuit or an inertia sensor (or a combination of the two) to determine when and how much current will go to the trailer brakes.

Inertia sensing units use a pendulum weight to detect the rate of tow-vehicle braking and to meter an appropriate amount of current to the trailer brakes to achieve a comparable level of braking to the tow vehicle. With the electronic controllers, following the manufacturer's instructions for adjustment of the unit is particularly important for proper brake performance. A variety of factors, including off-level mounting of the controller, must be dealt with correctly.

Brake controls that use timer circuits are less expensive—and fairly popular for that reason—but they do not offer the same level of braking performance during emergency stops that is provided by inertia-sensing units.

Use 12-gauge automotive-grade wire (or larger) to make the connection between the brake controller and the electrical connector. Circuit protection is essential. An automatic-reset circuit breaker should be installed in the black wire between the battery and the brake control to protect the brake control and vehicle wiring from short circuits. Use a 15-amp circuit breaker for two brake trailers, a 20-amp circuit breaker for four-brake trailers, and a 30-amp circuit breaker for six-brake trailers. The 12-volt feed for the brake controller should be attached directly to the battery, rather than being added to an existing vehicle circuit.

Trailer Breakaway Switches

A breakaway switch automatically applies the trailer brakes if the trailer becomes uncoupled from the tow vehicle while the vehicles are in motion. The switch is mounted on the trailer tongue, and a lanyard runs from the switch to the frame of the tow vehicle. If the trailer breaks away, the lanyard pulls a pin out of the switch, engaging the brakes. In this situation, power for the trailer brakes comes from the house battery through the breakaway switch.

Be sure the lanyard is connected to the frame of the tow rig, not to some part of the ball mount. Clean the inside of the switch with electrical contact cleaner on a regular basis, and lubricate the pin with light lubricant. Test the breakaway switch occasionally by pulling the pin and trying to drive the tow vehicle forward with the trailer hitched. If everything is working properly, the trailer brakes will be locked. Don't use this system as an emergency brake, which will overheat brake magnets.

CONVERTERS

Most RVs are equipped with power converters designed to transform 120-volt AC to 12-volt DC that can be used to operate DC appliances in the RV and charge batteries.

Converters can be divided into several categories:

Dual Output: Dual-output converters are most common because they are relatively low cost (Figure 10.13). They have two separate output circuits, one for battery-charging and the other to operate appliances. Battery-charge capability is often quite low, and the output for appliances often is "dirty"—subject to voltage surges and "ripple" that can damage sensitive appliances—because this output is not stabilized by an on-line battery.

Single Output: Also called "battery-floater" converters, these units are a step above the dual-output units in that they always have a battery on line, filtering ripple and surges (Figure 10.14). They may be of the older ferroresonant design or of more modern high-frequency switching design. Both designs produce a preset maximum voltage of about 14.0, which is not ideal because it is somewhat high for long-term use, but not high enough to provide complete charging and cell equalization.

Multi-Step: With several specific battery-charging programs, these units are the most effective battery chargers.

Charging Stages

The programs include:

- Bulk-Charge Stage: When a battery is partially depleted, the converter applies constant current, up to the converter output rating, for maximum recharging.

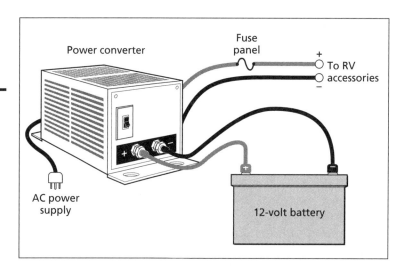

Figure 10.13
Power output of dual-outlet or "linear" converters is split, limiting battery recharge capability.

- Absorption-Charge Stage: Current is reduced while voltage is maintained at a specified absorption level. This delivers measured amounts of current to complete the charge without overheating or overcharging.

- Equalization Stage: This stage involves small current flow and elevated voltage (14.5 to 15) to remove all sulfate from plates. It is intended only for flooded-electrolyte batteries; gels or fiberglass mat batteries do not need this function.

- Float Stage: When a battery is at full-charge status and demands for power are light, the converter reduces the voltage level to about 13.2 and thereby cuts the level of activity inside the battery. This prevents excessive gassing and electrolyte loss in open-cell batteries and reduces electrical activity in sealed batteries.

One important feature of some of the sophisticated converters is temperature monitoring, or at least a setting on the converter that allows the operator to set operating conditions; this helps prevent overcharging. As an example of how desired charging voltage levels change with temperature, proper voltage at the completion of the charge cycle for a liquid-cell battery may be 14.2 at 80°F, but it increases to 15.5 at 0°F to overcome the battery's internal resistance to charging.

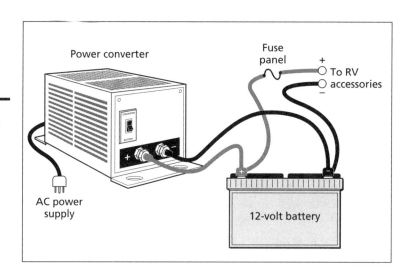

Figure 10.14
Entire output of single-outlet converters is available for battery charging.

Another important feature is a program setting to select for either flooded or gel batteries, which should be charged differently. Completed-charge voltage is slightly lower for gel batteries than for flooded batteries.

Converter Identification

How can you tell what type converter you have? The best way is to check the manufacturer's literature for information on charging profile. If it's a dual-output converter, ratings will be listed for the separate output circuits. Single-output converters will have but one output rating. Both types of units provide an automatic tapered charge rate.

If the unit is a multi-step charger, the various programmed phases of charging will be described in the owner's manual.

Regardless of the type, the converter should have at least 20 amps of output to be suitable for no-hookups camping during which an AC generator is operated for battery recharging, or generator running time will have to be excessive to make up for inadequate charging capacity. The battery-charge ratings of many dual-output "linear" converters range from 5 to 10 amps—not enough capability even for RVs with only one house battery.

Converter effectiveness may be measured with an ammeter, as described in Chapter 11. Simple troubleshooting can be performed with a multimeter. When a converter malfunctions, the result usually shows up as improper voltage output, which is relatively simple to check.

Whenever checking charge currents and voltages, make sure that at least one good house battery is connected to the converter. If the batteries are dried out, shorted or absent altogether, the charger may operate erratically, leading to false readings.

The rated output voltage should be listed on the identification label. The older single-output units usually are designed for 13.8 volts output, and newer ones may be set for 14.0 volts. These voltage levels will be reached when the converter has been operating long enough to bring the battery to a high state of charge. Voltage levels as low as 13.0 may occur when a converter begins charging a depleted battery.

The converter's output should be within 0.2 volt of its rating if the input AC voltage is 110 to 120 volts. If a converter rated at 13.8 volts produces about 14.0 volts, that shouldn't cause immediate problems. But any simple converter (not a multi-step) that produces more than 14.0 volts has the capability of causing excessive loss of battery electrolyte and shortened battery life in open-cell batteries if the converter is in continuous operation.

If battery voltage is lower than 13.8, the converter will not effectively replenish the battery's state of charge. Adjustment of output voltage must be handled by the converter manufacturer.

Incorrect input voltage to a converter can cause its output to vary if the converter is a dual-output type. If you see the converter's output drop to 12.5 or 13.0 volts, check input voltage and you'll probably find it low as well. If the converter is a single-output-type unit, its DC output should be unaffected by moderate changes in AC input.

With sophisticated multi-step converters, output voltage will vary according to the program; check the owner's manual for troubleshooting information.

INVERTERS

Inverters change 12-volt DC battery power to 120-volt AC power to operate household-type appliances without an auxiliary generator or "shore" power (Figure 10.15). They've become more popular in recent years, and range in size from 50-watt plug-in models to large wired-in units rated for up to 5,500 watts continuous duty.

Many inverters also contain excellent multi-stage battery chargers, making them good candidates for replacing a converter that is defective or lacks adequate battery charging capabilities while also acquiring the benefits of an inverter.

In considering the purchase of an inverter, there are several important factors to weigh:

- Output Waveform: Most early inverters produced a square wave output—essentially, a voltage that was either switched "full on" or "full off" at any particular

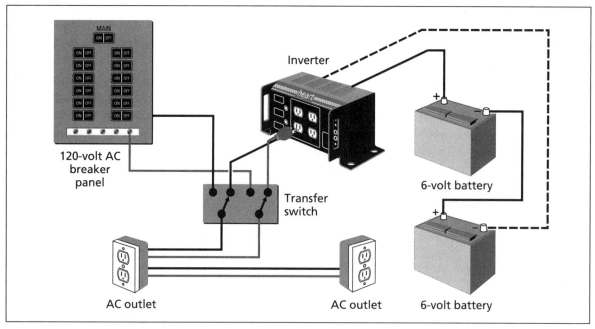

Figure 10.15
Inverters transform 12-volt DC power into 120-volt AC power for appliances
such as microwave ovens, televisions, and video players.

instant. To improve voltage regulation under varying loads, later models incorporated a "modified sine" waveform, in which the ratio of "on time" to "off time" (or duty cycle) is varied with different load conditions.

Although a modified sine wave doesn't look much like the smoothly rising and falling "true sine wave" voltage produced by commercial power sources and most AC generators, it nonetheless is close enough to operate most AC appliances satisfactorily. The few exceptions include some audio equipment (causing excessive hum), certain types of AC motors (reduced power and overheating), and some battery chargers for cordless power tools (overheating).

Inverters that produce a true sine waveform are now becoming more commonplace, and costs have dropped for some models to the point where they rival their modified sine wave counterparts. The quality of the power produced is actually better than most residences receive, and will safely operate any AC appliance as long as the inverter's power ratings aren't exceeded.

• Installation: Although the small plug-in inverters can be installed or removed in an instant, the larger models often require considerable planning. Large inverters require large battery banks, which means that the RV's existing batteries may be need to be upgraded. This may involve fabricating a well-ventilated battery compartment capable of supporting up to several hundred pounds of additional battery weight.

Furthermore, an inverter supplying 2,500 watts of AC power will draw at least 200 amps of DC current from the batteries. This places practical limits on how far the inverter can be separated from the batteries, even if very thick power cables, such as 000-gauge, are used to minimize voltage drop. Thus, some consideration must be given to finding an area large enough for both the inverter and any supplemental batteries.

Finally, some thought must be given to how the inverter's output will be wired into the RV's electrical system. Since there are some AC loads that shouldn't ever receive inverter power (such as air conditioners and two- or three-way propane refrigerators), a typical solution involves installing a "sub panel" of circuit breakers that are reserved for loads to be powered by the inverter. Most large inverters come with detailed installation instructions that include AC interconnection suggestions, as well as recommendations on battery, cable and fuse sizing.

- Performance and Convenience Features: Ideally, the inverter chosen should have an efficiency of at least 80 percent at most anticipated power levels. Inefficient inverters waste considerable power as heat, which leaves less battery power available for operating the load.

Also, the efficiency of some large inverters is poor when operating small loads, even though it improves considerably with large loads. Since many small loads are typically operated for long periods (such as TV sets, satellite receivers, VCRs, reading lamps, etc.), their use with an inefficient inverter can drastically reduce the time between battery recharges.

Many inverters designed for wired-in installation include a built-in automatic AC transfer switch. This allows the inverter to automatically supply AC power to the RV whenever outside power isn't available, and also prevents any possibility of outside power being back-fed into the inverter's output. If not included inside the inverter, an external transfer switch should be installed.

Most wired-in inverters are available with a remote control panel. Besides turning the inverter on and off from this location, the panel may also be capable of displaying other helpful information, such as battery voltage and DC amps being consumed or supplied by the inverter/charger. Some panels can also be used to adjust various inverter and battery charger parameters, and some models are capable of precisely measuring the battery's state of charge, based on battery bank size, voltage, electrolyte type, temperature, and amps consumed.

While electrical circuits in RVs are many and varied, an understanding of the basic principles of operation can help the owner solve problems. The tools described in this chapter are neither expensive nor difficult to use. Combined with a basic understanding of the RV and automotive systems, they should help you become more self-sufficient.

Chapter 11

RVING WITHOUT HOOKUPS

Is there life without hookups? Indeed, there is, although many RV owners are reluctant to travel self-contained to any extent. It's not for everyone, but it can be the most adventurous part of the RV lifestyle.

The modern recreational vehicle is truly an amazing machine. It can make us comfortable under widely varying conditions—in the desert under furnace-like temperatures, or at a ski resort where temperatures may fall well below zero. And, it can be done in comfort.

Even if we have no intention of exploring new climatic horizons, an RV still is our ticket to independence. It seems that many owners don't fully appreciate how much freedom their RVs can offer. Although campground hookups are convenient, they are not a necessity (Figure 11.1). Many RV owners who stay almost exclusively in commercial RV parks may believe they just can't survive without

umbilical cords connected to outside services. Some just prefer full-hookup campgrounds, which is fine.

For those of you who would like to do some "solo flying," this chapter will explain how. Certainly it's necessary to fill gasoline, water, and LP-gas tanks occasionally, but an RV can provide comfortable accommodations for several days without the need for the owner to add anything!

RV owners who take their self-contained RVing seriously are those who congregate on free or nearly free public land sites in the more temperate parts of the United States, notably in southern California, Arizona, and Florida. These people are ingenious adventurers who enjoy their freedom and independence to the utmost. Many have sold their homes and live on a fraction of their former living costs. This is not for everyone, but it proves that RVs can

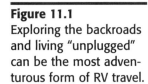

Figure 11.1
Exploring the backroads and living "unplugged" can be the most adventurous form of RV travel.

be used for full-time habitation for long periods with no hookups. All RVs aren't ideally suited to this kind of long-term use, but nearly all have self-containment capabilities that may extend well beyond their owners' expectations.

Following are discussions of the basic self-containment needs—electrical power, water, LP-gas, holding-tank capacity—and how to stretch self-sufficiency in an RV.

BOOSTING BATTERY POWER

The RV life-support system that offers the most challenge for RV owners who spend much of their time without hookups is the 12-volt DC system, including the batteries that are utilized for operation of RV accessories, the auxiliary (house) batteries (Figure 11.2). How much power is stored in a battery? How long is it liable to last? How can we quickly replenish batteries when they are depleted? Losing battery power may be a minor frustration on an occasional basis under moderate climatic conditions, but repeat occurrences can put a lid on our enthusiasm for unplugged RVing.

First, let's examine how to make the best of our factory-installed 12-volt DC systems.

Types of Batteries

The demands on batteries of "house" electrical components are different from that of engine starting. Thus, different batteries are needed:

Engine Starting: These batteries have numerous thin lead plates suspended in electrolyte (sulfuric acid combined with water, gel, or glass mat). They're designed to provide ample surface area exposed to the electrolyte and to give up large amounts of power in short bursts for engine starting; rarely are they depleted to any significant extent, and they are not designed for it. Starting batteries are rated in Cold Cranking Amps (CCA), reflecting the maximum load a fully charged battery can deliver for thirty seconds at 0°F while maintaining at least 7.2 volts.

Some starting batteries are maintenance free, but they usually are not of deep-cycle design and are not suited for powering RV appliances.

Deep Cycle: In contrast, these batteries have fewer plates, which are thicker and are coated

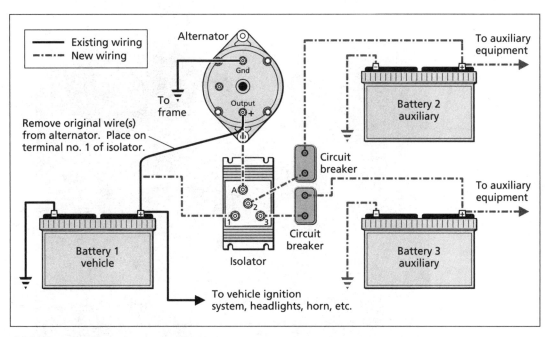

Figure 11.2
The auxiliary (house) batteries are the keys to comfortable self-contained RV use.

Figure 11.3
Conventional flooded-electrolyte batteries (left) must be serviced periodically by adding distilled water. Gel batteries are maintenance free. Battery on the left is a Group 24 size; the one on the right is a Group 27.

with antimony or calcium to increase hardness. Their design is intended to limit the amount of lead that is sloughed off into the bottom of the case with repeated charging/discharging cycles.

Deep-cycle batteries are available in three configurations:

1. Conventional flooded-electrolyte

2. Gelled electrolyte

3. Absorbed glass mat (AGM)

Flooded-electrolyte batteries utilize the technology that has been around for decades in which acid and water form electrolyte surrounding positive and negative lead plates. These batteries are most common in new RVs because they provide good reserve capacity at relatively low cost (Figure 11.3).

Gel-type batteries utilize a gel to immobilize the electrolyte and calcium on the plates to reduce the battery's tendency to give off gas (the gas is recombined internally). Absorbed glass mat (AGM) batteries are a type of gel bat-

Figure 11.4
Six-volt electric vehicle (golf-cart) batteries provide the best reserve capacity and long-term durability, although they require regular monitoring of electrolyte level.

tery in which the electrolyte is absorbed by fine glass mat, and this battery also recombines gases during charging. Both gel and AGM batteries are sealed, eliminating corrosion problems.

Golf-cart (electric-vehicle) batteries are a specific type of heavy deep-cycle battery of flooded-electrolyte design (Figure 11.4). They are rated at 6-volt output and in RVs are used in pairs, wired in series, to produce 12-volt output. They are particularly well suited to RV use because of their very substantial reserve capacity as well as resistance to deterioration caused by cycling (repeated depletion/recharge).

Eliminating Battery Handicaps

Some RVs are fitted with a single house battery (in addition to the engine-starting battery), while others may have two. Unfortunately, improper battery care takes its toll, especially on the house batteries, and they often don't supply the power they were capable of when new.

The first handicap that many RV owners incur is loss of battery capacity due to improper charging, and improper charging may result when the battery connectors and the terminals become corroded.

The advice that has been issued for so many years about cleaning battery connectors and terminals is more than just idle commentary; corroded connectors can derate a battery to a fraction of its original capacity. This is the most common cause of inadequate battery reserve power.

"I've been driving for at least four hours, but the battery didn't even get us through one night!" is a complaint heard frequently regarding insufficient RV-appliance power. The problem can be described in a water-system analogy: Although the pump (engine-driven alternator) had been functioning properly during the trip, the pipeline (wiring hookup) was restricted, and the tank (battery or batteries) was less than half full when the owner assumed it was filled.

At the basic level, battery-maintenance chores should include simple cleaning of terminals and connectors with a solution of baking soda and water to remove corrosion (Figure 11.5). Use this solution to clean corrosion off the battery tray and hold-down apparatus. Most corrosion occurs at the connection to the battery, but if problems persist, it's wise to check other connections as well. You might add these two steps to the typical cleaning procedure:

1. Use a wire brush or sandpaper to roughen contact surfaces.

Figure 11.5
Batteries should be cleaned periodically with baking soda and water to eliminate corrosion.

2. After reassembling, coat the exterior surfaces with grease or petroleum jelly to eliminate corrosion. Don't coat electrical contact surfaces because it can impede the flow of current.

Improper Battery Storage

Even when batteries are clean and connections are well maintained, significant self-discharge occurs during storage of flooded lead-acid batteries, particularly in warm or hot weather. Self-discharge is very low in gel and AGM batteries, and recharge of these batteries usually is not necessary during seasonal storage if the battery is fully charged at the beginning of the storage period; check with the battery manufacturer regarding self-discharge rates.

Self-discharge decreases with temperature. When temperature is under 50°F, a fully charged, conventional open-cell battery usually is okay for three or four months; in higher temperatures an effective charger should be used on the battery for at least three or four hours about once a month.

Battery Reserve Power

Continuing to visualize a battery as a water tank and the engine alternator as the water pump, we know the tank has a specific size. In battery terms this is known as reserve capacity. For example, a Group 27-size battery, the 12-volt battery most commonly used in RVs, may be rated at 160 minutes reserve capacity. This reserve-capacity rating describes how long the battery will sustain a 25-amp load at 80°F ambient temperature before voltage drops to 10.5. The 25-amp load does not usually represent the average RV load, which probably is closer to 10 amps, except in highline motorhomes. The difference is important because battery-reserve capacity is higher at lower discharge rates.

Helping to confuse the matter is the traditional ampere-hour rating, which has survived as a common battery descriptive term. The amp-hour rating is another measurement of a battery's reserve capacity. It is the amount of current that can be drawn from a battery for 20 hours before voltage drops to 10.5. Theoretically, a 100-amp-hour battery should sustain a 5-amp load for about twenty hours before voltage drops to 10.5, at which point most 12-volt appliances will not operate correctly, if at all. In actual practice it's best to subtract at least 20 percent from that to account for less-than-ideal charging practices and system losses, and because it's best to avoid full depletion. There is no accurate, universal correlation between the old amp-hour rating and the new reserve-capacity rating listed in minutes.

Most deep-cycle batteries are supplied by their manufacturers with data tables showing, by model, how long they will sustain a specific load. For example, a popular Group 27 battery

Table 11.1

Capacities of Typical 12-volt Deep-Cycle Wet-Cell Group 24 and 27 Batteries

Amps Draw	Based on peak performance, continuous power will be provided for (hours)	
	Group 24 battery	Group 27 battery
5	16.0	19.0
15	4.6	5.4
25	2.5	3.0

is rated to sustain a 5-amp load for 19 hours. That's 93 amp-hours minus 20 percent, or 15.2 hours for the practical purpose of calculating your 12-volt DC needs in a given period of time during which you expect to rely solely on battery power, and it's the information necessary to calculate your battery-capacity needs.

Depletion

How does the RV owner determine if a battery has been derated, other than assuming that's the case when the battery repeatedly goes flat prematurely? A depletion test can provide an approximate answer. Most battery manufacturers list performance tables for their deep-cycle batteries. House batteries should always be the deep-cycle type for anyone who expects to do much self-contained camping. The term deep-cycle means that the batteries are designed for deep or prolonged discharge, followed by recharge, without excessive loss of battery life and potential for storing energy that can occur when starting batteries are subjected to this type of use.

As examples of how deep-cycle batteries can be expected to perform, a popular liquid electrolyte Group 24 battery is rated at 125 minutes reserve capacity, and a Group 27 battery of the same type from the same manufacturer is rated at 160 minutes (Table 11.1).

By performing the depletion test described here, you can judge your battery's performance level against the rated performance of a typical battery. If you find that your battery will sustain considerably less load than the performance figures indicated here (or your own battery's performance figures), including the 20 percent reduction factor—check for corrosion and/or inadequate charging. You may recall that your battery sat in a discharged state for several weeks, incurring sulfation, which would explain the poor performance. If so, replacement is in order.

A Battery-Depletion Test

The average rate of power consumption for RVs may be 5 to 15 amps, with the exception of large, luxury motorhomes. Assuming that level of consumption, follow this test procedure to get an idea of how your batteries compare with performance specifications for new batteries:

1. The battery should have been charged for an appropriate amount of time to assure full-charge status. A multimeter is needed to conduct this test and is essential if you intend to understand and troubleshoot batteries and electrical systems.

2. With the battery fully charged, turn on interior lights to create a 5-amp load, measuring the load with the ammeter function of the multimeter. Note the time. Monitor time and voltage periodically until the voltage level drops to 10.5, ending the test. Compare your results with the performance specifications of your battery or with the figures listed in Table 11.1.

Accurate Battery Monitoring

The multimeter, a portable test meter, is essential for understanding, maintaining, and troubleshooting batteries and charging systems. It can perform a number of functions, including voltage measurement of both direct-current (DC) and alternating-current (AC) systems, as well as measurement of electrical resistance. For example, it allows you to monitor the state of charge of your batteries (Figure 11.6). The meter should include an ammeter function that will handle up to at least 10 amps so loads can be accurately measured for battery-depletion tests. Adequate multimeters are available from Radio Shack and other electronics-supply stores for $50 to $70. The accuracy of less-expensive meters may be questionable. Good-quality meters with digital readouts are most effective for accurate measurement of voltage.

One of the primary benefits of an accurate multimeter is the ability to monitor a battery's state of charge. If you want to know the state of charge, it's merely a matter of reading the battery's voltage according to Table 11.2.

These numbers must be interpreted based on experience. If the meter indicates your battery is 50 percent charged, you must estimate

Figure 11.6
A digital multimeter is essential in evaluating battery condition and state of charge.

how long it will sustain your typical needs based on your experience.

Note: Readings must be taken with no load on the battery and are not accurate if taken within twenty-four hours after the battery has been charged unless surface charge has been depleted by turning on a load of about 10 amps for five minutes. Specific gravity measurement is a method of checking the status of the electrolyte in conventional liquid electrolyte batteries. A temperature-corrected battery hydrometer (available on order at auto-parts stores) is needed for this testing method.

Proper Battery Charging

Battery charging occurs from two sources: the vehicle alternator or the RV's built-in converter, which is a device that transforms 120-volt AC power to 12-volt DC power for battery charging and to supply the needs of 12-volt DC appliances.

Our ability to properly charge batteries changes with the weather, which is why most vehicle alternators are temperature compensating; they raise output voltage as ambient temperature drops because a battery's willingness to accept a charge is reduced in low ambient temperatures. Higher voltage levels are more effective in cold weather. If wiring is cor-

Table 11.2

Open-Circuit Voltage, Open-Cell Battery

Charge Level	Voltage	Specific Gravity
100%	12.7	1.265
75	12.4	1.225
50	12.2	1.190
25	12.0	1.155

rect, the vehicle alternator is very effective in recharging the house batteries.

In contrast, electrical converters built into mid-line and low-line RVs are not totally efficient. Many of the units were improved in the 1990s, but most low-priced RVs still are equipped with marginally efficient units. Converters will be discussed in more detail later.

Aside from the question of adequate voltage output from the charging source—be it alternator or converter—the critical question is whether or not the voltage is seen at the battery, especially a battery located a considerable distance from the alternator. If alternator output is 14.2 volts, the voltage reading at the battery (which may be as much as 25 feet away) should not be lower than 14 when heavy charging is underway. The difference is known as voltage drop. Inadequate wire size (gauge) is the common cause of voltage drop in tow vehicle/trailer rigs, often exaggerated by faulty or corroded connections. Motorhomes usually are fitted with heavy cable (4 gauge or larger) for more effectiveness. However, corroded connections and inadequate attention paid to proper charging are typical causes of battery inadequacy in motorhomes. Just because you don't see corrosion on the exterior of the terminal doesn't mean it's not there, sandwiched between the terminal and the battery post. It's an excellent idea to get into the habit of removing terminals on batteries and periodically checking for corrosion.

Although most battery problems are caused by undercharging, the opposite also can cause damage. The result of excessive charging current is heat, which produces gassing and loss of water in a flooded battery, and can create the potential for a dangerous expulsion of electrolyte from a gel or AGM battery. Thus, it is important to make sure the charging method is appropriate for the type of battery used. Automotive alternators are regulated on the low side for flooded batteries and thus are suitable for gels. Nevertheless, an overcharge can occur even with an alternator when a battery or battery bank is drained excessively.

Total Battery Discharge

When batteries are "flattened," so to speak, they are especially vulnerable to damage from overcharging. Batteries should not be depleted beyond 80 percent discharge (10.5 volts under a 5-amp load). When overdischarge occurs, the acid will not rapidly recombine with the electrolyte medium. High current flow creates heat (anything over 120°F is damaging), and the battery can be permanently derated or ruined.

Thus, batteries should not be totally depleted. But, this sometimes happens when a couple of lights were inadvertently left on or some similar error. If this happens, the recharge current should be limited to capacity divided by 20, which is 5.25 amps in the case of a 105-amp battery, until at least 20 percent of the battery's capacity has been restored. That would be about four hours of 5-amp charging before heavier charging could begin. This gradual recovery process will prevent overheating and damage.

There may be no practical way to control this during a trip when the battery bank is inadvertently flattened overnight and driving is scheduled the next morning, or with a high-output converter that does not have manually adjustable voltage regulation. If so, don't be surprised if the battery's usable capacity has mysteriously shrunk. If possible, stop and check the batteries to see if they're getting hot. If so, dump a bag of ice in the battery compartment.

Testing for Charging Effectiveness

An accurate multimeter, used to measure voltage drop, will give a good indication of charging effectiveness. Different methods are used for vehicles with and without battery isolators. There are two types of battery isolators, and it's important to determine which kind your vehicle has. One is a mechanical battery isolator, which is a mechanical relay that makes clicking noises when the ignition key is turned on and off (Figure 11.7); the other is a solid-state isolator, which makes no sound (Figure 11.8).

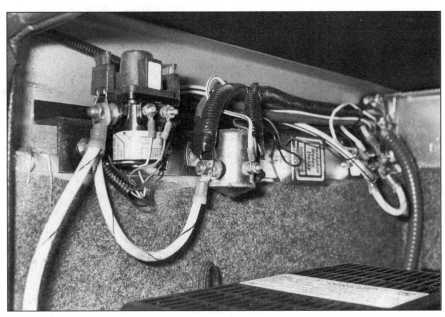

Figure 11.7
Most RVs are equipped with mechanical sole-noids to isolate house batteries from starting batteries when the engine is not running. The dual-battery solenoid is in the center; battery-disconnect solenoid (for vehicle storage) is at left.

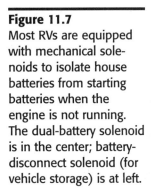

Figure 11.8
Solid-state battery isolators utilize diodes and have no moving parts to deteriorate with extended usage.

A Battery Voltage-Drop Test

To test for voltage drop, follow these steps:

• For vehicles that have no isolator or a mechanical isolator, turn on several interior lights to deplete the auxiliary battery(ies) to a voltage level of about 10.5. Set engine rpm to about 1,500 (approximately double idle speed), which initiates maximum charging, and check the voltage at two points: the alternator output terminal and the positive post of the auxiliary battery. The difference in the readings is the amount of voltage drop, or loss of efficiency, in the wiring and in the isolator, if one is used.

If the voltage drop exceeds 0.2 to 0.3 volt, wire size is inadequate, connections are faulty, or a mechanical battery isolator (relay) is creating resistance.

• Check for voltage drop across the isolator by checking the voltage at both the input and the outlet terminals while the isolator is carrying a heavy load. The readings at the two terminals should be almost identical.

• For vehicles with solid-state (diode-type) battery isolators, again use an auxiliary battery that has been depleted to 10.5 volts.

Test A: Set engine speed to about 1,500 rpm and check voltage at the output terminal on the alternator and at the alternator (A) post on the isolator. Voltage drop in this short line should not be more than 0.2 volt.

Test B: With engine rpm at about 1,500, check voltage at the auxiliary-battery output terminal of the isolator and at the auxiliary-battery lugs. Voltage drop should not exceed 0.3 volt.

Do not expect voltage levels taken in Tests A and B to be identical. Isolator diodes create a voltage drop of about 1 volt. However, the isolator causes alternator output to rise about 1 volt, compensating for the drop across diodes. For example, voltage at the alternator may read 15, compared to 14 at the output of the auxiliary battery terminal on the isolator.

- Recharge batteries when tests are completed.

Adding Battery Capacity

Now that we've discussed how to get the most out of what you have, let's consider increasing battery capacity to assure that adequate power will be available for accessories over long periods of self-contained camping. We'll base our needs estimate on battery amp-hour ratings because that's the terminology used to describe how power is used—i.e., if a television that draws 3 amps is used for three hours, it consumes 9 amp-hours of electricity.

Many RV manufacturers are using Group 24 batteries (11 inches long x 6¾ inches wide x 9⅝ inches long), rated at 80 amp-hours rather than Group 27 batteries (12¾ inches long x 6¾ inches wide x 9⅝ inches long), rated at 105 amp-hours, to reduce costs. The smaller batteries may be sufficient in RVs that don't have a large number of appliances or are not used extensively for self-contained camping, particularly in winter, when the furnace usually creates the largest power demand. The smaller battery probably won't sustain an RV for more than a couple of days even with minimal 12-volt DC needs in warm weather.

Calculating Correct Battery Capacity

Just how much capacity do we need? Arithmetic will provide the answer. We must estimate our total 12-volt DC needs during typical periods when neither the engine nor an AC generator will be used.

For example, a single, fully charged Group 24 battery ideally is capable of delivering about 80 amp-hours of power if the average depletion rate is 5 amps and the battery is in top condition. Reduce that factor by 20 percent and the available amp-hour figure drops to 64. That amount of capacity would be barely adequate for the sample twenty-four-hour cool-weather period (Table 11.3).

Further complicating matters in cool weather, low temperatures extend battery recharge time and reduce available capacity.

Assuming an average amp draw of 10, the least expensive improvement in this case is to replace the Group 24 battery with a Group 27, raising available amp-hour capacity from about 64 to about 84 (105-amp-hour battery minus 20 percent). If still more capacity is needed, a pair of Group 27 deep-cycle batteries can be connected in parallel to serve as the house batteries, providing about 168 amp-hours (at the 5-amp depletion rate), while a 12-volt starting battery is reserved to crank the engine. All three can be charged simultaneously through the use of a battery isolator, preferably a solid-state diode-type unit.

Table 11.3

Common RV Appliances and Their Power Requirements

Appliance	Amps	Running Time (Hours)	Amp-hours
Lights	4.5	4.0	18.0
Stereo	3.0	3.0	9.0
Television	4.0	3.0	12.0
Water pump	5.0	0.2	1.5
Furnace	7.0	4.0	28.0
		Total	**68.5**

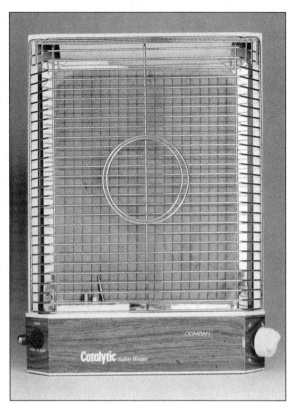

Figure 11.9
Catalytic heaters are well suited for boondocking because most require no 12-volt DC power.

Mechanical relay-type isolators function well when new, but their contact points gradually become corroded, causing electrical resistance.

The use of two 12-volt batteries in parallel is the common setup for RV use, even though it is not the best arrangement over the long term. A better auxiliary power setup consists of two 6-volt electric vehicle (golf-cart) batteries wired in series for 12-volt output. These batteries are not interconnected when they are at rest. Connected in series, the 6-volt batteries are rated at 225 to 245 amp-hours, depending on the brand and model, at 12-volt output. Derate the 225-amp-hour figure by 20 percent and the result is 180-amp-hours of usable power. This allows nearly three days and nights on our sample power load before recharging is necessary.

The 6-volt batteries are 10⅜ inches long x 7⅛ inches wide x 11³⁄₁₆ -inches high, which means they usually will fit in a compartment

designed for typical 12-volt Group 24 batteries, as long as there is additional height available (golf-cart batteries are about 2 inches taller, depending on the model). It will be necessary to build special accommodations if four batteries are to be used. Most motorized RVs are designed to accommodate two house batteries plus an engine battery.

Six-volt electric vehicle batteries are designed for the ultimate in deep-cycle abuse that occurs in golf carts. They have exceptionally thick lead plates in addition to special thick separator mats. The batteries weigh about 65 pounds apiece, compared to 55 pounds for a typical 12-volt deep-cycle battery.

With either battery setup, the ability to properly recharge the batteries is critical; wire size should be at least 8 gauge between the alternator and the batteries. Welding supply stores are a source for large-gauge wire and connectors.

CATALYTIC HEATERS

One of the best power-savers for boondocking is a propane-fueled catalytic heater (Figure 11.9), unless the camping location provides such a mild climate that little or no furnace operation is needed.

Non-thermostatically controlled catalytic heaters produce no flame (a catalyst is used to create combustion and heat); they require no electrical power and are are nearly 100 percent efficient in their use of fuel, since they require no flue.

Although these heaters do not meet construction codes for factory installation in new RVs, they have been demonstrated to be safe over many years of use. Available in camping supply stores under the Olympian brand, they're available in 2800-, 5800-, and 7600-Btu models with manual controls and in a 5800-Btu thermostatically controlled model that draws about 5 amps (DC) for less than a minute during the ignition cycle and about 0.5 amp during operation. The heaters are noiseless and they either eliminate the need for furnace operation or they greatly reduce furnace running time, depending on outside temperature and the RV's rate of heat loss.

AC GENERATORS AND POWER CONVERTERS

Most RV owners who intend to do much self-contained camping usually have an AC generator of sufficient size to operate one or two roof air conditioners. AC generators that are built into motorhomes typically are 4 kW or larger while portables used by trailerists and carried in the tow vehicle tend to be smaller.

The use of an AC generator for self-contained camping does not require extensive explanation, except to specify that most auxiliary generators do not have any 12-volt DC output for recharging batteries. However, they can provide plenty of 120-volt AC power for the RV's on-board converter for battery charging.

The converter is an automatic electrical device that transforms 120- volt-AC to 12-volt DC power. Some have little capability of recharging batteries, while others have reasonably good capability, and a few sophisticated units have excellent capability.

Ineffective converters are used in most low-priced RVs, and effectiveness tends to move up the scale with price.

Battery-charge ratings of common two-outlet "linear" converters range from 5 amps to 10 amps, which is not effective even for RVs with only one house battery if recharging with an AC generator is part of the camping menu. With these converters, the RV owner who runs his AC generator for extended periods for battery charging, possibly annoying his campground neighbors, usually is wasting time and fuel.

To evaluate your situation, inspect the converter's identification plate. It usually will specify battery-charging output. If the converter is the type with separate output for RV accessories and battery charging, it may be rated at 30 amps, but only 7 amps of that is available for battery charging.

In contrast, the converter with a single output is much more effective because the total output of the unit, minus the load from RV appliances being used at the time, is available for battery charging. Thus there will be no specific battery-charge rating—just the overall rating of the converter.

In either case, effectiveness may be measured with an ammeter. Turn on several interior lights for a couple of hours—sufficient time to partially deplete the house battery(ies). Place an automotive-type ammeter in the positive line leading from the converter to the house battery(ies). The ammeter on a multimeter usually won't be rated high enough to perform this task. Make sure all 12-volt DC appliances are turned off. Plug in the RV's power cord, which should automatically activate the converter. Check the ammeter; the charge rate should equal the rating listed on the converter/charger. If it is lower, inadequate wiring and/or placement by the manufacturer of the converter/charger too far from the battery(ies) usually is at fault.

If the charge rate is equal to or near the rating stamped on the converter, the wiring may be effective, but you still must decide if the output is high enough for your needs.

For rapid recharging in no-hookup situations, a converter with at least 20 amps of battery-charging capability is needed for a single Group 27 battery, or 30 amps for two such batteries. One of the more sophisticated multistage converters, sold in RV supply stores, is preferred (see Chapter 10). Installing such a converter as near as possible to the house batteries makes running an AC generator for battery charging worthwhile.

In absence of an effective converter, running the engine-driven alternator is the most effective way to recharge batteries, although it's impractical for the RV owner who spends considerable time without hookups. And, of course, it's inefficient to run an eight-cylinder engine for battery charging when it's possible to use a two-cylinder engine if you already have an AC generator.

INVERTERS

For maximum convenience and minimum AC-generator usage (noise), many RV owners install inverters that change 12-volt DC to 120-volt AC power, the opposite of the converter/charger discussed previously and in

Figure 11.10
Solar panels transform sunlight into electrical energy for battery charging. Several panels can be used to create charge rates of 10 amps or more in direct sunlight.

Chapter 10. Inverter output ranges up to 2,500 watts of AC power for most appliances, from microwave ovens to music systems, 120-volt televisions, videocassette recorders, and a wide variety of other items.

A popular role for the inverter is to supply power for a microwave oven, eliminating the need to crank up the AC generator every time the owner decides to warm a cup of coffee. Thus, the inverter, although not a necessity, greatly reduces generator running time. Check the oven's rating plate for the amount of power it requires, and size the inverter accordingly.

The only appliance that an inverter cannot handle is an air conditioner; an AC generator is still needed in climates where air conditioning is desirable.

POWER FROM THE SUN

The sun is a practical source of electricity for RV owners, and it's relatively easy (although expensive) to assemble a system that supplies all the electrical needs of the RV except for air conditioners.

Several manufacturers of solar panels offer a variety of panels that range in output from a trickle of power to amounts that are limited only by the number of solar panels that will fit on the roof of the RV.

The most cost-effective solar panels are the larger ones, rated at 100 to 120 watts, but size must depend on needs. A typical system capable of producing a substantial amount of power from the sun may consist of a single 120-watt panel or two 55-watt units (Figure 11.10), a charge controller, and deep-cycle batteries capable of storing adequate power for the owner's needs

Small solar panels are self-regulating, which means they do not require a charge controller and are suitable only for maintenance of batteries in storage. In contrast, the larger panels must be regulated by a charge controller to prevent battery overcharging (Figure 11.11). Several brands and types of charge controllers and batteries are sold by service firms for use in solar-panel installations.

Each motorhome owner's power requirements will differ, as will the power output of the panels in cloudy or partly cloudy weather. It's necessary to total the anticipated power usage to determine the needed solar panel output. This can be accomplished by multiplying the power usage by the number of hours and combining the totals. Example: A color TV rated at 4 amps is used for three hours, for a total power consumption of 12 amp-hours.

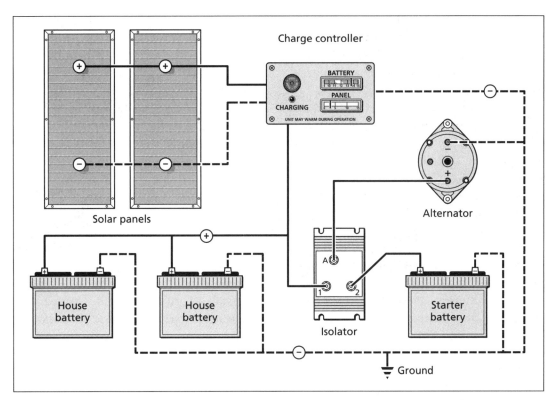

Figure 11.11
The output of solar panels must be regulated to prevent overcharging of batteries.

Table 11.4

Power Requirements for Typical 12-volt DC Appliances

Appliance	Amps
Incandescent light, each bulb	1.5
Fluorescent light	1.5
Color TV	4.0
CB radio (receive)	0.5
CB radio (transmit)	0.9
Videocassette player	2.5
Furnace	6.0
Water pump	6.0
Microwave oven (via inverter)	125.0

The amp-hour total is used to calculate solar panel needs based on estimates of available sunlight (Table 11.4).

A system consisting of a single panel rated at 100 to 120 watts output (or a pair of panels with the same combined rating) connected to a controller and then to a pair of 6-volt golf-cart batteries rated at 225 amp-hours (per pair), usually is appropriate for fairly aggressive self-contained camping.

Two 55-watt panels produce about 6.5 amps in direct sunlight, or a total of about 39 amp-hours per day assuming six hours of direct sunlight, while a 120-watt panel is rated at about 7 amps and will produce about 42 amp-hours of current in about the same period of time.

At the low end of the spectrum, the conservative RVer's power consumption might total only 20 amp-hours per day while the owner of a large motorhome equipped with appliances such as a microwave, satellite dish and others that are powered by an inverter might need 60 to 70 amp-hours per day. In the conservative situation, a single panel in the 55- to 80-watt range might suffice, while the owner of the big rig might consider two 100- or 120-watt panels, with appropriate controller and a large battery bank.

The panels are mounted on the roof, as near the refrigerator vent as practical, to minimize the length of wire needed to reach the charge controller installed inside the coach. For the amount of current involved, 12-gauge wire is specified. But many installation shops prefer larger wire to hold voltage drop to an absolute minimum.

Because the variables are so numerous, manufacturers of panels offer detailed solar-system guides and worksheets to help prospective customers calculate energy needs and estimate how sun-intensity variances affect power output of the panels in various sections of the nation. Solar panels are sold by many RV supply stores, which can also furnish the worksheets.

WATER—THE LIFE SOURCE

An RV owner's supply of water is another of the essential ingredients of comfortable, enjoyable, no-hookup camping. Of course, the more water we carry, the less we have to worry about running out. How much water is adequate? That's a question that must be answered individually because we all have different levels of efficiency when it comes to water conservation. Some RV owners may regard 30 gallons as adequate, while others may believe that 60 gallons are minimal. An "unplugged" camping trip or two will provide the answer.

Many RVs have water tanks of marginal size, and some of these tanks do not fill the compartments in which they are housed. In such cases it's wise to install the largest water tank that will fit in the compartment. Replacement tanks can be purchased from RV supply stores.

If the existing tank cannot be replaced with a larger one, it may be possible to locate another tank in a storage area that is not essential—under a dinette seat, for example. It's best that the tank fill be located on the same side as the fill for the original tank. Of course, the new tank must have an air vent so it can be filled properly. Inspecting the installation of the original tank will be helpful in installing the new one.

When adding water capacity, weight is an important factor. Some RVs are overloaded already, and adding water (8 pounds per gallon) adds to the overload. Weigh the RV before deciding to add water capacity (see Chapter 5). Be sure to weigh the RV laterally (side to side) to make sure that an additional water tank added to the heavy side does not create a side-to-side imbalance of sufficient poundage to cause vehicle handling/stability problems or tire overloading.

If water capacity is added, it doesn't mean the owner must travel with the tanks full. Twenty gallons might be an adequate amount until approaching the destination, when the tank(s) can be filled.

Conserving water may be an effective way to make do with what otherwise would be inadequate water capacity. During long periods of RV living in areas without hookups, separate portable wheeled tanks may be used to haul in water and haul out waste. Make sure you have separate tanks for potable water and waste water. Such tanks with dump-hose fittings are available in camping-supply stores in capacities up to 30 gallons.

LP-GAS

Although LP-gas, better known as propane, has been around for a very long time, it's still an amazing fuel when we take a moment to realize what it does for us. Our refrigeration, heating, and much of our cooking are made possible by this fuel, which is compacted into a relatively small cylinder or tank.

Except in winter, when furnaces place unusually high demands on propane supplies, propane storage capacity is not a problem. A normal rate of usage normally allows us to fill the tank(s) or cylinder(s) before we're in danger of running out.

In winter, however, the story may be a bit different if the RV tank is relatively small. The definition of "relatively small" will vary from one rig to the next, but 15 gallons is small for winter usage, unless the RV and its furnace are very compact. In a 25- to 30-foot motorhome or trailer, 20 gallons should be the minimum for RV usage. For truly large RVs, 30 to 40 gallons of propane would be sufficient for long-term self-contained usage.

If you find that the propane level drops rapidly and you're constantly monitoring the content, consider using a spare tank or cylinder. Ideally it should be at least a 7½-gallon DOT cylinder of the type fitted on travel trailers.

Note: *The cylinder must be transported the way it is designed to be used.* In other words, if it is designed to stand upright when connected to the gas system, it should be transported or stored that way. Instructions stamped on the cylinder's collar will identify the proper position. Don't store a propane cylinder in a closed storage compartment.

Although it requires more effort and planning, the ability to camp without hookups is the RV owner's ticket to a more adventurous RV experience.

Chapter 12

IMPROVING FUEL ECONOMY AND PERFORMANCE

Most RV owners range from very interested to mildly obsessed with fuel economy. Even though we may be able to afford to travel in a vehicle that gets 6 to 10 mpg, we're not satisfied with it; somehow, we thought mileage would be better.

Unfortunately, it takes considerable amounts of fuel to move large, heavy, aerodynamically challenged vehicles. Vehicle manufacturers have pursued technological advances such as computerized engine-management systems and electronically controlled overdrives, and the effort has paid off.

New engine designs have proven to be consistently more fuel miserly than the engines they replaced. For example, when GM introduced its new family of Vortec engines in the mid-1990s, they were noticeably more efficient and powerful than their predecessors, providing improved low-rpm torque. In the late 1990s, the Vortec 6000 replaced the Vortec 5700 in light-duty models with the Vortec 6000 offering a much broader operating range. For the 2001 model year, GM raised the bar still higher by introducing the Vortec 8100 (8.1-liter), which is a re-engineered Vortec 7400 (7.4-liter) engine, and a new turbodiesel, the Duramax 6600 (6.6 liters).

Likewise, Ford updated its engine family in the mid-1990s and introduced a new 5.4-liter V-8 and a new 6.8-liter V-10, both with improved (flatter) torque curves; the 6.8-liter engine replaced the venerable 7.5-liter (460 cid) V-8.

Dodge has relied on its 8-liter V-10 gasoline engine for a number years and on the 5.9-liter Cummins turbodiesel, which was upgraded to four valves per cylinder and higher torque ratings for 1999.

For those of us who are not prone to trade up and acquire the newer technology, there are steps we can take to make the best of what we have: increase the efficiency of the drivetrain and reduce wind resistance, rolling resistance, and weight. Any improvements made in these categories should yield increases in performance.

AFTERMARKET PRODUCTS DESIGNED TO IMPROVE MILEAGE AND PERFORMANCE

The automotive aftermarket offers a vast array of products designed to enhance mileage and performance, complete new or partial replacement exhaust systems with low-restriction mufflers, fresh-air intake systems, reprogrammed engine computers or chips, high-performance ignition systems, RV cams, roller rocker arms and lifters, special spark plugs, aerodynamic aids, energy-conserving oils and oil additives, low-rolling-resistance tires, and many more.

In examining ways to boost engine power or mileage, it helps to visualize the internal combustion engine as an air pump, with the goal to improve its efficiency. At the risk of oversimplification, anything that makes it easier for air to get through the engine should yield higher output (assuming the correct amount of fuel gets mixed with the air). Improvements in efficiency can be used to make the vehicle accelerate quicker and climb hills faster or to reduce fuel consumption while driving at the same comparative speeds.

It may be difficult to separate the valid systems from those that produce little, if any, improvement, but some products offer significant advances. However, the mileage and performance claims made by manufacturers of some products are exaggerated and sometimes even ridiculous.

While the list of mileage and performance boosters is lengthy, few have proven track records. Among those are kits for gasoline and diesel engines that reduce or remove restrictions in the intake air system while also improving exhaust flow.

Is It "Smog" Legal?

While some of the products can correct factory deficiencies, they may conflict with emission laws. Enforcement of such laws has grown more thorough, and it is best to make sure that any engine modification is emission legal. Products that have a California Air Resources Board (CARB) exemption or Executive Order

(EO) number are legal for use on the emission-controlled vehicles they are intended for use in all states. However, this only indicates that emissions were not significantly affected; it does not certify that the product will improve performance or fuel economy.

Because few products designed to improve fuel economy actually meet their advertising claims, the RV owner is wise to examine such products very carefully—especially in areas with strict emission regulations. Check closely on refund and warranty policies as well as the company's reputation. While the manufacturer of a miracle gas-saver gadget may offer what appears to be a very solid customer-satisfaction money-back guarantee, actually getting a refund may be difficult or impossible.

While some engines have deficiencies that can be corrected with aftermarket products, the more common problem is that the engine may be suffering from premature power loss although it's not ready for a complete overhaul. Most of us are aware of basic preventive-maintenance procedures; we change our oil every 3,000 miles and take it for granted that the engine should last for 100,000 miles. However, as we approach the halfway mark on the odometer, we may already begin to notice subtle signs of fatigue—reduced throttle response, more tendency to spark knock, and an increase in oil consumption.

This chapter will use two approaches to analyze fuel economy and performance:

1. How to make the best of what you have by making sure the engine meets its full potential

2. How to correct an engine's factory deficiencies with cost-effective modifications, if available

First, let's have a look at causes of engine-efficiency losses and discuss how to measure such losses.

EVALUATING ENGINE CONDITION

Timing Chains

Many engines begin to show signs of fatigue by the time odometer mileage reaches 50,000 miles. Engine-fatigue signals usually include reduction in fuel mileage and a subtle drop in

Figure 12.1
The timing chain is the engine component most vulnerable to premature wear, which will retard cam timing and reduce fuel economy and performance.

performance. As mileage climbs toward the 100,000 mark, a change in cranking compression may occur (variance between cylinders should not exceed 10 percent), and the engine may tend to run hotter. Oil consumption may also increase.

One cause of mileage and performance deterioration is wear of the timing chain (Figure 12.1). Such wear is quite prevalent in the older engines, especially the Ford 7.5-liter V-8. This chain's role is to turn the camshaft, and in many cases, the distributor and oil pump. As wear occurs in the chain's links, it lengthens, and camshaft timing is retarded, thereby reducing performance and mileage. Continued timing-chain wear will eventually result in "jumped" spark timing or the failure of the timing-chain assembly.

In most cases, timing-chain wear is within acceptable limits until the 50,000-mile mark. By the time the vehicle accumulates upwards of 100,000 miles, many timing-chain assemblies should be replaced. Timing chains on the Ford 7.5-liter V-8 and the Dodge 5.9-liter V-8s tend to show the most rapid wear. Premium-quality double-row timing-chain assemblies should be used in all applications. Timing-chain wear can be checked by using this simple procedure:

1. Remove the spark plugs and distributor cap, and rotate the engine by using a wrench on the vibration damper nut or bolt.

2. Turn the engine in the opposite direction of the spark-timing scale until you reach top dead center.

3. Ask an assistant to observe the distributor rotor. Rotate the engine, and watch the timing mark as it moves up the scale. When the assistant notices that the distributor rotor is beginning to move, stop turning the crankshaft and note the number of degrees of crankshaft rotation.

This number of degrees relative to movement of the rotor is a measure of timing-chain lash. Lash in excess of 4 degrees will begin to affect performance. At 8 degrees, the loss in performance will become evident, and at 12 degrees the timing-chain assembly is nearing failure and should definitely be replaced. Failure of a timing chain often causes major engine damage when pistons strike the valves.

Fuel Injectors

Fuel injectors must spray a very fine mist of fuel into the engine (Figure 12.2). Over time, this mist spray pattern deteriorates because solid deposits from the fuel build up inside the nozzles until the engine begins to run roughly. Power, fuel economy, and emissions suffer.

Modern fuels contain additives that retard the formation of deposits; fuel injectors on late-model vehicles are designed to resist clogging. However, this problem can still occur, and it happens so slowly that a person who drives the vehicle regularly won't notice the decline in perfomance.

On gasoline engines, injector clogging usually manifests itself as a "lumpy" idle, surging, hesitation, and, in bad cases, as a slight mis-

Figure 12.2
Spray pattern from fuel injectors may deteriorate with time, due to deposits in the injectors, which must be cleaned or replaced.

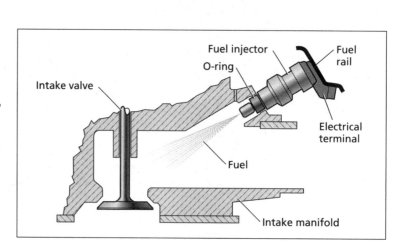

fire. Diesel engines may be more difficult to start when cold; they may also make an unusual knocking or pinging sound under light accelerator settings and may produce more black smoke than normal or even make some white smoke.

Most gasoline and diesel-fuel injectors can be cleaned and tested and returned to service. Sometimes they leak or are damaged, in which case they can be replaced by new or rebuilt units.

Unfortunately, it's not easy to be sure a drivability problem is caused by injector deposits without removing them and bench-testing each one. Slightly clogged injectors are not detected by conventional diagnostic equipment. Many shops decide to check the injectors when the other systems check out okay, but the engine still doesn't run properly.

However, there are some guidelines to help you to know when to suspect injector problems. Generally, injector clogging doesn't occur at very low mileages. Before replacing injectors, make sure the engine is properly tuned and the compression is up to specifications and is uniform. Insure that ignition cables are in good condition and all fuel and air filters are clean. Also see if the "check engine" light is on or any computer trouble codes are stored in memory.

Injectors may be chemically cleaned on the vehicle. This can be done with chemicals added to the fuel tank or by connecting a special apparatus to feed the chemical directly to the injectors in place of fuel. The engine is then operated until the cleaner is consumed in the combustion process.

Additives placed in the fuel tank are greatly diluted and therefore less effective than the concentrated direct chemical feed to the fuel line. This latter method can be effective and is less expensive than removing injectors. The drawback is that it provides no method of testing the degree of clogging or the success of the cleaning process.

Some fuel-injection specialists have off-the-vehicle injector cleaning and test machines. These units are the costliest but most accurate method of servicing injectors. Injectors can be flow-tested before and after cleaning, and the volume and spray pattern can be checked. Injectors can be matched for flow rate, and any injectors that fail the tests may be replaced.

Cylinder Pressure

When performance or mileage begins to sag, a compression test is in order. Always perform compression tests with the throttle held open,

Figure 12.3
Poor performance and fuel economy may indicate low cylinder compression, which should not vary more than 10 percent from one cylinder to another.

and allow two or three compression strokes of each piston being tested. Compression readings should not vary more than about 10 percent between cylinders (Figure 12.3). If a higher variance is noted, inject a few squirts of motor oil into the low cylinder and into the one adjacent to it, then retest both. If the retest figures show that the cylinders are closer in compression, this indicates ring sealing is a problem. If cylinder balance remains about the same as the first test, a valve-leaking problem is indicated. When a piston-ring problem is indicated, recheck the compression after changing the oil and driving for about 300 miles. In some cases, rings may be sticking or a cylinder wall may have been washed down due to excessive fuel from cold starts or flooding (see Chapter 13).

Oil Consumption

The amount of oil used by an engine is directly related to how the engine is used—i.e., heavy or severe service will result in higher oil consumption than occurs with less strenuous use. The rate is roughly proportional to fuel consumption, which usually is a direct indicator of how hard the engine is working.

Ford's "Motorhome Chassis Service Manual" notes that vehicles over 8,500 pounds GVWR should go at least 900 miles per quart of oil, but that vehicles subject to severe duty may use more oil.

GM's shop manual for the 5.7-liter engine states that oil consumption of as much as a quart in 1,000 miles is regarded as acceptable.

In any engine, heavy throttle usage produces more oil consumption. For older engines, a GM engineer described as acceptable the use of a quart for every 150 gallons of fuel consumed. At that rate, a vehicle getting 7 mpg would go about 1,000 miles per quart of oil consumed.

Keep a record of mileage points at which oil is added and a list of oil changes by date and odometer mileage so you can have an accurate reading of the engine's oil consumption. In addition to the natural consumption of oil past the piston rings, leakage through valve guides and seals is common in older engines.

There are two other methods of determining if oil is passing through the valve guides or past the intake manifold. After shutting down a hot engine and allowing it to sit for thirty minutes or more, restart the engine without using the throttle. Observe the tailpipe; if blue smoke is emitted upon startup, the oil is more likely passing through the valve guides and seals than leaking past an intake-manifold gasket.

Another method is to check for oil smoke after coasting down a long grade and applying throttle at the bottom. Oil smoke will increase immediately upon applying throttle and will disappear or greatly reduce in a few seconds if continued throttle is applied.

If uncorrected, excessive oil consumption can create carbon buildup in the combustion chambers and may foul spark plugs, causing misfire. This will result in further loss of power and economy and an increase in exhaust emissions.

Crankcase Pressure

When engine wear is suspected, it's advisable to check for excessive crankcase "blow-by," which indicates combustion leakage past the pistons and rings. One method of checking this is:

1. Bring the engine to normal operating temperature.

2. Place the automatic transmission in park or the manual gearbox in neutral.

3. Apply the parking brake.

4. Block the wheels.

5. Remove the oil-fill cap.

6. Run the engine at approximately 2,500 rpm. If a substantial flow of oil vapors appear from the oil-fill opening, the pistons and/or rings are not sealing properly.

7. If the oil vapors are light, chances are that valve seals or guides are causing the excessive oil consumption.

If you are unsure of how much vapor should be present, perform this test on a known, well-functioning engine for familiarization.

Cylinder Leakdown Tests

Prior to engine teardown, always have a cylinder leakdown test performed. This test injects air pressure into each cylinder with the valves closed and measures the rate at which it escapes, expressed as a percentage. It will also pinpoint leaky valves or pistons/cylinders; the sound of air escaping through the intake manifold indicates intake valves are leaking; if it escapes out the tailpipe, exhaust valves are the cause; and if hissing can be heard in the oil-filler tube it means piston rings are worn.

Oil Pressure Test

If low oil pressure is a concern, double-check the stock gauge or light by temporarily using an aftermarket mechanical oil-pressure gauge. Checking with such a gauge will eliminate the chance of having a faulty sending unit or a voltage problem giving a false reading. As a general rule, oil pressure should be at least 7 psi at hot idle.

Distributor Function

Fully electronic ignition systems have minimized the role of the distributor on most new engines by relegating the control of automatic spark advance to the vehicle's electronic control module. However, distributors on some engines built well into the 1990s still contained mechanical spark advance equipment, and malfunction of that equipment is among the many causes of premature power loss.

To determine if a particular distributor has mechanical weights, read the emission-control label. If it indicates that ignition timing is nonadjustable, the distributor does not have mechanical advance weights.

Neither do late-model vehicles have vacuum spark-advance systems, but in an older vehicle that does (a diaphragm attached to the distributor with a vacuum line connected to it), idle the engine and temporarily make and break the vacuum-line connection (using a source of manifold vacuum). It should cause an easily noticeable difference in engine rpm as the vacuum advance affects spark timing.

General Motors trucks up to 1987 models and motorhome chassis up to 1990 models used a system of mechanical spark-advance weights in a distributor in which an inner shaft tended to bind, causing chronic ignition-related problems. The binding caused the automatic spark-advance system to stick, resulting in power and mileage loss and/or starter kickback and pinging.

On vehicles with conventional distributors, the automatic spark-advance system is easy to check. To do so, remove the distributor cap and twist the rotor against spring tension (Figure 12.4). Spring tension on the centrifugal advance weights should return the rotor fully to the rest position. If it does not, the distributor must be disassembled, cleaned with solvent and fine emery paper, relubricated, and reinstalled.

Inspect the distributor cap and rotor for evidence of carbon tracking (leakage of electrical current). Don't be concerned that the tip of the rotor or the electrical contacts inside the cap appear to be burned; it's not advisable to clean the carbon from those surfaces. Use a light coat of electrical silicone compound instead. Although silicone is an insulator, it does not impair the distributor's function, and it prevents burning of the contact surfaces.

Take the vehicle to a local auto-repair shop equipped with an oscilloscope and have a mechanic check the secondary ignition system (spark plugs and spark-plug cables). These components are a common source of engine problems. Make sure the mechanic loads the engine on a dynamometer or while running engine in gear (foot on brake, and hand brake set) while checking for secondary electrical-ignition breakdown. This checkup will show bad spark-plug cables, spark plugs, or other ignition components. Primary voltage should also be checked, especially on Chrysler vehicles.

Carburetor Function

All late-model RV engines use electronic fuel injection, troubleshooting for which is covered in Chapter 10, but carburetors were used on some vehicles, including motorhomes, into the late 1980s. Carburetors on GM vehicles were equipped with nitrophyl (plastic) fuel-bowl floats, which gradually become saturated

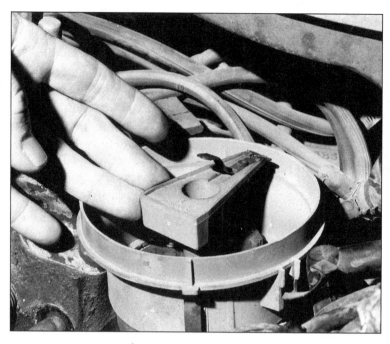

Figure 12.4
After twisting the distributor rotor against spring tension, it should freely return to its original position.

with fuel, raising the fuel level. The floats should be replaced every two years. An increase in weight compared to a new float is an indication of float saturation. The saturation causes excessive fuel use, stalling on corners and on abrupt stops, and hard starts while the engine is warm.

Holley carburetors, common on Ford engines of the early and mid-1980s, were equipped with power valves for fuel enrichment. Internal-gasket failure, vacuum leaks, and backfiring of the engine through the carburetor can cause the valves to leak. To check for leakage, bring the engine to operating temperature, shut it down, and allow it to sit for thirty minutes. Without touching the accelerator pedal, have an assistant start the engine while you watch for excessive black smoke; if present, it indicates a faulty power valve. Excessive fuel consumption is another indication. Use of a Holley 6.5 power valve and new gaskets for the metering body and fuel bowl are advisable.

Improper operation of the choke can adversely affect engine performance, as well as reduce engine life. An over-rich choke allows excessive fuel to wash cylinder walls, causing accelerated wear. It also loads the spark plugs with carbon.

Most carburetors have choke systems with pull-off diaphragms that open the choke when the engine starts. These vacuum-operated diaphragms are fairly easy to check and adjust. The choke diaphragm is located on the outside of the carburetor and is connected via linkage to the choke butterfly. Before a cold startup, remove the air cleaner and observe the linkage that opens the butterfly. Start the engine to check that the linkage partially opens the butterfly immediately. If the diaphragm is faulty, remove it and take it to a parts supplier for visual confirmation that the new part you are buying is the same as the old one. The choke should progressively open and be fully open when the engine is up to operating temperature.

Secondary metering tubes in Quadrajet carburetors tend to loosen and drop into the secondary fuel bowl, causing a lean condition and power loss during heavy throttle. Checking for this problem requires the removal of the air horn (top) of the carburetor; the tubes are pressed into the air horn. If they have dropped out, reinsert them with a light coat of epoxy glue to hold them in place.

Also, check pressed-in plugs in the bottom of the fuel bowl for evidence of leakage. Layer epoxy glue on top of the plugs if leakage is suspected.

Fuel Volume and Pressure

Adequate fuel volume and pressure must be available whether the vehicle is fuel injected or carbureted. Check fuel filters; you should be able to blow freely through them. Fuel starvation can exist, creating a lean condition under a sustained load, without clear indication to the driver. This is especially true of fuel-injected engines. Fuel pressure and volume specifications are listed in shop manuals, along with testing procedures.

Generally, with carbureted engines, if volume is okay, pressure is acceptable. The fuel pump of a carbureted engine should produce a pint of fuel under free-flow conditions in fifteen to twenty seconds. Check the factory specifications for fuel-injected engines; sometimes they are supplied by two pumps and only one will fail. This leads to drivability problems, such as stalling or surging, and may mimic vapor lock. Ford in-tank pumps have been problematic during hot-weather driving.

Air Filter

Inadequate fuel pressure, restricted filters, and other problems usually will be identified by the computerized codes. Beyond these items, it's especially important to make sure the air filter is in good condition.

In fuel-injected engines, proper maintenance of the air filter is crucial, especially on engines where fresh-air ducting is used. Although carbureted engines are also affected by restricted air filters, filter maintenance is much more critical in fuel-injected engines because fuel flow is controlled mainly by throttle position rather than airflow through the venturi of a carburetor. Therefore, any restrictions in the air filter will dramatically affect fuel mileage. The air-filter element should be inspected every 10,000 miles. Also, look for restrictions in the fresh-air inlet tube. Hoses sometimes collapse, and foreign matter can partially block the inlet.

Valves

General Motors V-8s have adjustable valve lash, and they should be checked about every 20,000 miles. Valves of other popular V-8 and V-10 RV engines are not adjustable. After valves are initially adjusted, audible valve noise is an indication of valve-train problems. Set GM valve adjustment to one-quarter turn down from zero lash, rather than the one full turn recommended by the factory. The valves should be adjusted with the engine idling. Rocker-arm adjusting nuts on GM vehicles are the friction type; be sure there is resistance to turning during the adjustment procedure. If no resistance is felt, replace the nut.

With the valve covers off, visually compare the movement or lift of one valve stem with another. They should be uniform. If one is low, it indicates a worn cam lobe or a bad lifter. Special clips are available from performance equipment shops that block oil splash during valve adjustment. Worn lobes are especially common with small-block Chevy engines. Compression checks performed with each tune-up will provide information about overall valve condition.

TESTS THAT REQUIRE TEARDOWN

Cylinder-Wall Taper

When substantial oil consumption is a problem and a leak-down test indicates faulty pistons/rings or walls, cylinder-wall taper should be checked. This requires the removal of the cylinder heads. If less than 0.004 inch of taper (wear) is found, proper honing of the cylinders and installation of moly piston rings may extend engine life.

Rod bearings should be inspected and may need to be replaced; piston-pin fit and connecting-rod alignment should also be checked. The main bearings should be inspected, but they seldom need replacement. Valve lifters should be removed (keep them in proper order for replacement in their original positions) to permit visual inspection of the camshaft. The engine should be rotated so all cam lobes can be inspected for pitting and wear. The bottom of each lifter should also be inspected for wear and pitting.

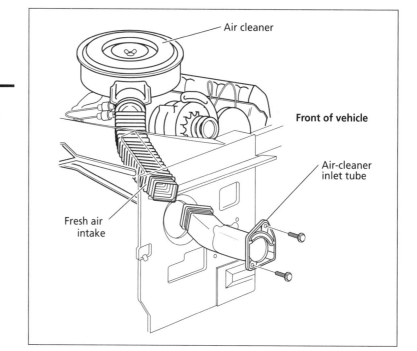

Figure 12.5
Unobstructed engine air intake should be positioned ahead of the radiator to avoid preheating.

Manifold Inspection

During the process of checking cylinder-wall taper, also inspect the intake manifold. Observe the gasket surface at the lower side of each intake port for signs of oil leakage past the gasket. Faulty gaskets, milled heads and/or improper torquing are common causes of this problem.

Check for manifold warpage. Thoroughly clean the manifold and place a light coat of oil on the surface contact areas. Cover the contact areas with a piece of glass. The coat of oil will contact the glass, and any warped areas will be evident because the oil will not adhere evenly to the glass. A warped manifold must be replaced.

The manifold must also be inspected for cracks. Having the manifold professionally cleaned and inspected is an excellent practice. If oil leakage past the intake gaskets is discovered, use particular care with the gaskets and sealant during reinstallation. First, use an effective gasket sealer/adhesive over the cylinder-head surfaces after these surfaces have been thoroughly cleaned, unless the gasket is a type that must be installed dry (follow gasket maker's instructions). Put the gasket in place. Prior to installation of the manifold, apply a light coat of silicone sealer around each port and in each corner of the gasket. Immediately install the manifold, and torque to factory specifications.

If the valve seals must be replaced on a high-mileage engine, the heads should be disassembled and the guides should be remachined to accept Teflon-type free-floating seals. Pioneer and Perfect Circle are two effective brands, available at auto-parts stores. These seals are to be used along with the standard seal. With the heads off the engine and all of the carbon removed, it's also logical to inspect valve guides and perform a valve job.

AFTERMARKET MODIFICATIONS

Properly selected aftermarket engine modifications can increase the efficiency and durability of the engine and drivetrain. The net result can be more power and/or better fuel economy. It's important to select components that work together. For example, if a higher-output camshaft is selected, it's important to have low-restriction intake and exhaust systems to go with it.

Connect vacuum gauge to manifold vacuum

Figure 12.6
A manifold vacuum gauge can be used to measure restriction in an engine's air-intake tract.

Air Intake

Air ducting designed to feed an engine intake from ahead of the radiator rather than the air preheated by the radiator is standard on most late-model engines and is essential for engine performance in hot weather. Such a system can be added to an older engine if it was not standard. An engine will perform better on cool air, which is denser than hot air (Figure 12.5). Make sure the potential for improvement is not counterbalanced by a restriction in the air ducting; it should be at least 4 inches inside diameter, with no sharp bends.

Air-intake tracts of many engines are restricted, which causes performance and fuel-economy losses while operating under heavy throttle. Restriction can be measured with a manifold vacuum gauge (Figure 12.6). The restriction may exist in the cool-air ducting, in the air-cleaner housing, or in both. It's possible to measure the restriction by accelerating or climbing a hill under full throttle at about 3,500 rpm while monitoring vacuum at the intake manifold. Vacuum readings should not exceed 1 to 2 inches Hg (mercury). Test with

the intake system intact, and retest with the cool-air ducting disconnected from the air-cleaner housing to determine the adverse effect of the ducting.

Many air-cleaner housings are inefficient and can be improved, as can the air filters themselves. Effective aftermarket air-induction kits designed specifically for RV engines are available from companies that service the RV industry; their ads usually can be found in RV magazines such as *Trailer Life* and *MotorHome*.

While it may seem overly simple, neglect of air filters can cause mileage and performance losses. Restrictions in the air filter will dramatically affect power and fuel mileage; therefore the air-filter element should be inspected every 10,000 miles. Also, look for restrictions in the fresh-air inlet tube. Hoses sometimes collapse, and foreign matter can partially block the inlet. Whether or not the intake tract is modified, the use of a high-performance air-filter can is an effective addition. Typically, this will add several units of horsepower.

Auxiliary Transmissions

Vehicles that are expected to move a lot of weight usually do so with multiple gears. Not so with most RVs, which usually are limited to four speeds forward. Highline motorhomes are the exception, with 5- or 6-speed transmissions as components of their relatively sophisticated chassis.

Older vehicles with 3-speed automatics are the primary beneficiaries of additional gear ratios, which can be added in the form of auxiliary transmissions. Two primary brands, U.S. Gear and Gear Vendors (Figure 12.7), are available for installation at many RV repair shops and at the national chain Camping World.

The two units differ in that the U.S. Gear unit can be purchased either as an overdrive or as an underdrive, while the Gear Vendors unit is an overdrive.

In an underpowered vehicle—one, for example, that has a 3.21:1 axle ratio when the load it is towing suggests the need for 3.73:1 gearing—use of the U.S. Gear unit in underdrive mode more than makes up for the difference. The unit's underdrive ratio is 1.25; when applied to a 3.21:1 axle ratio, the effective ratio becomes 4.01:1. Used as an overdrive, the U.S. Gear unit's ratio is 0.80:1.

Use of the Gear Vendors unit (0.78:1 ratio) in a vehicle with a 4.56:1 ratio brings that ratio to an effective 3.55:1 ratio. However, the widespread use of 4-speed overdrive transmissions with 0.7:1 overdrive ratios has reduced the potential fuel-economy benefit of auxiliary overdrive units. It is not effective to run an overdrive ratio on top of another overdrive ratio in most RV situations. Thus the primary benefit of overdrive units is to serve as gear-splitters, providing intermediate gear ranges between first and second and between second and third gears, improving hill-climbability by enabling the driver to keep engine rpm in the best power range.

Camshafts and Valve Gear

Special rocker arms with higher ratios (1.6:1 instead of 1.5:1) have proven to be effective in popular V-8 RV engines. Roller rocker arms and lifters can reduce internal friction substantially, and this can lead to more power and better fuel economy. Roller rocker arms can be added to an existing camshaft but lifters cannot. Since the cam determines how long each valve is open and closed—and the timing in relation to piston movement—a cam change can improve some engines. Cam-replacement is labor-intensive, especially on motorhomes, because the job requires substantial disassembly work. Thus, a cam replacement requires close scrutiny of advertised results to insure against disappointment.

Computers and Chips

Replacement computers and chips designed to recalibrate electronic fuel-injection systems are offered for gasoline engines, and several companies offer emissions-legal computers or chips that are advertised to provide both measurable performance and fuel-economy gains.

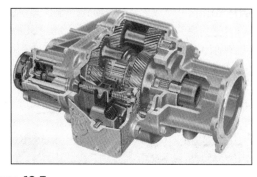 

Figure 12.7
Auxiliary transmissions such as U.S. Gear (left) and Gear Vendors (right) units can be used to add gear versatility for better performance.

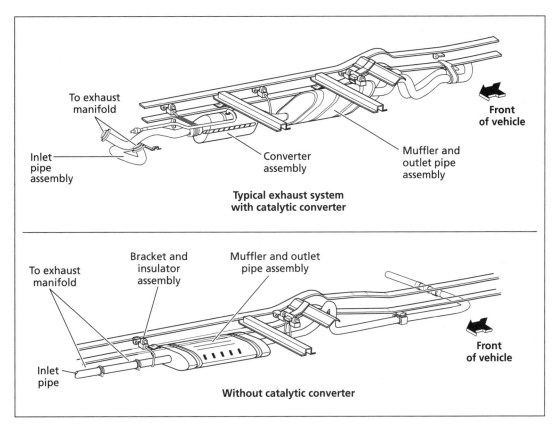

To exhaust manifold

Front of vehicle

Inlet pipe assembly

Converter assembly

Muffler and outlet pipe assembly

Typical exhaust system with catalytic converter

To exhaust manifold

Bracket and insulator assembly

Muffler and outlet pipe assembly

Front of vehicle

Inlet pipe

Without catalytic converter

Figure 12.8
The amount of exhaust restriction varies from one vehicle to the next, and can occur at any point from engine to tailpipe.

The on-board computer or electronic control module, as it's often called, contains the program that controls air/fuel ratios, spark timing, and the operation of items such as the exhaust-gas recirculation system. Later models also control the automatic transmission shifting.

The potential for improvement varies from one vehicle to the next, depending on the design effort devoted to each at the factory. Some vehicles have relatively effective reprogramming units while others are in need of improvement. Products designed for heavy-duty operation like trailering and motorhoming are essential rather than those designed for passenger-car use. Be sure to inquire if the product requires the use of premium fuel, which adds to the overall cost.

Typically, reprogramming units offered for gasoline engines may raise power 5 to 15 percent, if at all, and fuel economy gains range from zero to 10 percent. Such programs usu-ally work better when combined with other improvements like a free-flow exhaust system. Diesel engine reprogramming units, by themselves, may add so much fuel flow under heavy throttle (the easiest way to get more power from a diesel) that they create excessively high exhaust gas temperatures. When accompanied by modifications designed to improve air flow, properly programmed increases in fuel flow can produce dramatic torque and horsepower gains.

Intake and Exhaust Improvements

RV engines have varying degrees of restriction in their intake as well as exhaust systems (Figure 12.8), which supports a large and active aftermarket for smog-legal tow vehicle and motorhome systems. Virtually all RV engines benefit substantially from the installation of high-performance aftermarket headers

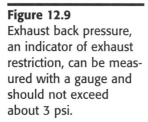

Figure 12.9
Exhaust back pressure, an indicator of exhaust restriction, can be measured with a gauge and should not exceed about 3 psi.

and exhaust systems with free-flowing mufflers, and some more than others. The best systems include free-flowing exhaust headers with larger-diameter mandrel-bent (to prevent size reduction in bends) exhaust tubing and less restrictive mufflers. Those systems also include modifications and special equipment for the intake air tract to reduce restriction and to prevent entry of air that has been preheated by the radiator (cooler air is more dense and enhances performance).

Similar air-flow-improvement systems boost performance of diesel engines as well, although they do not replace exhaust manifolds.

Complete systems for gasoline engines can yield as much as 10 percent better fuel economy and up to 80 percent better rear-wheel horsepower at peak output; lower but very substantial horsepower gains are achieved in more typical cruising rpm ranges, 2,500 to 3,000. Kits for diesel engines include improvements for exhaust and intake tracts as well as provisions for additional fuel flow, creating torque gains of as much as 40 percent.

Even though most engines can benefit from exhaust system improvements, exhaust back pressure can be measured at a point downstream from the exhaust manifolds to evaluate the need. A fitting must be welded in an exhaust pipe so a pressure gauge can be attached (Figure 12.9). If the system is to remain intact from the converter forward, measure back pressure immediately behind the converter. While accelerating or climbing a grade under full throttle at about 4,000 rpm, exhaust back pressure should not exceed about 3 psi. It can range upward as high as 10 psi in various applications, greatly restricting performance.

Gear Ratios

Sale of vehicles for trailer towing that have improper axle ratios is fairly common even though the motor companies publish guides that suggest engine/axle ratio combinations for specific amounts of trailer weight.

Still, a salesperson is prone to push vehicles that exist on the sales lot, rather than encouraging the prospective customer to order a vehicle with specific equipment. The result is tow vehicles with axle ratios that may be numerically too high, 4.10:1 or 4.56:1, for example, when 3.73:1 may have been adequate, or the opposite, a 3.21:1 axle when 3.73:1 is proper.

When ratios are numerically too high, fuel economy suffers because the engine is turning higher rpm than necessary to move the weight. This is less prevalent with 4-speed automatic transmissions with overdrive top gears. More common is the opposite: numerically low ratios that do not provide enough torque multiplication, which creates inadequate power and excessive downshifting.

Axle ratios can be changed, although ever-tightening emissions laws have caused most dealerships and many independent shops to decline the business. Off-road vehicle magazines still advertise gearsets and many off-road specialty shops still perform this work on selected vehicles. Many 1996 and later models have Onboard Diagnostics Version II (OBD II) self-diagnostic systems that may signal a fault (activating the "check engine" light) if gear ratios or tire diameters are changed.

Ignition

Many modifications of a standard electronic-ignition system designed to increase spark output or character don't help RV engines noticeably. The OEM systems are good enough for moderate rpm duty. Manual spark-control units available in performance shops offer the ability to control initial spark timing with a dash-mounted control while on the road. The driver can adjust initial spark timing in response to changing road, fuel, or altitude conditions, which can affect timing at all speeds and therefore performance and mileage.

The factory-recommended initial spark-advance setting may be somewhat conservative, depending on individual driving conditions, and two additional degrees may add a noticeable measure of throttle response. Factory specifications for spark advance found on stickers affixed under the hood list a specific initial spark-advance number, but factories usually allow variance of plus or minus 2 degrees. Use the factory setting if the vehicle is prone to spark knock (ping) occasionally,

which indicates the engine is calibrated as aggressively as possible for the grade of fuel being used.

Superchargers

Superchargers are bolt-on units that consist of blowers that are belt-driven by the engine's crankshaft to pressurize the intake tract of a gasoline engine, force-feeding more air and fuel than the engine is capable of otherwise ingesting under full throttle. The result is a substantial boost in power, usually accompanied by increased fuel consumption and the need for premium fuel to prevent spark knock.

For the RV owner who seeks the maximum power, the supercharger is the answer. Smog-legal kits are available for several GM and Ford engines. A free-flowing exhaust system is needed for the engine to utilize the full advantage of the supercharger. The manufacturers usually include computer programming to modify fuel delivery, ignition timing, and transmission shifting characteristics. Check to make sure the reprogramming is also smog legal.

Turbochargers

Marketed primarily for diesels of 1980s and early 1990s vintage that were naturally aspirated, aftermarket turbochargers are available for the Ford 6.9-liter and early 7.3-liter engines and for the GM 6.2-liter engine. The bolt-on units contain the necessary hardware to reroute the engine's normal air-intake tract through an exhaust-driven blower, creating up to about 9 psi of boost pressure and dramatically increasing engine power output by as much as 60 percent. The turbochargers also tend to reduce maximum exhaust-gas temperatures despite the dramatically increased power output. Purchasers of turbo systems should also invest in a pyrometer (exhaust-gas-temperature gauge) to make sure temperatures do not exceed levels recommended by the turbocharger-kit manufacturer.

ON THE ROAD

In an ideal world, we could have maximum fuel mileage and maximum performance at the same time. But we'll have to settle for one or the other. Those of us who want the best possible fuel economy must be prepared to make the speed sacrifices necessary to get it. Those who want to maintain a brisk speed must pay the fuel-economy penalty. We may vary between one of these preferences and the other during the same trip.

Cruise control can improve fuel mileage on fairly level roads, especially compared to a driver who is not concentrating on driving for economy. On the other hand, the use of cruise control often reduces mileage in mountainous terrain when we don't think ahead and increase speed a few more miles per hour while descending one hill and facing another. Cruise control also may apply heavy throttle to maintain a set speed, whereas the driver may choose to let speed drop a few miles per hour and use less throttle.

Regardless of your driving style, knowledge of your engine's torque and horsepower curves are helpful in getting what you want. The power curves illustrate an engine's specific output of torque and horsepower. Torque is a twisting force, in this case produced by the engine and measured in pound-feet. Horsepower is a unit of work over time, calculated by multiplying engine torque by rpm and dividing by 5,252.

An engine is most efficient, doing the maximum amount of work on a given amount of fuel, at its torque peak. Therefore, the most efficient pulling power occurs at or near the engine's torque peak. In exceptionally light-load situations, operation below the peak torque rpm reduces fuel consumption.

When passing another vehicle or climbing a mountain grade, additional power is needed, so we downshift. As the engine speed goes above the torque peak toward the horsepower peak, the amount of force delivered per revolution drops off, but there are more revolutions, so horsepower continues to increase up to a point. Beyond the horsepower peak rpm, performance drops; the most practical, usable operational range for normal driving is between the torque and horsepower peaks.

Several power curves are provided here for reference (Figure 12.10), and it's obvious that performance characteristics of the newer engines have changed. Many of the latest models have very high peak horsepower rpm, which translates to extended operational range, and they have relatively flat torque curves, which means that they deliver almost the same torque across the entire range. These engines have excellent performance in low-rpm ranges as well as at the top end. If the power curve for your engine is not among those included in this chapter, check with a dealer or call the manufacturer's customer-service hotline.

Fuel Economy

Many factors combine to produce the fuel consumption profile for a specific vehicle, including weight, aerodynamic drag, engine and chassis efficiency, and how the vehicle is driven. The nature of the fuel itself is yet another factor, beyond our control. The introduction of reformulated (oxygenated) gasoline in many areas of the nation in 1995 took a bite out of fuel efficiency, estimated to be 2 to 5 percent. While we can improve all the design factors, making a real difference in any of them can be difficult and costly. We do, however, have immediate control over how the vehicle is driven.

On-the-road rules for best fuel economy are relatively simple:

- Maintain the minimum cruising speed that you find tolerable, creating minimum wind drag.

- Operate in higher gears when possible; avoid downshifting until you're using heavy throttle and cannot maintain your desired minimum speed.

- Accelerate gradually, with minimum pressure on the pedal.

- Maintain constant cruising speeds; varying speeds wastes fuel.

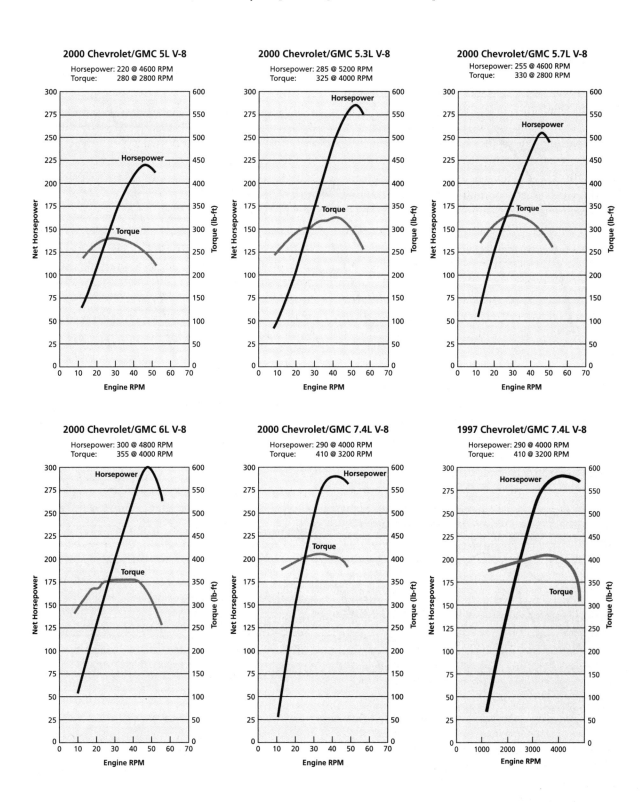

Figure 12.10
Engine power curves published by vehicle manufacturers indicate rpm ranges where
best horsepower and torque, measured in pound-feet (lb-ft), occur. Curves shown are a
sampling from popular engines in tow vehicles and motorhomes.

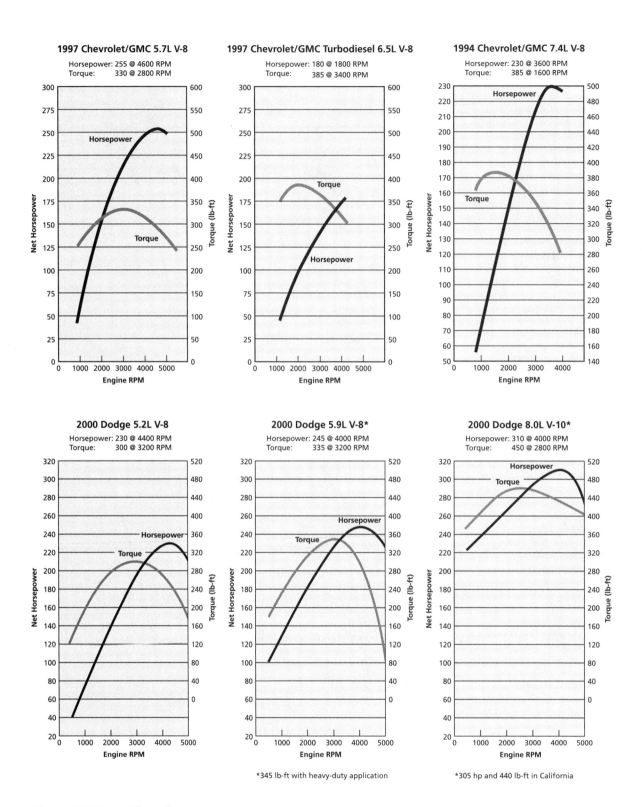

1997 Chevrolet/GMC 5.7L V-8

Horsepower: 255 @ 4600 RPM
Torque: 330 @ 2800 RPM

1997 Chevrolet/GMC Turbodiesel 6.5L V-8

Horsepower: 180 @ 1800 RPM
Torque: 385 @ 3400 RPM

1994 Chevrolet/GMC 7.4L V-8

Horsepower: 230 @ 3600 RPM
Torque: 385 @ 1600 RPM

2000 Dodge 5.2L V-8

Horsepower: 230 @ 4400 RPM
Torque: 300 @ 3200 RPM

2000 Dodge 5.9L V-8*

Horsepower: 245 @ 4000 RPM
Torque: 335 @ 3200 RPM

2000 Dodge 8.0L V-10*

Horsepower: 310 @ 4000 RPM
Torque: 450 @ 2800 RPM

*345 lb-ft with heavy-duty application

*305 hp and 440 lb-ft in California

Figure 12.10, *continued*

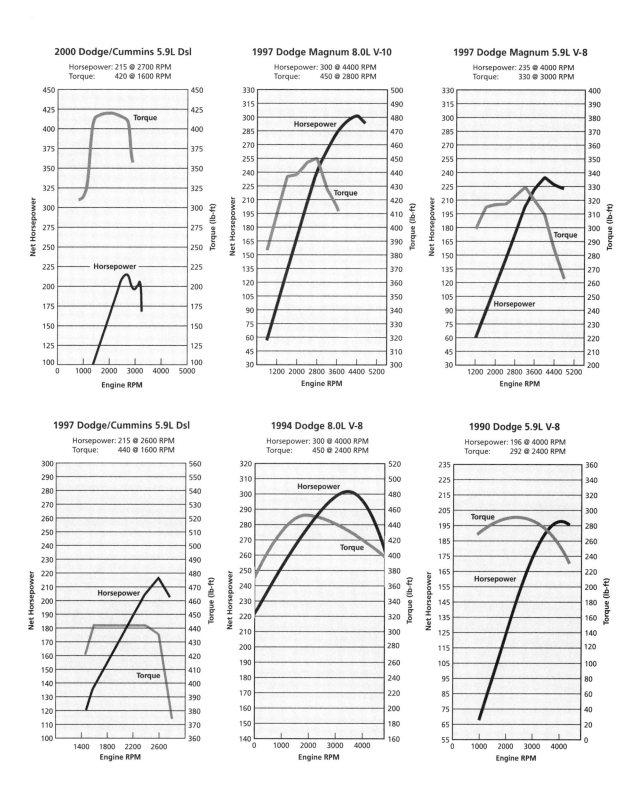

Figure 12.10, *continued*

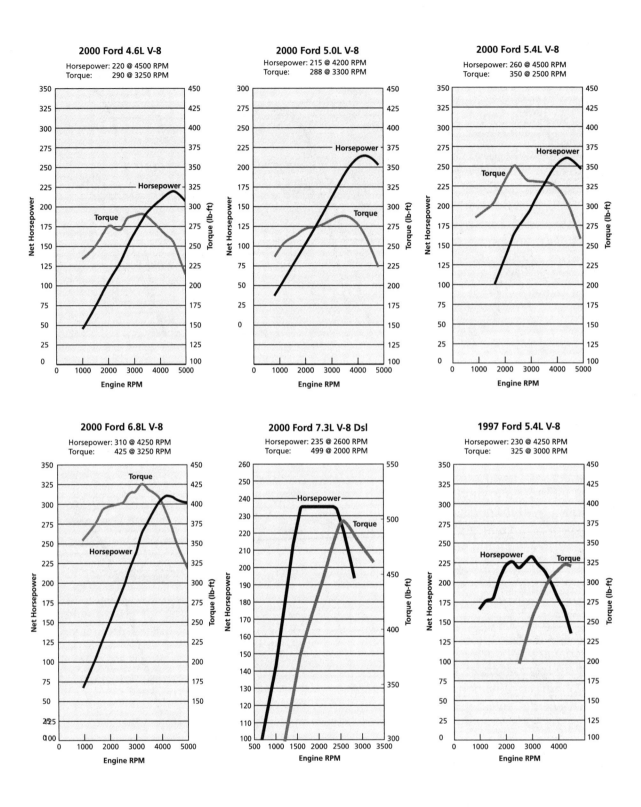

Figure 12.10, *continued*

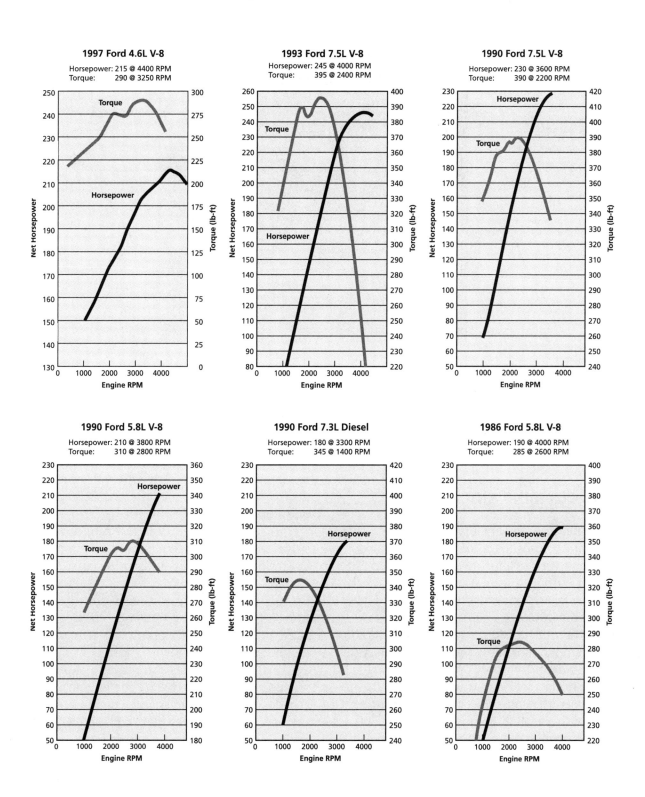

Figure 12.10, *continued*

Figure 12.11
A tachometer is essential in operating an engine at its highest potential.

Beyond those procedures, your fuel economy will depend on the vehicle type, the chassis equipment selected, and the level of chassis maintenance regularly performed.

HILL CLIMBING AND PASSING

Whether priorities are for fuel economy or performance, knowledge of an engine's power curve is very helpful in putting the engine's power output to its best use. How the accelerator pedal and transmission are handled determine the outcome.

If the transmission is left in drive, its shift program will not allow the engine to over-rev, even under full-throttle operation, although at times it may sound that way. In fact, the programmed transmission upshift point for vehicles with gasoline engines usually is 500 to 1,000 rpm below the engine's redline. Additionally, most current engines with electronic controls will cut power automatically; all diesels are protected by an rpm-limiting governor.

During full-throttle passing we don't always note the speedometer and the automatic upshift point. Thus it's necessary to stage such a maneuver in a nonpassing situation so you can note the upshift speed without a tachome-

ter, and calculate engine rpm using the formula included in this chapter. This produces only a rough approximation, because your transmission may shift slightly early or late, rpm-wise. Thus it's better to have a tachometer (Figure 12.11), which will tell you at a glance where you are in the engine's torque and horsepower ranges.

During your full-throttle test run, note the vehicle's ability to gain speed. It might be strong throughout the entire rpm range, or it may seem to diminish before it reaches the upshift point. If a gasoline engine upshifts before 4,000 rpm, the transmission programming probably is not working properly or the engine has an unusually low horsepower peak. With diesel engines, automatic upshifts should occur slightly before the engine's governed rpm limit, which can be determined by manually selecting a gear and accelerating until the engine reaches the rpm limit.

If, in a situation with a gasoline engine, the transmission upshifts sooner than 4,000 rpm, shift to second gear and perform another run, noting rpm or road speed and releasing the throttle when you notice that the rate of acceleration has begun to diminish. This will identify your "best power" point. If you have noted the road speed, you can calculate the rpm in second gear at that speed.

When climbing grades, there are a couple of different approaches you can use:

1. *Conservative.* Allow road speed to drop until the engine is in its peak torque range. That will be a narrow range for some gasoline engines—200 to 300 rpm—and a rather broad one for some others and for most diesels. For example, the torque peak of an early-1990s Ford 7.5-liter V-8 occurs at 2,400 rpm and drops off sharply above and below that level. If your road speed at that rpm is satisfactory, hold at that level because it is the most efficient use of engine power. Torque falls off rapidly above 3,000 rpm.

   By comparison, the torque peak of the 2000-model Ford 6.8-liter V-10 occurs at 3,250 rpm, and falls off very little on either side, providing a broad range of torque output from 2,000 to 4,000 rpm. You may be able to allow rpm to drop to about 2,000 rpm before downshifting.

   However, if it appears that the grade is steep enough that you will not be able to avoid dropping below the peak torque rpm, downshift before you reach that point or the loss of vehicle momentum will carry you below the peak torque rpm, requiring a downshift to an even lower gear.

2. *Performance-oriented.* This approach involves downshifting at whatever road speed will raise engine rpm to your previously established "best power" point or slightly above. Downshifting a gasoline engine from third to second at 3,000 rpm will raise rpm to about 4,000. This allows the driver to maintain the best possible vehicle momentum and have the option of backing off a bit for a slightly slower pace, less engine noise and better fuel economy.

Maximum RPM

If your "best power" rpm level seems too high, it isn't, assuming the engine is being cooled properly. When necessary, all popular gasoline engines used in RVs can be operated up to their redlines, which usually are a few hundred rpm above their rated peak horsepower rpm points, to get maximum performance. In fact, the engines are tested at full throttle at peak horsepower rpm for extended periods to determine durability. Marine conversions of the GM big-block engines, for example, are rated to run continuously at full throttle in their peak horsepower range, 4,200 to 4,600 rpm. The marine durability test involves running the engine at peak rpm for 300 hours at full throttle.

Figure 12.12
An exhaust gas temperature gauge (left) is valuable in monitoring diesel engines.

Many external components are installed for marine use, but the internal balance of the engine and the strength of its block and reciprocating parts are not altered. Thus these engines are virtually identical to their counterparts in light trucks and motorhomes from the standpoint of suitability for high-rpm operation—assuming that engine operating temperature is not excessive.

Diesel engines are tightly controlled by governor mechanisms, which simplifies the performance equation if automatic transmission shift points are set properly. The following simple tests will determine if they are:

Test 1. Shift to second gear and accelerate under full throttle from about 40 mph until the governor limits rpm. Note the rpm level.

Test 2. Shift to third gear, begin at 40 mph, and floor the accelerator, allowing the transmission to upshift automatically. If the transmission upshifts at or about the rpm level noted in Test 1, transmission programming is correct. If it upshifts early, you can get better uphill and passing performance from your diesel by manually controlling the upshift point to coincide with the governed rpm.

Operating any engine under heavy throttle at high rpm assumes that engine-coolant temperature does not rise beyond about 225°F and that spark knock (gasoline models) does not occur. It also assumes that the owner is using top-quality oil and changing it at proper intervals.

Calculating rpm Versus Road Speed

Engine rpm can be calculated for various road speeds. This is very useful for predicting the effect of different gear ratios or tire sizes before purchase:

$$rpm = \frac{R \times M \times MPH}{60}$$

R   = Transmission gear ratio multiplied by axle ratio.*

M   = Tire revolutions per mile (see Chapter 7 for a method of calculating this factor)

MPH= Road speed

60   = A constant

Most overdrive transmissions have a direct gear ratio (1:1) in third gear; top (O/D) gear is around 0.70:1.

A list of engine rpm/road speed figures can also be posted near, but not obstructing, the driver's field of vision if you don't have a tachometer.

USEFUL INSTRUMENTATION

Air/Fuel Ratio Monitors (Gasoline Engines Only)

Several aftermarket manufacturers now offer air/fuel ratio monitors. These units generally employ an automotive oxygen sensor mounted in the exhaust and a small microprocessor that illuminates light-emitting diodes (LEDs) on a monitor panel. The LEDs indicate what the air/fuel ratio is at the moment. This allows the driver to know if the engine is getting the proper fuel mixture and at what point fuel enrichment occurs.

Air/fuel ratios of engines at normal operating temperature typically range between about 11.5:1 under full load to slightly higher than 15:1 during light throttle and coast conditions. A ratio of 14.7:1 during part throttle cruise is considered ideal for low emissions and good fuel economy.

Monitoring air/fuel ratios can be especially helpful with the reformulated fuels now on the market. If an engine is getting too much fuel (too rich) it will waste gas, develop carbon deposits, and may ruin the catalytic converter (if so equipped). If an engine is not getting enough fuel (too lean), it may backfire, surge, or stumble, and eventually may burn valves and pistons.

Boost-Pressure Gauges (Turbocharged and Supercharged Engines Only)

A boost gauge is a welcome addition to engines with pressurized intakes. These instruments generally measure intake manifold pressure in psi (metric gauges use Bar; one Bar equals about 15 psi). Boost gauges allow the driver to monitor the output and effectiveness of the turbocharger or supercharger. Some diesels also don't have an automatic wastegate to limit pressure; with a gauge the driver can limit boost by varying the accelerator. By avoiding excessive boost, a driver can reduce stress on the engine.

Exhaust-Gas Temperature Gauges (Diesels Only)

Exhaust-gas-temperature gauges (Figure 12.12) monitor the heat present in the exhaust gases. This temperature varies directly with load and is a good indicator of how hard a diesel engine is being "worked." At idle, exhaust temperatures of diesel engines are typically around 300°F. Under full load, temperatures can soar to well over 1,300°F.

Most diesel-engine manufacturers recommend that peak EGT should not exceed about 1,200°F; check and follow the recommendation for your engine. If EGT approaches this maximum, ease off the accelerator enough to stay below the redline temperature to insure engine durability and long service life.

Manifold Vacuum Gauges (Gasoline Engines Only)

Manifold vacuum gauges are useful tools for driving more efficiently and for monitoring the operational status of the engine (Figure 12.13). The gauge is connected to the intake passages of a gasoline engine by a small hose so it can monitor the varying levels of pressure (partial vacuum) inside the manifold. These levels, measured in inches of mercury (Hg), change in relation to throttle position and load. By positioning the gauge where it's easy to see, the driver has a constant reminder of throttle position, and is prone to drive with a steadier and lighter foot on the accelerator pedal.

A vacuum gauge also can signal restriction in the engine's air-intake tract. Ideally, vacuum gauge readings at full throttle should be zero, although that is rarely the case. A reading of 2 to 3 inches at full throttle would sug-

Figure 12.13
Manifold vacuum gauge indicates throttle usage, and is helpful in driving for best possible fuel economy.

gest that the owner investigate intake tract improvements such as those provided as part of a performance improve kit that also includes replacement exhaust equipment.

Electronic fuel-injection systems gradually enrich fuel mixtures in response to heavier throttle so there is no single transition point (indicated in vacuum-gauge readings) where a significant change occurs. Electronic fuel-injection systems gradually enrich mixtures by increasing the dwell period (time during which the injector is spraying fuel into the engine).

However, there is a definite important enrichment point with carburetors. All carburetors have fuel-enrichment systems that allow lean mixtures to be used for light- to medium-throttle conditions and richer mixtures for heavy throttle. Four-barrel carburetors have three such systems: cruise, primary power, and secondary power. Two-barrel carburetors have two: cruise and power.

The four-barrel carburetor of an engine propelling an RV on relatively level highways in low altitude (below about 5,000 feet) operates in the cruise range at light to medium throttle, producing vacuum readings between 8 and 12 inches. The readings are affected by such things as the weight of the vehicle, efficiency of the engine, and effective gear ratios.

When moderate hills are encountered, vacuum readings may drop into the 4- to 8-inch range. Therein lies the opportunity for fuel-economy improvement. The transition in most carburetors between the cruise fuel-metering system and the primary power-enrichment system occurs at 6 to 7 inches of manifold vacuum, and with some carburetors it may occur as low as 4 to 5 inches. It's possible for the driver to maintain vacuum readings above 6 inches rather than slightly below that level for significant fuel-economy improvement.

Although it might follow logically that downshifting early to maintain vacuum levels above 6 inches would also improve fuel consumption, that's not entirely true because the engine uses additional fuel at higher rpm. It's simply best to hold vacuum above about 6 inches as long as possible, then use heavier throttle until vehicle speed drops to a comfortable downshift point.

The secondary metering system of a carburetor further enriches air-fuel ratios, but the vacuum gauge is less useful in monitoring its action, which occurs near full throttle.

The vacuum gauge will not single out any particular transition point in fuel metering. However, it's useful as a reminder of throttle position.

During efforts to improve fuel economy and performance, one should establish reasonable goals and make changes that are designed to work together. For RV use, it's more important to increase low- and mid-range torque and horsepower than to gain power at high rpm. Improvements in performance and fuel economy can be elusive, but with a well-thought-out plan, it should be possible to make noticeable gains.

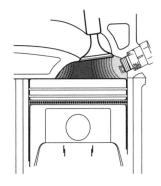

Chapter 13

MAKING A VEHICLE LAST LONGER

Vehicles, being rather complex assemblages of parts that work in close tolerances, have the unfortunate tendency to wear out. Indeed, the only thing that keeps many of their parts from wearing out posthaste is a microscopically thin film of oil or grease that separates the metal parts and carries heat away.

The engine is the most expensive single vehicle component and usually requires the most maintenance. It isn't uncommon that some engines give outrageously good service, while others are quite mediocre. Although the original design and quality of the engine are major factors in longevity, the owner can get long-term durability—extended life of any engine—by using the wide variety of techniques listed in this chapter.

DEVELOPING PROPER VEHICLE STARTUP AND DRIVING HABITS

Even engines of the highest quality can be adversely affected by poor driving habits. A common bad habit is a tendency to start the engine, rev it a couple of times, drop the transmission into gear, and roar away. An engine needs a few seconds for oil to get into full circulation, particularly to the valve train, which is the last to see oil flow. When the engine is revved right after starting, the valve train, as well as other surfaces, may be marginally lubricated (Figure 13.1). Engine oil is supposed to prevent metal-to-metal contact, but cold starts are a particularly vulnerable time. Revving the engine creates more metal-to-metal contact during this period, and thousands of cold starts accumulate to cause serious wear.

Similarly, revving the engine just as it's shut off causes unneeded wear and stress. Turbodiesel drivers should also allow their engines to idle for several minutes after a hard run before shutdown to allow the turbocharger to cool down. This helps prevent "coking" of the oil in the turbo and saves the bearings.

The type of driving we do usually cannot be altered significantly, but it's interesting to note that city driving is estimated to be about 17 percent less efficient than steady highway cruising; short trips of 3 miles or less increase fuel consumption due to the fact that the engine has not had time to fully come up to normal operating temperature.

Cold Starts

When starting a fuel-injected engine, it's not necessary to touch the accelerator pedal. Without touching the pedal, engine rpm will rise to a preset fast-idle level that is best for initial oil circulation.

The proper method of cold-starting a carbeurator engine is to depress the accelerator pedal about halfway to set the choke, and release the pedal. This will result in a fast idle (about 1,500 rpm) when the engine starts. Giving the engine too much throttle while cranking usually will result in initial revving to 2,000 rpm or higher, which is hard on the marginally lubricated parts of a cold engine.

To properly cold-start diesel engines, turn on the ignition and wait until the preheater or glow-plug timer light indicates it's okay to start the engine. Do not pump the throttle. If the engine doesn't start within about ten seconds, turn the ignition off and on again to recycle the cold-starting device. Allow the starter to cool after prolonged cranking.

Regardless of the type of fuel system or engine, when cold-starting an engine, run it at a fast idle for about twenty seconds, allowing oil to circulate to the most remote sections of the engine (such as the valve train), before placing the transmission in gear. This small delay will assure good oil circulation. Keep engine rpm low and avoid heavy acceleration until the engine has reached its normal operating temperature.

Extended idling of the engine during warmup is not a good practice because fuel vaporization is poor and cylinder pressures are relatively low. Warmup occurs more rapidly if the vehicle is driven soon after being started.

Stop-and-go driving creates many more opportunities for wear, especially in cold weather when fuel enrichment occurs with each restart. This kind of driving is known to

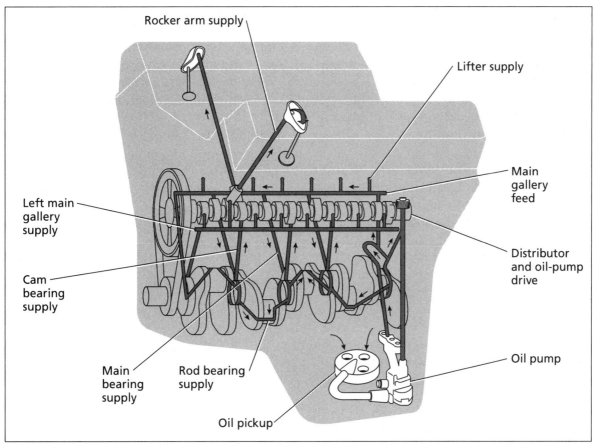

Figure 13.1
Oil flows under pressure to lubricate all of the engine's moving parts. The valve train is the last item in the system to receive lubrication after a cold start.

be hardest on engines. The driving situation that creates the least engine wear is light-load cruising. RV driving undoubtedly qualifies somewhere in between these two extremes, at least in moderate weather. When weather is hot, RV trips can produce high engine-oil temperatures and an increased tendency for gasoline engines to spark knock (ping or detonate). RVing typically is classified by motor companies as heavy-duty service, requiring accelerated engine-oil change intervals.

Cylinder Washdown

A significant cause of accelerated wear of gasoline engines during cold starts is gasoline—too much of it. On carburetor engines, chokes produce rich fuel mixtures; raw gasoline then floods into cylinders and washes the microscopically thin film of oil from the cylinder walls. All liquid fuel engines do this to some extent. This allows metal-to-metal contact between piston rings and cylinder walls. Cylinder washdown can cause accelerated piston ring and cylinder wear, leading to the loss of the ring seal, the reduction of compression, and excessive oil consumption.

During a cold start, the engine should not backfire, stall, or stumble. If it does, readjust the choke pulloff to a richer setting, which will improve driveability. On the other hand, if the engine chugs or produces black smoke from the tailpipe, lean the choke adjustment.

On fuel-injected gasoline-powered vehicles, cold-start enrichment circuits are more accurate and normally do not cause too much enrichment.

With any system, waiting about twenty seconds for oil to circulate and avoiding heavy acceleration until the temperature is up are important.

Avoid extended engine idling, during which fuel vaporization and combustion temperatures are not ideal. The result is less lubrication and a higher level of cylinder washdown, causing accelerated wear, as well as an increase in carbon deposits.

On the Road

Most engines are designed to be operated for short periods at speeds slightly beyond their peak horsepower rpm, such as in passing situations when the accelerator pedal is "floored" and the transmission downshifts. Horsepower/torque graphs featured in Chapter 12 identify peak horsepower rpm for various engines. For example, the Chevrolet/GMC Vortec 6000 (6-liter) engine's peak horsepower occurs at 4,800 rpm. This represents the engine's upper limit for best performance while passing other vehicles or hill-climbing when maximum performance and speed are desired. Engine rpm levels above 4,000 rpm may seem high for V-8 engines, but in fact engineers say the engines can be operated even above the peak horsepower rpm if the driver needs to extend the operational range for maximum speed in lower gears for short periods of time.

A complicating factor in operating an engine under heavy throttle at any rpm, but especially at high rpm, is heat. Engine-coolant operating temperature may climb to 230°F or higher, and engine-oil temperature may approach or exceed 300°F, depending on the engine's and vehicle's design and mechanical condition. Heat also raises the engine's fuel-octane requirements, leading to another serious factor, detonation (engine ping), which can quickly damage engines. Thus, heat may bring an engine into a crisis situation that might be repeated several times a day.

Barring an increase in operating temperature beyond the upper end of the normal operating range (about 225°F), engines that are in good condition can be operated continuously under heavy throttle at their peak horsepower rpm. More conservative owners may want to limit rpm to 80 percent of peak horsepower rpm.

ENGINE COOLING

The need for adequate engine cooling cannot be overemphasized, despite the fact that engine metallurgy and oils have been greatly improved during the past decade to withstand more heat. In the 1970s, it was not uncommon for heat to cause oils to thicken, due to oxidation, into something resembling hot asphalt that would not drain from the crankcase. Good-quality oils (identified by the American Petroleum Institute starburst symbol) are much better now, but quality may still vary. High temperatures create tremendous heat loads on lubricants, which may reduce their ability to prevent metal-to-metal contact. It's wise to make sure cooling systems are in the best possible condition and that engine temperature gauges are accurate.

Cooling systems of late-model vehicles are usually able to restrain temperature rise under severe operating conditions. Most systems keep engine-coolant temperatures from exceeding about 230°F through use of viscous-clutch fans designed to go into high-speed modes when temperatures reach 215°F to 225°F. The fans freewheel until engine temperature reaches a certain point, and then the fan clutches more fully engage, raising fan rpm for maximum airflow.

An engine that tends to incur a noticeable temperature rise (possibly accompanied by a tendency to spark knock) needs help. It may require additional cooling capacity such as a thicker radiator, a slight reduction in initial spark timing, higher octane gasoline to prevent spark knock, or something as simple as unclogging the exhaust gas recirculation (EGR) passages.

Late-model engines are designed to operate at relatively high temperatures, 195°F to 205°F, to help vaporize fuel and reduce pollution. These temperature levels are intended to control emissions and to contribute to better fuel economy. The thermostat is regarded as a component of the emissions-control system, which means that it is covered by general prohibitions against tampering.

On the opposite end of the spectrum, running an engine too cool can cause accelerated

Figure 13.2
Proper engine cooling depends on the correct operation of the viscous-drive fan clutch which is belt-driven by the engine.

wear and increased combustion deposits inside the engine. General Motors estimates that cylinder wear increases eightfold with coolant temperature at 100°F compared with the normal 195°F. Thermostats sometimes stick in the open position, evidenced by gauge readings that do not rise to normal except in hot weather or under heavy load.

The ingredients of a healthy cooling system include:

- Radiator of adequate size, maintained properly

- A 50–50 mix of antifreeze and distilled water, changed every two years unless extended-life coolant is used

- Engine fan of adequate size that goes into high-rpm mode (makes more noise) when engine temperature rises to around 225°F to 230°F

- Effective fan shroud

- Unrestricted airflow through radiator

Inoperative fan clutches are a common cause of excessive operating temperatures. When engine-coolant temperature exceeds 210°F to 230°F (calibration differs according to type of engine), the fan should go into its high-speed mode, dramatically increasing airflow through the radiator.

Most cooling systems designed for 14 to 17 psi of pressure will not boil out (release pressure from the radiator cap) until the temperature reaches approximately 260°F to 270°F. But that's far too hot if you expect the engine to live very long. Peak operating temperature even under very high ambient conditions should not exceed 230°F, and even that is high enough to push many engines to spark knock. A coolant temperature of 230°F is the highest point at which the engine fan should go into its high-speed mode to arrest temperature rise. When the fan locks in, a higher level of fan noise should be audible. If it isn't, and if temperature climbs steadily, the fan clutch (Figure 13.2) may be in need of replacement.

When antifreeze is added, it should be mixed with distilled water rather than tap water. The reason is that tap water contains minerals. When the water is heated in the cooling system, the minerals deposit on the surfaces of the cooling system, particularly on water passages inside the cylinder heads and the radiator. Thus, the engine gradually builds up a coating of mineral deposits that retards the transfer of heat into the coolant, increasing combustion-chamber temperature and the tendency of the engine to detonate.

It's important that cooling-system maintenance never be neglected because the effects are difficult or nearly impossible to reverse.

Certainly, the radiator can be reconditioned, but deposits and corrosion inside of the block usually are permanent.

ENGINE OIL

The search for the best engine oils has led in many different directions and has been underway for about as long as vehicles have occupied America's roadways. Advertising claims ballyhoo one brand against another. The consumer's only accurate guide, other than long personal experience with a particular brand and grade, are the ratings by the American Petroleum Institute (API) for quality and performance. Two symbols indicate the rating, an API service symbol, which includes the viscosity rating (Figure 13.3), and a starburst symbol, which indicates that the oil is rated as having a positive effect on fuel economy, compared with other oil grades. (Figure 13.4). Both symbols insure the oil has passed API's performance tests, and are displayed on the container.

Current Engine-Oil Ratings

Following are the current ratings for engine oils:

- SJ for gasoline engines in cars, vans, and light trucks

- SH for gasoline engines in cars, vans, and light trucks. (This category was no longer valid inside API's service symbol after August, 1997.)

- CH-4 for high-speed four-stroke diesel engines

- CE and CD ratings for diesel engines were discontinued after 1995

Multigrade oils include a complex package of additives designed to extend suitability for operation in widely varying temperatures as well as other performance functions.

In order for an oil to qualify for the highest rating, it must pass a series of performance tests. Each test is used to evaluate a specific characteristic of oil, such as protection against wear, corrosion, rust, and oxidation due to heat. For example, an oxidation/wear test is

Figure 13.3
The circular API service symbol indicates viscosity and grade of oil, which must match recommendations of the vehicle manufacturer.

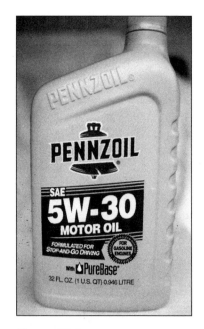

Figure 13.4
The starburst symbol indicates gasoline-engine usage and energy conservation capability.

conducted for sixty-four hours with the oil at 300°F to measure the oil's tendency to permit excessive wear and to measure thickening, sludge, and varnish formation. Resistance to these deteriorating factors is an important aspect of the classification. All SJ oils are assumed to have passed the 300°F test.

Selecting Oil Grades

Automotive companies universally specify multigrades in owner's manuals, and SAE 30, which was the preferred oil for GM's 7.4-liter engine in the company's motorhome chassis for many years, is no longer listed as suitable.

Owner's manuals for Ford motorhome chassis and light trucks, for example, list 5W-30 as preferred for gasoline engines in all temperatures and 10W-30 as suitable for temperatures above 0°F. GM light truck manuals specify SAE 5W-30 as preferred and 10-W-30 as acceptable for temperatures above zero. GM recommends against using any other grades of oil, specifically 20W-50.

Engineers suggest that the viscosity spread of 20W-50 is too great, requiring too many additives. Many years ago GM advised against use of SAE 10W-40 for the same reason, although other motor companies continued to approve that grade.

Federal fuel-economy regulations also motivate manufacturers to recommend relatively low-viscosity multigrades. Also, there is the possibility that the vehicle owner who uses a heavier oil may neglect to change to a lighter oil for cold-weather driving. Single-grade oils such as SAE 30 do not circulate well immediately after a cold-engine startup in temperatures below 40°F, creating the possibility of accelerated wear. Single-grade oils create additional resistance to movements of engine components under all conditions, compared to multigrades with lower reference numbers. These companies apparently do not believe most motorists are conscientious enough to avoid misusing single-grade oils.

In support of the recommendations, engineers admit that they are motivated by fuel-economy considerations in vehicles under 8,500 pounds GVWR, but add that they are convinced the latest lightweight multigrades carrying the starburst symbol will protect engines under extreme operating situations. One veteran engine-design manager admitted he had always favored thicker oils for hot-weather situations but was won over by his own engine durability testing with the lower viscosity oils.

Synthetic Oils

Most manufacturers, including Mobil, recommend following the vehicle manufacturer's oil-change intervals, since additive packages in all oils are neutralized by the combustion byproducts that form inside an engine.

Few engine manufacturers specifically recommend synthetics, although they are included in lists of approved oils if they carry the latest ratings—and providing the vehicle manufacturer's oil-change intervals are observed.

Modern synthetics may be mixed with conventional oils, although it dilutes the properties of the synthetic. Motor companies insist that regular oil changes are mandatory for engine durability because contaminants that are absorbed by the oil must be flushed from the engine. Good synthetics are generally recognized as having higher performance levels than petroleum-based oils due to:

- High-temperature stability
- Cold-temperature performance
- Improved protection against engine deposits

Among these attributes, better tolerance for high temperatures may be a primary advantage for RV owners whose engines pull heavy loads under sustained heavy throttle and high engine rpm, often during hot weather. Although the heat resistance of conventional oils has been improved steadily during the past few years, true synthetics still apparently have a definite edge. They resist oxidation, which means high resistance to varnish formation and thickening.

Some oils are a blend of synthetic and conventional oils. The oil's characteristics will depend on the percentage of each type plus

What a Multi-Viscosity Oil Includes

A multi-viscosity additive package includes the following:

- **Pour-point Depressants** Straight mineral oils tend to congeal into waxlike consistency in low temperatures. Special additives keep the oil molecules from joining, thereby keeping the oil liquid.

- **Oxidation and Bearing-Corrosion Inhibitors** These compounds are designed to slow the rate of oxidation and to provide a coating for bearings.

- **Rust and Corrosion Inhibitors** Water-laden air enters engine crankcases, and the water condenses when the engine cools. It mixes with the oil and causes formation of acids. Additives are needed to neutralize the acids and help coat metal surfaces to keep acids from attacking them.

- **Detergent/Dispersant Additives** Combustion byproducts must be kept in suspension so they can be drained out with the oil. It's important to note that these additives will not clean sludge and varnish out of an engine; their primary role is to prevent sludge formation. The role of these additives is one of the reasons new oil tends to darken soon after an oil change. As these additives are used up, they perform their function, which is why the oil must be changed.

- **Foam Inhibitors** Oil is subjected to high pressure and engine components that are rotating at high speeds, so it mixes and becomes aerated. Because aerated oil does not work very well, these inhibitors, mainly silicones, are used to reduce foaming.

- **Viscosity** Oil viscosity (thickness) changes with temperature, and since many engines are operated in widely varying temperatures, oils that maintain fairly consistent viscosity can provide good circulation during cold starts, while also affording proper lubrication under high temperatures. Polymers are used to provide this versatility in multigrade petroleum-based oils. For example, SAE 10W-30 is listed by many motor companies as suitable for use in an ambient temperature range from 0°F to an excess of 100°F, while SAE 30 is listed as suitable for a range of 40°F to in excess of 100°F.

- **Extreme-Pressure Additives** Certain chemicals that tend to be attracted to metal surfaces are known as boundary lubricants. They help prevent metals from galling or from welding to each other under high temperatures when the oil film is very thin, such as in the cam-to-lifter contact area.

the quality of the base stocks. Blends may not have the same capability to protect at high-temperature as true synthetics.

The base compounds used for synthetic oils vary among brands. Most synthetics use polyalphaolefins and esters for the base stock, combined with an additive package. The molecules are of consistent size and shape, while molecules of conventional mineral oils vary widely in size and shape. They tend to clump together and thicken at cold temperatures. Under high temperatures, the smaller molecules tend to boil off, thickening the oil.

Energy-Conserving Oils

Oils that are categorized as energy conserving carry the starburst symbol. The designation is carried by most popular 5W-30 and 10W-30 oils.

Use of oils with the starburst label, indicating energy conservation, is estimated to improve fuel economy by 2.7 percent or greater. These estimates apparently refer to passenger-car driving; less improvement may occur in heavily loaded engines in severe service.

Oil Additives

With the complex package of additives present in modern oils, no additional ones are needed—despite the advertising claims for a broad variety of oil additives. Some additives are merely viscosity improvers and others claim to reduce friction. Engineers at the motor companies consistently maintain that modern oils have all the additives they need and that additional additives serve no useful purpose. Indeed, in some cases, additives are said to seriously degrade the oil's performance. Manufacturers of aftermarket oil-improver products usually are not able to provide authoritative analyses by independent testing laboratories to back up their claims of reduced engine wear.

Oil Cooling

Any oil can benefit by operating under reasonable temperatures. An oil film only 0.001-inch thick must lubricate, seal, and cool engine components in areas where combustion temperatures range from 2,000°F to 3,000°F. The oil must soak up as much as 20 percent of the engine's heat output (Figure 13.5). While the coolant mixture circulating through the engine's water jacket cools the upper part of the engine (including cylinder heads, cylinders, and valves) the oil must cool the crankshaft and connecting-rod bearings, the camshaft and its bearings, the timing gears, the pistons, and other components.

In racing situations, coolers are used to keep temperatures in the low 200s, helping engine components withstand extreme high rpm levels under full-throttle conditions.

In contrast, oil temperatures in RV engines usually run 250°F to 270°F during summertime driving and may exceed 300°F on grades in hot weather. Modern oils are designed to resist breakdown at high temperatures, but operating conditions approaching 300°F under hot-weather hill-climbing conditions provide a severe test for an oil's ability to resist breakdown. Engine manufacturers say that temperatures up to 285°F are within their design parameters.

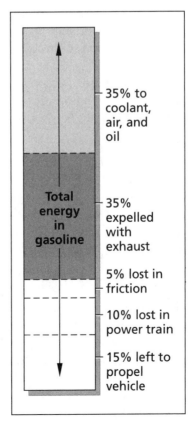

35% to coolant, air, and oil

Total energy in gasoline

35% expelled with exhaust

5% lost in friction

10% lost in power train

15% left to propel vehicle

Figure 13.5 Engine oil must absorb up to 20 percent of the engine's heat output.

Oil cooling has obvious benefits for RV engines, but the vehicle owner must weigh the cost of adding an oil cooler against the amount of driving that will be done under hot-weather conditions. Owners who frequently drive mountainous terrain in hot weather and routinely see temperatures that exceed 275°F (in the sump) are prime candidates for additional oil cooling. Oil coolers that are suitable for most RV engines are available at performance-equipment stores and RV supply stores.

AUTOMATIC TRANSMISSION FLUIDS

The use of extended-service transmission oil fluids has stretched recommended fluid change intervals. For example, the use of extended-life Dexron III in GM light trucks has promoted the manufacturer to recommend fluid changes at 50,000-mile intervals in some light trucks, even for heavy duty service such as trailer towing. The fluid-change interval is more frequent for other vehicles, and it's necessary to at least adhere to the manufacturer's maintenance schedule for the particular vehicle, while giving consideration to more frequent change intervals if driving conditions are severe (mountainous terrain in hot weather).

Dexron III also is designated for Ford vehicles that use Mercon V fluid, but neither it nor Mercon V are are to be used in Fords that require Type F fluid. Dexron III is preferred for vehicles that required its predecessors, Dexron II and Dexron fluids.

ATF+4 is the high-performance standard for the latest Chrysler vehicles, although it's not necessarily usable as a replacement for the earlier fluid, ATF+3.

The color and odor of Dexron III are not as reliable for the indication of overheated fluid as was the case with fluids of older design. The fluid may take on a brownish color without having deteriorated.

Over the past couple of decades, much emphasis has justifiably been placed on deterioration of transmission fluid from excessive heat, but the new high-performance fluids have improved resistance to oxidation from heat. GM's new optional transmission temperature gauge on 2000-model-year trucks suggests that Dexron III has raised the definition of "hot." The gauge, which monitors temperatures in the transmission pan, indicates the "hot" mark at 265°F; at 275°F, the owner is instructed to pull off the road and allow the transmission to cool down by fast-idling the engine with the hood up.

Synthetic fluids that meet the requirements of most transmission manufacturers are excellent candidates for use in towing vehicles. Superior stability allows high-temperature operation without varnishing valves and clutches, while also possibly improving shifting characteristics in extremely cold weather.

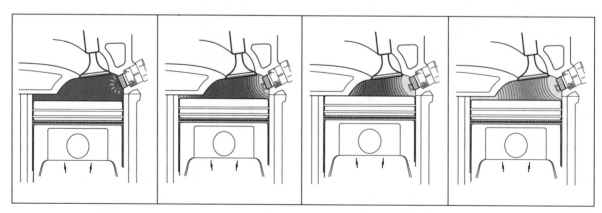

Figure 13.6
Detonation occurs when two abnormal flame fronts meet in the combustion chamber, creating shock waves and the sound of spark knock or "ping."

MANUAL TRANSMISSION OIL

Standard transmissions (and four-wheel-drive transfer cases) have no gauges or warning lights and often are ignored until it's too late. Check the fluid level every time the engine oil is changed, and change the oil in the gearbox at the intervals recommended in the maintenance section of the owner's manual. Use the correct viscosity, such as 80W-90, for the expected climatic conditions.

Synthetic gear lubricants are now available and generally offer reduced operating temperatures and longer component life. Read the owner's manual for the manufacturer's recommendations on use of synthetics in limited-slip differentials.

Even with proper cooling, conventional automatic transmission fluid and the filter should be changed about every 20,000 miles in RV use. If cooling is marginal and/or the fluid has been overheated, the transmission fluid should be changed every 10,000 miles during the period when high temperatures occur.

DETONATION AND PREIGNITION

Spark knock is the audible portion of either detonation or preignition. It can be caused by different conditions, but the results are similar: extreme stress and heat leading to engine damage. Detonation occurs when a rapid rise in temperature or pressure ignites the air-fuel mixture. This premature combustion pushes the piston down violently while it's still being pushed up by the crankshaft and connecting rod. Preignition has the same result, but the abnormal flame front may be ignited by a glowing piece of metal or carbon (Figure 13.6).

Engine ping typically occurs under heavy loads and high temperatures. Although a slight ping on initial acceleration or at the moment of upshift under heavy load is not cause for alarm, continued and heavy pinging may do damage. As the combustion-chamber temperature increases beyond normal in an engine that has a tendency to ping, higher fuel octane may be needed. If spark knock is allowed to continue, the abnormal combustion that results can in severe cases burn holes in tops of pistons. Piston-ring seal may be disturbed, and valve and valve-seat wear is accelerated.

Late-model cars and light trucks are equipped with sensors that detect engine ping or spark knock, telling the computer to retard the spark timing. If your engine is not equipped with a knock sensor (usually those engines without electronic control of spark advance), it's important to recognize that detonation can substantially shorten the life of your engine.

In addition to excessive temperature and inadequate fuel octane, excessively lean air-fuel ratios can cause ping. Whatever the cause, the problem must be avoided. Cures include improved engine cooling, improved exhaust flow, higher fuel octane, exhaust gas recirculation system repair, and reduction of initial spark advance.

COOL DOWN

When an engine is operated under heavy throttle for an extended period, such as while climbing a mountain grade, temperatures should be allowed to restabilize before shutdown. Turbochargers and exhaust manifolds are particularly at risk to hot shutdown, but it also can compromise gasket sealing and other parts such as intake manifolds. Hot shutdown can cause coolant after boil and fuel percolation (engine flooding) in carburetor engines.

The most severe high temperature shutdown situation occurs in hot weather after climbing a mountain grade that has a turnout at the top. When stopping in such situations, allow the engine to idle for three to five minutes in park (or neutral, with manual transmission) before shutdown, preferably with the hood up to improve air circulation.

REFORMULATED GASOLINE

The federal government mandated the use of reformulated gasoline nationwide in 1996.

The result is fuels that include alcohol or other agents to promote cleaner combustion and reduce emissions. Another result was lower heat content and a change in air/fuel ratios in vehicles without electronic feedback fuel systems, which are designed to maintain preprogrammed air/fuel ratios regardless of changes in fuel.

Thus the only vehicles that are vulnerable to damage are those with carburetors. Leaner fuel mixtures create more heat and increase the tendency of the engine to spark knock. Problems can range from a drop in fuel mileage and deteriorated rubber parts in the fuel system to cracked manifolds, burned exhaust valves, broken piston rings, and damaged pistons.

If the engine runs too lean, it's necessary to have the carburetor recalibrated internally (different metering rods and jets) based on chassis dynamometer testing with an exhaust gas analyzer monitoring fuel mixtures.

ENGINE-SERVICE INTERVALS

Even while we search for new ways to stretch engine life, engineers say that one of the primary causes of engine wear is poor engine maintenance. Many owners apparently stretch service intervals through inattention or by misreading the owner's manual. Most manufacturers of engines specify two sets of maintenance intervals—one for typical use and another for severe use.

General Motors, for example, recommends oil changes every 3,000 miles or three months for severe service (trailer towing) rather than the 7,500 miles or twelve months prescribed for normal driving.

Severe service is defined as operating in dusty areas, towing a trailer, extended idling and/or frequent low-speed operation such as in stop-and-go traffic, operating when outside temperatures remain below freezing, and when most trips are less than four miles. Motorhomes always are in the severe service category.

OIL FILTERS

Filtration of oil is critical to remove abrasive particles that come from engine components, as well as those that may leak through the air-filtration system. The standard pleated paper filters are designed to catch particles down to about 25 microns in size (Figure 13.7). A micron is about $\frac{1}{25,000}$ inch. For greatest engine durability, you should use a name-brand filter and change it according to the vehicle manufacturer's recommendation.

AIR FILTERS

The air-filter element should be inspected every 10,000 miles or less if the vehicle has been used in dusty conditions. Also, look for restrictions in the fresh-air inlet tube. Hoses sometimes collapse, and foreign matter can partially block the inlet.

PUMPING LOSSES

Engine efficiency affects more than fuel economy and performance, it also affects longevity. Parasitic losses occur in several ways, at least one of which may be altered by the owner. Such inefficiencies include pumping losses—excessive suction on the intake side of an engine and excessive back pressure in the exhaust chambers. Others include piston-ring drag and friction in bearings, cams, lifters, valve steps, and seals.

All engines must create a partial vacuum with the intake stroke of the piston in order to draw in air or an air/fuel mixture. But, when a piston must act against excessive partial vacuum (restricted air intake), the partial vacuum adds to the load of the piston. More horsepower from the crankshaft must be used to move the piston on its intake stroke.

Likewise, excessive exhaust back pressure causes excessive pumping loss as the piston exerts pressure on the gases to force them out the exhaust. Again, horsepower from the crankshaft must be used to overcome back pressure and create exhaust flow. The energy

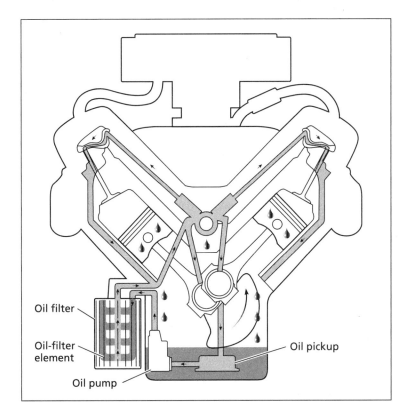

Figure 13.7
Standard pleated paper oil filters are designed to remove contaminants down to approximately 25 microns in size.

for these pumping losses must be provided by fuel. The pumping losses add to loads on pistons, cylinders, and bearings. Reducing pumping losses allows the engine to devote more energy to propelling the vehicle. Methods of checking for excessive pumping losses and correcting them are discussed in Chapter 12 on improving fuel economy and performance.

EFFECTS OF STORAGE

Some RVs, particularly motorhomes, are stored for long periods during winter months. Long-term storage can be hard on an engine if preventive maintenance is not performed.

The engine oil and filter should be changed immediately before the vehicle is put into storage. This prevents the acids in the oil from doing corrosive work on bearings during the storage period. Also, proper amounts of fuel additive should be poured into the gasoline tank to prevent fuel deterioration and formation of varnishes on surfaces in fuel systems, particularly injector nozzles and carburetor

components. This is particularly important with oxygenated fuels. Fuel-storage additives are sold in auto-parts stores.

The vehicle should be driven for a few minutes to circulate the oil and the additive-protected fuel. Just prior to parking the vehicle, idle the engine and inject enough light oil into the carburetor or EFI intake to produce smoke from the exhaust. This coats the cylinders to prevent rust. Boating-supply stores sell oil in aerosol cans designed for this purpose. Shut the engine down after the smoke appears. During the storage period the engine should not be started because this wipes away the oil coating in the cylinders and also causes formation of water in the crankcase and exhaust system due to condensation.

Be sure to use enough fuel additive to protect the entire contents of the tank. It's best to store the vehicle with the fuel tank full to minimize water formation due to condensation. A complete chassis lubrication and check-out should also be performed. Tires should be inflated to normal pressures for travel. Provisions should be made for battery charg-

Figure 13.8
On most late-model diesel engines, a single unit serves as both fuel filter and water separator.

ing once a month unless the battery is a gel type that does not self-discharge as rapidly as an open-cell battery.

DIESEL ENGINES

Dependability, durability, and economy of the diesel engine is unquestioned. The heavy-duty diesels in commercial truck service routinely go beyond the 400,000-mile mark before requiring a major overhaul. Many engines used in motorhomes—Cummins, Caterpillar, Detroit Diesel—have the same kind of longevity. The lighter-duty turbocharged engines, such as the GM 6.5-liter, the Ford/Navistar PowerStroke 7.3-liter and the Cummins 5.9-liter used in Dodge pickups, should provide 250,000 or more miles before major repair is needed.

This longevity does not occur from simply owning a diesel; a strict regimen of thoughtful preventive maintenance, coupled with sensible operating habits, is essential to realize this potential.

Diesel-Fuel Systems

Preventive maintenance of diesel-fuel systems is basically simple, but very small tolerances are used in injector pumps and components. For example, if the plunger and bushing were separated from a Detroit Diesel injector in a room with 65°F ambient temperature, and the plunger was held in a person's hand for two minutes, it could not be reinserted in the bushing due to thermal expansion. And the sweat from your hand could damage the lapped surface if not cleaned off within a few minutes. This serves to illustrate why the cardinal rule in fuel-system care is to "keep it clean." A microscopic bit of sand can render a $200 injector useless. Yet this same injector could last the service life of the engine with good preventive maintenance.

Some diesel-fuel systems include two filters for protecting the injection pump and the injectors, but most have one, a combination water separator and final filter (Figure 13.8). Other engines have water separator/primary filters in the suction side of the fuel-transfer pump, and a final filter between the fuel-transfer pump and injection pump.

Sediment filters have the capability of removing particles as small as 80 to 100 microns (.0032 inch to .004 inch), and the final filter can be as fine as 5 microns (.0002 inch). The better sediment filters have a glass or clear plastic bowl that enables you to see how much water or other crud has accumulated. The only problem with the plastic bowls is that when the sediment filter is mounted outside the frame rail and near the ground, road debris can abrade the plastic so badly it becomes opaque. If you do have one mounted, place it where it is protected and visible. "Out of sight, out of mind" can apply when a sediment filter is hidden from view.

Some sediment filters also have sensing devices that trigger a light on the dash, warning of high water level. Don't rely on the light to tell you when to drain or clean the filter. It should be checked, either by visual inspection or draining, at least weekly. If you travel in the boondocks and must buy fuel from local suppliers, check it daily, preferably at the

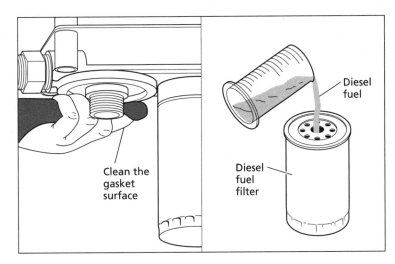

Clean the gasket surface

Diesel fuel filter

Diesel fuel

Figure 13.9
Priming the filter can make a diesel engine easier to start following a filter change.

day's end, at least an hour after shutdown. You may be surprised how much trash you find in it. You could take on a load of contaminated fuel 12 miles or twenty-two minutes after a scheduled filter change. Carry a couple of spares, know how to install them, and know how to bleed the fuel system. Changing a filter need not be a frustrating experience. Just remember, clean.

Most manufacturers do not recommend filling a new filter with fuel prior to installation, to reduce the chance of fuel contamination. However, when done right, there is little chance of getting dirt in the fuel. Priming a new filter can make a restart much easier. Some engines will reprime their fuel systems easily; some will not.

To prime a filter (Figure 13.9), fill a clear plastic container with fuel, cover it, and let it sit for at least an hour to allow any sediment or water to settle to the bottom. Then slowly pour this fuel through a clean drip coffee filter into another clean nonmetallic container. After removing the old filter, clean the filter base to reduce the chance of any dirt falling into the new filter. Unwrap the new filter, fill it with the priming fuel, wait a few seconds to let the filter media absorb the fuel, then finish filling it. Coat the filter gasket with clean grease or petroleum jelly and install the filter. Do not overtighten, or you may crush the gasket and cause a leak. Fire it up and check for

leaks. You may get a burp or two, then the engine should run smoothly. If it does not start, loosen the vent on top of the filter base and have your helper crank the engine until an uninterrupted stream of fuel comes from the vent, then close it. The engine should now run smoothly.

Bacteria

Warm, humid weather can cause fuel problems. A bacterial growth nicknamed "fuel fungus" or "black slime" grows in the interface between the fuel and any water that may be in the tanks or filters. This microbial growth is not algae, as algae needs light to grow, but it closely resembles it. This slimy mess that can completely plug a filter causes power loss and can even shut down the engine. Once formed, it is difficult to eradicate and is more prevalent in storage or fuel tanks that sit idle for a week or more, especially in warm weather.

The best prevention is not getting water into the tanks in the first place, but this is sometimes inevitable. The next-best solution is addition of a fungicide formulated for diesel fuel. Regular fuel additives, or antigel agents, usually do not have a fungicide in them, and the fungicide can be hard to find on the open market. The addition of kerosene, gasoline, or acceptable alcohols does not help. If you plan on going into the boondocks, you may have to buy fuel wherever you can get it, and your chances of getting water and other contaminants in the fuel are good. Be prepared: Find a supply of the biocide and carry it with you.

Diesel Lubrication Systems

Diesel engines are much harder on oils than gasoline engines due to the larger amounts of carbon that get into the oil. Carbon is responsible for the dirty, black appearance of the oil and the sulfur/sulfuric acids formed during the combustion process. The carbon is from incompletely burned fuel, and the sulfur comes from the fuel, too. The carbon is not, in itself, very harmful to the engine, other than building up in the various nooks and crannies in the engine and leading to more rapid filter clogging. The sulfur, on the other hand, corrodes iron and bearing metals. The only way to combat these contaminants is through frequent oil and filter changes and by using the best oils available.

Engine condition is also a factor in how fast your oil gets contaminated. An engine with well-seated rings that does not burn a lot of oil doesn't have the ring blow-by that leads to rapid oil contamination. Manufacturers' recommended oil-drain intervals should be followed to the letter, along with use of specified oil grades recommended by the engine manufacturer.

Fortunately, improvements in oil and filtration quality have caused Cummins, for example, to recommend a 15,000-mile oil change

A Diesel-Engine Prestart Checklist

- If the vehicle has been in storage, perform an engine-oil check when the engine is cold, using the dipstick scale for a cold engine. The rig should be level (very important with Ford/Navistar engines). If the oil level is below the bottom marker, add enough oil slowly to bring it to the bottom marker. In some engines, or in cold weather, it takes a long time for the level to stabilize. Recheck oil level when the engine is fully up to operating temperature and add oil as necessary to bring it to the top marker.

- A coolant check should be performed with the engine cold. Check the level in the coolant overflow tank, but also check radiator level; add coolant as needed. If you do not have any coolant mix handy and you must use water, add the same amount of antifreeze at the earliest opportunity; if you have a small leak and must continually add water, you are weakening the coolant protection. If you let small external leaks go until you get around to fixing them, they have a nasty habit of becoming gushers.

- Check the automatic transmission. Most manufacturers recommend checking fluid levels while the transmission is at normal operating temperature, and this is good advice. Most dipsticks have a hot and cold level on them, but some folks overlook this (Figure 13.10). If you look at the wrong marker at a cold check, you may add fluid when it's not needed; the fluid expands quite a bit as it reaches operating temperature,

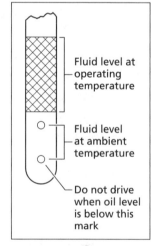

Figure 13.10
Some dipsticks have different levels for hot and cold operation. Checking the oil level when the engine is hot is preferable.

interval using SAE 15W-40 oil for its ISB and ISC (5.9- and 8.3-liter) engines, suggesting that the multigrade reduces deposits, improves oil flow in cold climates, and improves lubrication during high-temperature operation. Synthetic oils are also approved. Oil analysis as a method of justifying extended oil-drain intervals is specifically not recommended by Cummins for any oil.

Name-brand filters should be used because filter quality varies; Caterpillar, Cummins, Navistar, Ford, and General Motors all assure the effectiveness of their filters. Oil additives are not recommended.

Diesel-Engine Coolant

Maintenance of engine coolant is critical for any engine, but especially for diesels. Many diesel-engine manufacturers require special coolant additives to prevent cavitation and pitting of cylinder liners. Follow the engine manufacturer's recommendation on types of coolant, additive, and the change interval. Some manufacturers also require low-silicate antifreeze. Use distilled water in 50–50 percent solution with the coolant, unless the coolant is premixed and needs no water added. Refer to the instruction label.

Diesel Air-Intake Systems

Any engine requires a given volume of air to burn a given amount of fuel. If that air supply is impeded, performance suffers. The air-intake filter must clean this air without starving the engine, and this takes a big, efficient

and has been known to overflow out of the dipstick tube onto a hot exhaust pipe or manifold, and may catch fire.

- Perform a power-steering-fluid check. On dipstick-equipped systems, the stick will have hot and cold levels; again, don't overfill the reservoir. Check your owner's manual to determine if your system calls for automatic transmission fluid (ATF) or power steering fluid. ATF and steering fluid have different additives.

- Check all drive belts and hoses. Loose belts cause slippage; overtightened belts can cause bearing damage. If you have a loose belt, and you have the correct gauge for measuring tension, great; most folks don't. If you must make a field adjustment, tensioning the belt to 1/2-inch deflection of the belt between two pulleys will allow you to go on until you can have the belt adjusted properly. Check coolant and any hydraulic hoses for leaks, bulging, soft spots, loose clamps, or leaking fittings. Carrying a spare set of belts and coolant hoses is also considered good preventive maintenance.

- Check for leaks. Drips on the ground mean something; any leak is a cause for concern. If you have an engine that is a habitual dribbler and you know the leak source and how often you need to attend to it, fine. But don't be lulled into a false sense of security by the old, familiar dribble.

Note: When starting the engine after prolonged storage, watch the oil-pressure gauge and shut down immediately if pressure doesn't register within fifteen seconds. Check the manufacturer's recommendation.

filter—more so on diesels than on gasoline engines, whose air intake is restricted by an air-intake throttle valve. Diesels draw in much more air than gas engines, especially at lower power settings.

Filter types and cleaning methods vary, but regardless of which kind you have, it must be serviced according to the conditions under which the vehicle is used. Many diesel air filters have indicators that signal when service is needed. Most owner's manuals list a cleaning interval, either in miles, hours, or both.

In regular service, this interval may be good enough. But drive through a dust storm, and the recommended interval goes out the window. Frequent inspection is the most foolproof method. If the filter looks dirty, service it; if it doesn't look dirty, but it has been some time since it was last cleaned, check and clean it anyway. If you have the disposable type, carry at least one spare.

Some of the cleanable diesel-engine air filters that come with some aftermarket turbo kits are supplied with one aerosol can of a special oil to re-oil the element. This aerosol can last about three cleanings; then you must locate more. If that proves difficult, make your own oil: Mix your favorite engine oil 50–50 with diesel fuel, and use an empty window-spray bottle to apply it. Whatever type of cleanable filter you have, handle it gently; it is somewhat fragile and banging it on a work bench to dislodge the bugs and dirt can distort it or damage the gasket, causing an improper fit, with resultant leakage. Compressed air should not be used on these. A leaking filter is the same as no filter.

ON THE ROAD WITH DIESELS

Anyone who believes in good preventive maintenance knows that a thorough prestart check can prevent a lot of headaches. If the diesel rig is used every day, there should be a daily walkaround inspection routine. The following checklist is not all-inclusive, since all rigs are not the same, but it's a good start.

Startup and Idling Diesels

If everything is okay in the engine house, let's fire it up. Diesels, especially turbocharged diesels, should be run at the slowest speed at which they will idle smoothly until oil pressure stabilizes. Some of the turbos are mounted so they are the last component to receive oil. Since the turbine will spin at startup, high startup rpm may spin the turbo at excessive speed, and premature wear will result. It does not do rods or main bearings any good either.

Contrary to legend, extended idling of a diesel engine is detrimental to longevity. Some idling is inevitable, but letting the engine idle for hours is not conducive to long service life. Ideally, you should start the engine, check your instruments to insure everything is A-okay, let the engine idle for a minute to stabilize pressures, then take off at reduced engine speed until temperatures reach normal operating level.

Diesel Cool Down

Allowing a turbocharged diesel engine to idle for three to five minutes before shutdown is essential if the engine has been operated under heavy throttle just prior to stopping. The idling period permits cool down of super-heated components. The flow of lubricating oil through the turbocharger's bearings is halted during a hot shutdown, and the oil may be oxidized by excessive residual heat. In most cases it's not necessary to idle the engine for three to five minutes after arriving in an RV park, which annoys neighbors.

Cold-Weather Care for Diesels

Starting a diesel in cold weather can present some unique problems, particularly at subzero temperatures. The glow-plug-equipped engines, such as Ford/Navistar and General Motors, usually will start at -20°F with little trouble if the engine is in good condition. Other brands such as Detroit Diesel, Caterpillar, and Cummins may not have glow plugs (cold-starting devices). In these instances, other starting aids may be required if a 120-volt AC preheater cannot be used. The popular Cummins 5.9-liter engine is equipped with a fuel heater that is controlled thermostatically for cold starts.

Ether-based starting aids, sold in aerosol cans, will get the engine started, but they can damage engines if used in excess; Cummins and several other manufacturers prohibit their use and/or recommend only ether-metering devices. Even when used properly, ether puts a lot of strain on engine parts.

If you must use hand-administered ether, there are right and wrong ways. Removing the air-cleaner cover, firing a long squirt of ether down the engine's throat, then racing back to the cab to hit the starter is not the right way. In this method, you may get a heavy dose of ether into one or two cylinders whose intake valves are open, and little, if any, in the other cylinders. Have someone crank the engine while you fire short bursts of ether into the air intake. This will give each cylinder a more balanced dose. You may have to give the engine a couple more short bursts to keep it running.

There are other ways to get the balky engine started in an emergency. If you have 120-volt AC power available, using a hair dryer can help; set it on the hottest setting and direct the airflow into the air intake.

Diesel Storage

Some folks "lay up" their diesel rig in winter for three to six months with little preventive care. A biocide agent should be added to diesel fuel before storage. On all models, the oil and filter should be changed, and tire pressure should be checked. The fuel tanks should be topped off to minimize air space with resultant condensation. With the engine and oil warm, run the engine at about half speed, and while still running, squirt a liberal quantity of a light oil, preferably a preservative oil, into the intake. Shut the engine down while it is still smoking to create a thin film of oil on the cylinder walls and exhaust system to prevent rust. Seal off the intake and exhaust pipes before the engine cools. Be sure to remove the seals prior to restarting!

Charge batteries in the vehicle once a month (every six months with gel-type batteries), or remove them for storage in a heated area. Use a maintenance-type float charger to keep the batteries up.

In summary, getting the best longevity, dependability, and fuel economy from an engine requires effort. If you give the engine the care it deserves, it will repay you with trouble-free, dependable performance.

Chapter 14

TROUBLESHOOTING RV ENGINES

Be Prepared ■

Troubleshooting Engines ■

Diesel Engines Only ■

Vehicle breakdowns on the road are at least vexing and can be expensive, frightening, and even hazardous. The best prevention is a comprehensive scheduled maintenance program and thorough pretrip inspection, which can save you time and money in the long run. However, with even the best maintenance, the possibility still exists that your RV may balk unexpectedly.

To loosely paraphrase an old saying: An ounce of diagnosis is worth a pound of money. This chapter, with its accompanying troubleshooting procedures, covers the most common vehicle failures, whether the rig is powered by diesel or gasoline. It will provide helpful suggestions designed to get you going again. Certainly there are many things that could go wrong on the road, but failures in the systems covered here—fuel, ignition, and cooling—account for most on-the-road troubles.

BE PREPARED

To make the troubleshooting procedures work, a basic set of tools should be on board. It does not have to be a full-blown set weighing hundreds of pounds and costing thousands of dollars; just the basics will do. Be sure to get the right types of tools for your vehicle. Older American-built vehicles use standard (fractional inch-based) tools; all imported and late-model American-built vehicles use metric sizes, and many American-built vehicles use a combination of metric and standard fasteners. A good set for travel should consist of:

- Combination wrenches, (both open and box end) standard from ⅜ to 1 inch or metric 8 mm to 24 mm

- Several common sizes each of flat-blade and Phillips screwdrivers

- A ⅜-inch-drive ratchet set with sockets from ⅜ inch to ¾ inch or 6 mm to 19 mm

- A ½-inch-drive socket set from ½ inch to 1 inch

- A set of Torx bits

- Needlenose and regular pliers, plus slip-joint "water-pump" pliers

- Locking pliers such as Vise Grips

- A 1-pound hammer

- A pocket knife

- Spark-plug socket (check your engine's size, either ⅝ inch or ¹³⁄₁₆-inch)

- A good set of high-quality, long, heavy-duty jumper cables

- An electrical test light, or better yet, a digital multimeter (volt-ohmmeter)

- Lengths of spare electrical wire in several gauge sizes, a wire crimper, butt connectors, and wire splicers

- A flashlight with spare batteries

- A shop manual

Every RVer should carry along a few spare parts as well, including:

- Spare engine drive belts. Whether your rig is a $250,000 diesel coach or a $20,000 gasoline-powered pickup truck, it can't function without a simple and inexpensive drivebelt.

- Spare fuel filter(s). One tank of dirty or water-contaminated fuel can render the rig helpless.

- Extra upper and lower radiator hoses, hose clamps and at least four feet of spare heater hose

- A can of radiator stop-leak

- A spare distributor cap and rotor for engines that have not yet been converted to totally electronic controls

- A roll of duct tape and a few clean rags

- Spare fuses that not only fit the 12-volt DC RV accessories, but will fit any engine or chassis circuitry. Spare fusible links are also invaluable.

- It's also a good idea to carry a couple extra quarts of motor oil and automatic transmission fluid, plus an unopened can of brake fluid.

- A roll of insulated 12-gauge wire

Although this is a basic "bare-bones" spare-parts assortment that will probably get you going in event of emergency, these supplies and tools can be absolutely invaluable. Even if you are not the mechanical type, you may be able to get another RVer or a shop to install a part that you have carried, which was not available in the area of the breakdown.

TROUBLESHOOTING ENGINES

If the Engine Fails to Start

For your engine to run, three systems must operate in harmony, assuming it hasn't experienced a major internal failure like a thrown rod. 1. The starting system must be able to crank the engine; 2. The fuel system must supply the proper amount of fuel to the engine; 3. The ignition system (gasoline engines only) must supply sufficient voltage to the spark plugs to initiate combustion. The troubleshooting procedures in Figure 14.1 will take you through each of these areas and give you points to check in order to single out the culprit.

Since many more problems occur than can be listed here, the procedures cover only the most common problems—those that lend themselves to roadside repair.

Checking the Battery

If an engine won't start, we must systematically eliminate possible causes. If the engine simply fails to crank or cranks too slowly, check the battery terminals for corrosion and/or looseness. If the terminal connections are heavily corroded, they should be removed and scraped clean with a knife. Or, purchase a battery brush/terminal cleaner and keep it in the toolbox. Sometimes a starter will begin working or crank faster after it cools.

Caution: *When working around the battery, acid can cause burns to skin and eyes and ruin clothes. Take care to avoid exposure, and if it occurs, immediately wash the area with water and, if it has affected eyes, seek medical attention.*

To insure that the failure to start is not caused by dirty battery components, thoroughly clean the battery and terminals.

Next, try to start the engine. If there is no activity from the starter, turn on the headlights and check them for brightness. If they are dim, the battery charge is low and will require a jump-start, battery recharge, or battery replacement. Some RVs, mainly large motorhomes, have battery-boost circuits that allow you to bring the vehicle's auxiliary battery(ies) into parallel with the starting battery by pushing a switch. This is invaluable, especially if chassis accessories such as the headlights were inadvertently left on. If you don't have a battery-booster switch circuit, use a set of top-quality jumper cables to connect the auxiliary battery to the engine battery. Wear eye protection.

If, after cleaning the terminals and attempting a jump-start, the engine still fails to crank, the problem is probably in the starter itself or its circuitry. On automatic transmissions, the neutral safety switch may be out of adjustment. Hold your foot on the brake and try operating the starter while you move the shift lever through all gears. Troubleshooting beyond this point will probably require the aid of a professional mechanic with specialized test equipment.

Checking the Ignition and Fuel System

If terminal cleaning and jump-starting bring the starter to life, but the engine still fails to start, new tactics are needed. When the engine is gasoline-powered, the trouble can be narrowed to the ignition system or fuel system. If the engine is diesel, the fuel and pre-heating systems are the only places to look since diesels don't have ignition systems.

First things first. Check the fuel gauge! If there is any reason to doubt the fuel gauge, tap on the tank and listen for an empty, hollow sound. Remove the filler cap and listen for a whoosh that indicates a possible venting problem. This may seem obvious, but even

Troubleshooting Gasoline Engines

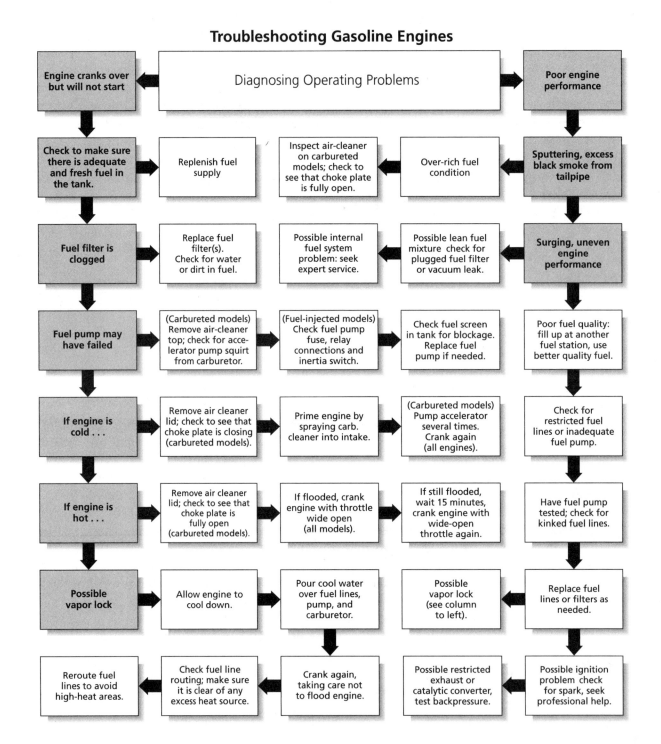

Figure 14.1
Locating the source of a problem with a gasoline engine requires
a step-by-step troubleshooting process.

many professional mechanics have wasted time troubleshooting a vehicle that fails to start or run without first checking the basics.

Electronic ignition systems are normally reliable and maintenance free. When they fail, usually only the replacement of faulty components will get you rolling. However, there are a few things a novice mechanic can do. Look for any burned or damaged wires around the ignition components. Remove the distributor cap if the vehicle has one and check for cracks inside. Check the rotor, and closely examine the wires connected to the ignition pickup and module; often they break internally due to constant flexing. Also check the coil for cracks or damage. Try unplugging and replugging connectors. Inspect them for corrosion or loose or bent prongs.

Checking for Fuel Delivery

If the fuel tank appears to contain enough fuel, check to see if the fuel is getting to the engine. In gasoline-carbureted engines checking for fuel delivery is easy, but in diesel or fuel-injected gasoline engines it can be more difficult.

1. First, remove the air-cleaner cover to expose the air horn of the carburetor or throttle body of a fuel-injection system (this procedure not applicable to port-type fuel-injection systems).

2. If the engine is carbureted, use a flashlight to look into the carburetor throat. Hold the choke plate open, and have an assistant slowly depress the throttle. Check for fuel squirting into the primary carburetor bores—the bore(s) that have

An Ignition-System Checklist for Gasoline Engines

When checking the ignition system of a gasoline engine, follow these steps:

1. Remove a spark-plug cable from a plug, or remove the center cable from the distributor cap. Some ignitions may not have a center cable to the distributor cap because the coil assembly is actually built into the distributor.

2. Turn on the ignition switch, and have someone crank the engine while you hold a spark-plug cable against a good ground (Figure 14.2), which is any metal engine part. Some ignition systems have ignition coils mounted atop the spark plugs. If this is the case, it may be necessary to remove the plug, reattach the coil and then crank the engine to check for spark. There should be an obvious spark every other engine revolution. If there is a strong spark, the source of the problem probably is in the fuel system. If no spark is present, remove the distributor cap and make sure there is no moisture inside. If you are near 120-volt-AC power, or if you have an AC generator, you can dry the distributor with an electric hair dryer. If that's not possible, dry the cap and as many ignition components that you can with paper towels or a clean, absorbent rag.

3. Replace the dry cap and try the spark test again. If no spark is present, replace the spark-plug cable and determine whether your system is electronic or the old style with breaker points.

choke plates. Squirting fuel is the result of the action of the accelerator pump. If no fuel squirts when the throttle is pumped, the fuel bowl of the carburetor is probably empty, or the accelerator pump may be defective.

3. In the case of a carbureted or throttle-body fuel-injected engine, have the assistant turn the ignition key on and off a couple of times while you look into the throttle body. If no fuel is present, crank the engine for two or three seconds, and repeat the check for fuel at the carburetor or throttle body. If still no fuel is present, the fuel pump may be inoperative, the fuel filter may be clogged, or vapor lock may be the culprit, especially if ambient temperature is high.

4. If your RV has an electric fuel pump inside the fuel tank, check the owner's manual for the fuse location and inspect the fuse. Also check the owner's manual for the location and reset procedure for a fuel pump cutoff switch (these are common on Fords with fuel injection). Have an assistant turn the ignition key on for a few seconds and then off (but not to the start position) while you listen for the sound of the pump running.

If the fuse is okay but the pump still doesn't run, the fuel pump relay may be faulty. Have a professional mechanic check the fuel system.

5. If the fuel filter is suspected, it is usually easily changed. Many carburetors have inlet filters that can be removed, while other vehicles may have in-line filters between the pump and carburetor or between the tank and pump. Check carefully along the length of the chassis where the fuel lines are routed. Wear eye protection, and be especially careful on fuel-injected vehicles because they often retain pressure even after they're shut off. Hot engine parts combined with fuel leakage can spell disaster. Make sure precautions are taken to prevent fire when working with the fuel system. Allow the engine to cool, keep a fire extinguisher handy, and by all means, no smoking!

6. If the engine may not be getting fuel, spray a little aerosol carburetor cleaner into the intake. Crank the engine. If it now starts and runs briefly, the problem is somewhere in the fuel-supply system.

Figure 14.2
To check for spark, insert a spare spark plug in any spark plug cable, and hold it against a metal part while the engine is cranked.

Checking for a Faulty Fuel Pump on a Carbureted Engine

1. Disable the ignition system so the engine will not start. The best way to do this is to remove the 12-volt lead to the coil or the distributor.

2. Remove the fuel line from the carburetor. Hold a container at the end of the open line at the carburetor and have someone briefly crank the engine. Fuel should pulsate from the line. If it does not, the pump is bad, the filter or fuel-tank pickup is clogged, or the engine is still vapor locked. Again, be aware of fire danger.

3. Look at the fuel in the container to see if it has water or dirt in it. Also sniff it to determine if the vehicle may have been misfueled with diesel fuel.

Checking Fuel Delivery to Gasoline Fuel-Injected Engines

Fuel delivery to electronic fuel-injection (EFI) systems is more difficult to diagnose. Fuel pressure typically ranges from 9 psi to 45 psi, depending on the model, versus 5 psi to 7 psi for carbureted engines. This creates the possibility that significant volumes of fuel can be sprayed in the engine compartment if you make an error during pressure testing. If your EFI-equipped engine has a fuel-delivery problem, see Chapter 10 (electrical systems) for a method of checking pressure. Beyond that, contact your dealer or a professional mechanic who is proficient in the repair of EFI systems.

Fuel-Tank-Cap Problems

Fuel-tank-cap problems can plague RV engines. The wrong cap or a clogged or damaged one can cause the engine to starve for fuel, especially under high-demand situations like climbing steep grades. If the cap is not properly vented, air cannot enter the tank, and a partial vacuum forms, making it impossible for the fuel pump to do its job. If frequent fuel-starvation problems are noted, make sure that the gas cap is the right one. An easy way to test the cap is by loosening it and driving the vehicle under the same conditions that usually cause trouble. If the problem is solved, get a new, correct cap. On most 1996 and newer vehicles, a loose or missing gas cap can cause the engine malfunction indicator lamp to be illuminated.

Vapor Lock (Gasoline Only)

Hot weather can cause vapor lock by boiling the gasoline before it can reach the fuel pump, or after it has passed the pump on the way to the engine. Pouring cool water over the fuel lines and pump will condense the fuel back into its liquid state. Vapor lock is far less likely with fuel-injected systems because fuel in the entire system is under pressure, raising the vaporization point. However, it can occur on some fuel-injection systems, particularly upstream of the fuel pump. Also, some electric fuel pumps slow or quit when they get hot.

A vapor-lock problem is indicated if your engine surges or quits during warm-weather operation but runs well when under cool conditions. However, ignition problems can mimic vapor lock. Check for spark immediately after the engine quits; if there's no spark or a weak spark, check the coil and electronic components in the ignition system.

If vapor lock is a persistent problem, heat buildup in the engine compartment is likely, due to poor ventilation, or the fuel lines may be exposed to heat radiation from the engine (especially exhaust components), causing the fuel to vaporize in the line. Make sure fuel lines are insulated and routed well away from any excessive heat source. Use procedures described on page 211 to check for fuel delivery.

Flooding in Gasoline Engines

So much for lack of fuel; what about flooding of gasoline engines? The first sign that an engine is operating under a high fuel-to-air ratio (rich condition) is the presence of black smoke from the exhaust. Make sure that you don't confuse it with blue smoke, which is a sign the engine is burning oil. Black smoke is accompanied by sluggish performance and very poor fuel economy.

If your RV is equipped with a carburetor, a choke plate that is stuck closed or is not adjusted correctly is the most common cause of an over-rich condition. Remove the air-cleaner lid and inspect the choke plate with the engine at normal operating temperature. The plate should be in a vertical (open) position to allow free flow of air through the carburetor. If the plate is closed on a warm engine, it partially blocks the airflow, causing the rich condition. The plate should be nearly closed when the engine is cold to enrich the fuel mixture.

If the plate refuses to open when the engine is warmed, it's possible to keep it open by temporarily wiring the choke linkage in the open position. This is a temporary fix that allows you to drive the vehicle, albeit with difficult cold starts. Make sure that your temporary choke wiring cannot cause the throttle linkage to jam, which could cause engine overspeed and a dangerous situation. Other causes of an over-rich condition cannot be easily corrected as they involve other internal circuits of the carburetor.

Other Causes of Flooding

Other fuel problems may be caused by incorrect float adjustment. This allows excess fuel to spill into the engine, causing an over-rich mixture. Carburetors equipped with plastic floats can become saturated with fuel and raise fuel levels, allowing too much fuel into the engine. In addition to the float, a faulty needle and seat or a stuck or blown power valve can cause difficulties. Check with a mechanic if problems with these items are suspected.

Flooding Diagnosis

If you suspect a gasoline engine is flooded but are not sure, remove a spark plug and inspect the firing tip. If it's wet and smells of gasoline, the engine is probably flooded.

Starting a Flooded Gasoline Engine

An engine that is flooded may be difficult to start. When a flooded engine starts, it will emit black smoke from the tailpipe. Don't pump the accelerator pedal, which only floods the engine more. On a gas engine, hold the throttle to the floor (wide open) to allow the maximum amount of air to enter the engine. This will tend to dilute the rich fuel mixture. Crank the engine with the throttle in this position for no more than twenty seconds at a time. Continual cranking may overheat and damage the starter motor and will deplete the battery in a short time. If there are no signs of life, wait fifteen minutes and attempt to start again with the throttle held wide open. If results are negative, it may indicate fuel-soaked spark plugs or ignition trouble. It may be necessary to remove all the spark plugs and crank the engine for about twenty seconds to clear fuel out of the combustion chambers.

EFI Troubleshooting

Over-rich mixtures may also occur in EFI systems, but the causes are different. The electronic fuel-control system monitors oxygen content of the exhaust, engine temperature, incoming airflow, and throttle position, just to name a few. A problem with one of these sensing systems can feed the computer incorrect information. For example, a defective temperature sensor may send the computer a signal that the engine is cold, even though it may not be. The computer's reaction is to tell the fuel-injection system to send more fuel, resulting in an unnecessary amount of fuel in the cylinders.

If your EFI engine isn't operating properly, look for any loose, cracked, or missing hoses or damaged wiring. There is little else that can be easily done to analyze the situation since testing of these specific components requires sophisticated equipment and professional knowledge of the particular EFI system. Difficulties in EFI systems are best handled by knowledgeable mechanics.

Overheating in Diesel and Gasoline Engines

There are many causes of engine overheating, some of which can be quite elusive. The following troubleshooting procedures cover the most common overheating causes, many of which can be handled at roadside. Diesel engines seem to have less tendency to overheat compared to gasoline engines, partially because most diesels are outfitted with large, heavy-duty radiators, and less combustion heat is created at idle and part throttle.

First, let's define overheating. When is an engine too hot? Technically, an engine is not overheated until it continually boils coolant out through the overflow. But high temperature will cause an engine to operate poorly at temperatures well below the point at which boil-out occurs.

Accurate temperature gauges are needed for proper diagnosis of engine temperature. The gauges installed at the factory often are not precisely calibrated. If your RV has an "idiot light" rather than a gauge, or a gauge that is not calibrated in degrees Fahrenheit, install a top-quality gauge calibrated so you can read temperature accurately.

By the time a hot-engine warning light is activated, overheating is in advanced stages, which may result in loss of a considerable volume of coolant or even engine damage. When overheating occurs, pull off the road immediately, activate the warning flashers, shift the transmission to "park" or "neutral," set the parking brake, set the heater control on maximum, open the hood, and run the engine at a fast idle (1,500 rpm). If a hose has burst and coolant is pouring out, shut the engine off immediately. Otherwise, if in two or three minutes the temperature has not dropped, it's best to shut the engine off anyway and let it cool.

Once the engine is shut down, coolant loss may be experienced due to after-boil caused by heat soak. When the engine is stopped, the coolant pump and airflow movement provided by engine operation cease, resulting in residual engine heat "soaking" into the stationary coolant, causing it to boil. If coolant is lost every time you shut off the engine, it may mean a defective radiator cap, a weak antifreeze to water ratio or an engine that typically runs hot, requiring repair.

The troubleshooting procedure for overheating cites points in the engine compartment as possible culprits. Make sure the engine accessory-drive belt(s) are tight and in good condition. A loose belt can cause loss of coolant circulation and reduced radiator-fan speed. Belts should be tightened so that moderate pressure with one's thumb causes about a ½-inch deflection in the middle of the belt. Make sure all hoses and clamps are checked regularly. Carry spare hoses and belts in your tool set.

A daily walkaround inspection of your RV should include the cooling system. Pop the hood and look at all hose connections and the hoses themselves for signs of leakage. Check the radiator for road debris. It's easy to pick up such things as insects and plastic bags that can block most of the radiator's airflow. Continual neglect can lead to clogging with dirt, bugs, and other debris.

Thermostatic fan clutches must function properly in hot weather. It's usually obvious when the clutch engages, as fan noise increases dramatically. Sometimes it sounds like the transmission downshifted. If your RV is overheating and you have a fan clutch, it should engage as the temperature rises and disengage as the temperature drops. If you don't hear the cycling action of the fan, the clutch may be defective.

If you're trapped in stop-and-go traffic and the engine starts to overheat, idle speed may be set too low. Slow idle speeds mean poor coolant circulation and slow airflow past the radiator. Turn off accessories, such as the air conditioner, since it adds heat load to the cooling system. Shift to the neutral position when stopped and run the engine at a fast idle speed (1,500 rpm). If you can stand the heat, set the heater on maximum—but not on defrost, which runs the air conditioner compressor.

Incorrect engine ignition timing can also contribute to overheating. If ignition timing is excessively retarded (which may have been done to get through an emissions test or to reduce the engine tendency to spark knock), overheating at low speeds may result. The cure may be to use middle grade or premium fuel so the timing can be returned to the normal setting.

In a few instances, overheating may occur at highway speeds. This is sometimes caused by the collapse of the lower radiator hose. At high pump speeds, there is a strong suction on the inlet to the water pump. Make sure your lower hose is equipped with an internal wire coil designed to prevent collapse.

Radiator-Cap Problems

It's not commonly known, but a defective radiator cap can cause boil-over. The boiling point of the coolant is raised 2.5°F for every pound of pressure added to the system. Most cooling systems use 15-psi caps. Under this pressure, a 50-50 mix of water and ethylene glycol coolant has a boiling point of 265°F. If the cap seal is defective, or if spring pressure is insufficient, the pressure is reduced, allowing the coolant to boil at a lower temperature. Have the cap tested (Figure 14.3).

Water-Pump Failure

Water-pump failure can cause coolant to leak, reducing coolant flow through the engine and radiator. The first sign that the water pump is failing may be slight leakage or bearing noise. The noise is a grumbling sound that may be heard at all speeds and may be particularly noisy at idle. Loss of the water-pump bearings leads to the loss of the water-pump seal, or vice-versa, leading to coolant leakage around the water-pump shaft.

The water pump can also cause overheating. A broken or corroded pump impeller (or one that slips on the shaft) may fail to circulate enough coolant to transfer heat from the engine to the radiator. The reduced ability of the water pump can be checked in the field only by removing the pump and visually inspecting the impeller. With this much work involved, it may be wise to install a new or rebuilt pump.

Other Causes of Overheating

Other not-so-obvious overheating causes can be more serious and may be difficult to detect. Blown head gaskets, cracked cylinder heads, cracked blocks, and coolant leaking into the intake system dictate professional attention. A simple check with a combustion leak detector can spot the presence of exhaust gases in the coolant, which indicates a blown gasket or crack that allows the gases to infiltrate the system. The test will not tell exactly where the leak is occurring, but most often it's a blown head gasket or a crack in the cylinder head, either of which is an expensive item to repair. Leak-detector chemicals, introduced in the radiator, change color to indicate presence of combustion gases. The cooling system must be drained free of antifreeze for the leak detectors to function properly.

Figure 14.3
A tester is used to check the radiator cap, as well as the entire cooling system, for pressure retention capability.

Figure 14.4
Trouble with diesels usually can be traced to dirty or water-borne fuel. The water separator is visible at the bottom of this Racor unit.

The key to preventing overheating is maintenance. Neglect of the cooling system allows rust and scale to form on heat-transferring parts that rid the engine of heat buildup. Use a 50-50 mixture of ethylene glycol and distilled water, unless your vehicle is a late model that requires extended-life coolant and dictates an extended change interval (General Motors vehicles, for example, which require Dex-Cool and stipulate a coolant change every five years or 150,000 miles). Normal coolant should be changed every two years. At coolant-change time it's also a good idea to backflush the cooling system to remove any accumulated sediment. The system-flushing procedure applies to gasoline as well as diesel engines. Diesel owners should check the coolant filter system if the engine is fitted with one. The filter collects debris that may form between changes and when backflushing the system, and it should. Also check your owner's manual for antifreeze specifications, such as silicate content and anti-cavitation additives.

DIESEL ENGINES ONLY

Checking for Lack of Fuel

If the RV's engine is diesel fueled, lack of fuel is almost always caused by a dirty filter. Diesel systems have one and sometimes sometimes two filters. Primary and secondary filters are usually connected in series. Some systems use a special water trap just ahead of the primary filter to collect large amounts of water that could find its way into your fuel tank from a service station's supply tanks (Figure 14.4).

Lack of fuel is first evident in lack of performance. Diesel-engine power output is directly proportional to the amount of fuel that is injected into the cylinder. Instead of controlling the airflow and fuel flow to the cylinders as a gasoline engine does, diesels control just the amount of fuel that is injected when the piston reaches the top of the compression stroke.

A transfer pump brings fuel from the tank to the filter housing. Then a high-pressure positive displacement pump draws its supply from the filter housing and supplies fuel to the fuel injectors. If fuel filters become clogged, they will pass only a fraction of what is necessary to keep the engine operating at peak performance. The engine may idle and run at low speed properly, but at full throttle, performance may drop off. The solution is usually to change both the primary and secondary fuel filters.

If the Diesel Engine Fails to Run

Diesel engines do not require ignition systems. But most diesels do require a preheater, ether injection, or glow plugs to assist in cold starting. If the engine cranks over normally and has fuel but still fails to start or run, the next logical place to look is the electrical system.

Checking the Diesel's Glow Plugs

A diesel uses the heat of the compressed air in the combustion chamber to ignite the fuel. The high compression ratios associated with diesel operation normally heat the air in the chamber enough to ignite the fuel sprayed into the chambers by the injectors.

When the engine is cold, some engines use glow plugs to add enough heat to the combustion chamber to make for easier ignition of the fuel. With age, glow plugs may deteriorate or burn out.

Owners can use a test light to determine if power is getting to the glow plugs during cranking. If no power is getting to the plugs, check for a burned-out glow-plug fuse. Glow plugs may be tested in the field with an ohmmeter; disconnect the glow plug from the circuit and measure the resistance between the terminal on the glow plug and ground. If the resistance is roughly 1 ohm the glow plug is probably okay. If there is an open circuit (infinite resistance), the glow plug is burned out.

Glow-plug circuits can be checked with special testing equipment to determine the condition of the controller and plugs. A diesel-service shop should be able to do this.

Flooding in Diesel Engines

Although flooding usually is associated with carbureted gasoline engines, diesel engines can become flooded too. This usually happens when the driver holds the accelerator pedal down too far while starting a cold engine. It also may occur if the driver doesn't allow the glow plugs or other starting device to warm up before attempting to start the engine.

Typically, a flooded diesel will produce white exhaust smoke during cranking. Because diesel engines have such high compression, the combustion chambers are very small. Therefore, flooding may cause a hydraulic lock in the engine, which may damage the engine. Avoid flooding by following the recommended starting procedure in the owner's manual.

To start a flooded diesel, operate the preheater or glow plugs and crank the engine without stepping on the accelerator pedal. If a diesel is badly flooded, you may have to remove the injectors or glow plugs and crank the engine to clear it.

Checking Diesel Fuel Delivery

At least 95 percent of all diesel engines that quit on the road are disabled by fuel-supply problems. These breakdowns are usually due to blocked fuel filters, and this is the first item you should check. Remove the filter and see if it's full of clean fuel. Often, the engine will gradually lose power, which is noticed first while climbing grades. Unlike a gasoline engine, a diesel with a fuel-filter blockage will usually run smoothly, but may only run at idle or slightly above. When the blockage gets worse, the engine won't run at all.

Checking and Draining Water Traps in the Diesel Fuel System

If water is found, remove the filter(s) and pour their contents into a container. Install fresh fuel filter(s) and follow the instructions in the owner's manual to prime them. Some systems must be primed by a hand pump, and others are primed by cranking the engine. If you fill the filters with diesel fuel prior to installation it will make priming and starting easier.

Look for sediment and give the fuel a "sniff" test. Sometimes diesels are misfueled with gasoline; if this is the case the entire fuel system must be drained.

On mechanically injected diesels, if no water is found, the filter(s) are full, and the

Troubleshooting Diesel Engines

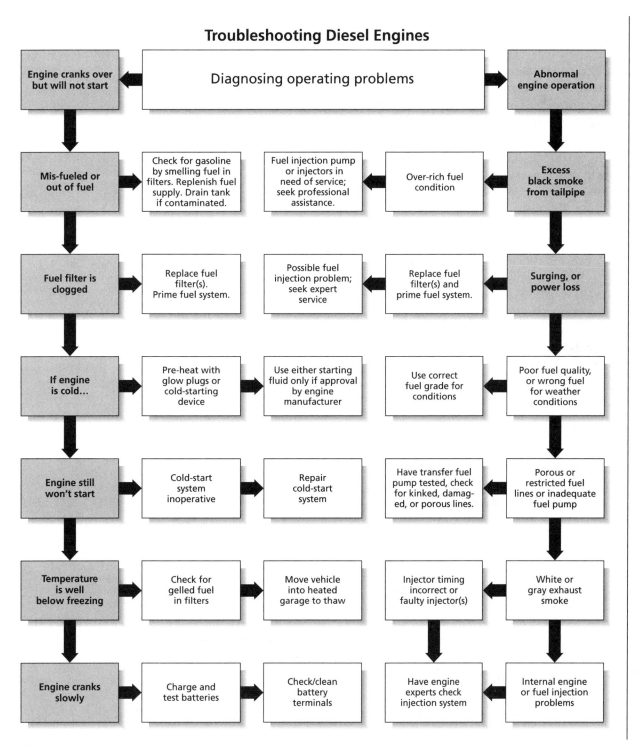

Figure 14.5
Diesel-engine troubleshooting focuses primarily on fuel problems.

engine still won't start, check for fuel delivery at the injector lines. This procedure does not apply to electronically controlled diesels. Wear eye protection and gloves. Have an assistant step on the accelerator pedal about ¼ inch and operate the starter, while you use a wrench to slightly loosen the fuel-line fitting at an injector. If fuel is getting this far, you will observe a squirt of fuel every other revolution of the crankshaft. If fuel is squirting from the injector line, it indicates fuel is getting through and the problem probably lies elsewhere. If fuel isn't getting through, carefully check the entire fuel system from tank to injection pump.

If you have followed the previous procedures on checking the fuel filters, for fuel delivery at the injectors and for flooding, yet the engine still won't start or run properly, there are a few more items to check. If the engine seems to crank over slower than normal, the battery may be weak, the starter may be faulty, or the cables or connections are bad.

If these systems are working and the engine cranks over fast enough, there may be an internal problem such as low compression or jumped timing. See Figure 14.5 for diesel troubleshooting procedures.

In cold weather the glow plugs, ether injector, or fuel preheater (if applicable) may not be working, or the fuel or oil are too viscous. Diesel engines do not usually suffer from over-rich conditions. If excessive black smoke is evident, the air filter may be plugged or the pump and/or injectors may need repair or adjustment. Professional help should be sought.

This chapter has covered basic on-the-road trouble situations so you can diagnose malfunctions, which should be informative whether you attempt to repair the problems or seek help from a professional mechanic. Many detailed automotive troubleshooting books are available at dealerships, in libraries, and bookstores. Shop manuals from the manufacturer for the specific vehicle are great to have; even if they are too advanced for you, often they can be of use to a mechanic if a breakdown occurs where there is no franchised dealer. Being informed is important. While most mechanics are honest, the motorist who is totally ignorant of the causes of a mechanical breakdown is a more likely target and may pay for unneccessary repairs.

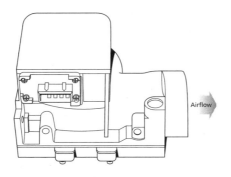

Airflow

Chapter 15

ELECTRONIC ENGINE CONTROL SYSTEMS

Fuel Injection Components

Dodge OBD I Troubleshooting

Ford EEC IV

General Motors Fuel Injection

"No Code" Drivability Problems

Vehicle Emission Control Information Labels

Test Equipment

Emission System Component Warranties

The under-hood environment on late-model vehicles can be downright intimidating to the do-it-yourselfer. Engines are often obscured by a maze of vacuum hoses, wires, and cables, and covered with a variety of unusual-looking components. An onboard computer monitors and controls vital engine and vehicle functions such as fuel delivery, ignition timing, and a multitude of other tasks including climate control, cruise control, and traction control. Initially, it would appear that diagnosis and repair must be left to experts who are trained and specially equipped to deal with such high-tech equipment. These procedures require expensive scan tools, scopes, and exhaust-gas analyzers.

Not quite. The home mechanic can still do a considerable amount of troubleshooting and repair, given specific information and a few simple tools. Even if you don't intend ever to touch your computer-controlled carburetor or electronic fuel-injection (EFI) system, knowledge of its principles and how the components work can be valuable in diagnosing on-the-road problems and finding help, not to mention improving your ability to assess the validity of a repair estimate or bill.

Onboard Computers

The onboard computer is commonly called an electronic (or engine) control module (ECM) (Figure 15.1). These computers are also variously known by acronyms such as powertrain control module (PCM) and Dodge calls one type a single module engine control (SMEC).

The computer is the brain of the engine-control system. It is usually contained in a metal box located within the dash, behind a kick panel, under the driver's seat, or in a protected location in the engine compartment. Some vehicles have other computers to control various body systems like anti-lock brakes, etc.

An ECM may go into a "limp-in" mode if the signals from certain critical sensors are outside of preset design parameters. In some cases the computer will substitute fixed average values and disregard the out-of-range information the faulty sensor provides. The "check engine" or "malfunction indicator lamp" (MIL) will come on, and power may be reduced. Problems of this nature should be corrected as soon as possible.

Most intermittent problems are caused by loose or corroded connections, damaged wiring or components that malfunction when they change temperature. The most common way to locate such problems is to duplicate the conditions that caused the problem. With OBD II systems, malfunctions that set a code also store "freeze frame" records of the malfunction, which can be reviewed to help duplicate the conditions. Note any recent repairs or maintenance, which may have disturbed connections. Onboard computers don't fail very often. In fact, they are one of the least common causes of engine malfunction. Statistics show that if the computer lasts the first six months, it will probably outlast the vehicle. Since the computer rarely fails and you suspect it has, get a professional to check it before you buy a new one.

Computer-Controlled Carburetors

Carburetors rely on the difference between atmospheric pressure and the lower pressure (or so-called partial vacuum) inside the intake manifold to meter and atomize fuel. From the late 1970s through the late 1980s, many cars and light trucks used computer-controlled carburetors to reduce exhaust emissions. These systems used a fairly conventional carburetor, with the notable exception that it had a fuel-mixture solenoid. The computer would vary the engine's fuel mixture with this solenoid, based on information from the oxygen sensor. When the engine warms up, the solenoid should make a buzzing sound that indicates that it's getting a signal and that it's working. These systems were an interim measure between the conventional carburetor and the feedback-type fuel-injection system.

Figure 15.1
The electronic control module (ECM) controls all aspects of engine operation, and is located inside the vehicle or in a protected location under the hood.

Fuel Injection

Fuel injection, a system designed to meter the correct amounts of fuel into the engine during varying modes of operation, has been with us for a long time. In fact, airplanes have been equipped with it since the dawn of aviation with the Wright brothers in 1903. These early systems were rather crude, mechanically controlled devices. With the advent of solid-state electronics, electrons and transistors have taken over the job.

Electronically controlled fuel injection has gradually replaced carburetion and mechanical fuel injection as the system of choice because of its greater precision in providing the correct ratios of fuel and air under a wide variety of operating conditions. Gasoline engines will run on a broad range of air-fuel ratios, varying from about 8:1 to 20:1 by mass. However, the ideal (stoichiometric, for you chemistry buffs) mixture for low emissions is about 14.7 pounds of air for every pound of gasoline. This ratio allows reduction catalysts to work efficiently. Any more or less than this and emissions rise substantially.

How Does Gasoline Fuel Injection Work?

Fuel-injection sprays (injects) fuel under pressure into the airstream entering the engine, hence its name. Manufacturers use various types of fuel injection; however, the popular types all have much in common. Each uses a number of sensors to determine the operating conditions of the engine. A computer receives the signals from the various sensors and tells the fuel injectors how much fuel to spray, and also switches power to actuators that operate emission-control functions like exhaust gas recirculation and canister purge valves.

On gasoline engines, as the driver steps on the accelerator pedal, throttle plates in the throttle body open, allowing additional air to enter the intake manifold. As the air rushes into the manifold, the inside air pressure changes. Sensors detect this change instantly and pass the information on to the computer. When the computer gets the signals, it orders the fuel injectors to spray more fuel.

The first electronic gasoline fuel injection systems in the late 1950s through the late 1970s metered the fuel much like the current ones, but they didn't monitor the exhaust. Increasingly stringent emission and fuel-economy regulations have prompted the vehicle manufacturers to introduce computer-controlled feedback systems, first on cars (most 1980 models had them) and later on light trucks, sport utility vehicles (SUVs), motorhomes and vans. These systems use oxygen sensors to sniff the exhaust and tell the computer whether the fuel-metering program has missed the mark and the engine needs more or less fuel for a certain amount of air. Many of the early feedback systems used computer-controlled carburetors.

Think of an electronically controlled feedback fuel-delivery system as a circle or loop. When the engine is started, the oxygen sensor in the exhaust is cold and therefore unable to tell the computer what is happening. Until the oxygen sensor warms up, the engine runs on preset mixture values in the computer's memory. This condition is known as "open loop" because the circle is incomplete.

When the engine warms up to normal temperature, the oxygen sensor starts working (at about 600°F tip temperature), and the feedback loop is completed. The computer uses the information from the oxygen sensor(s) to constantly adjust the fuel mixture. This is known as closed loop.

The oxygen sensor(s) "sniff" the exhaust, and if they find less oxygen (because a rich fuel mixture used it up), the computer uses this information to decide to cut back on the amount of fuel being sprayed into the engine.

This monitoring occurs rapidly and constantly. Each time the oxygen sensor detects a rich fuel mixture, it signals the computer to reduce the amount of fuel being injected, and vice versa. Corrections occur many times per second, allowing very accurate control of fuel flow. This precise metering is necessary to allow reduction-type catalytic converters to work efficiently in ridding the exhaust of oxides of nitrogen, carbon monoxide, and unburned hydrocarbons.

Throttle-Body Versus Port-Type Fuel Injection

Two basic fuel-injection designs are commonly used on gasoline-fueled domestic cars, light trucks, SUVs, motorhomes, and vans:

1. Throttle-body (TBI, or single-point, or central) fuel injection (Figure 15.2)

2. Port-type (also called multi-port or multi-point) fuel injection (Figure 15.3)

Both types work on the same basic principles. However, throttle-body systems more closely resemble carburetors in appearance and function, with the fuel being mixed with air in the throttle bore.

A third type of fuel injection, direct injection, is being adopted in at least a few automotive applications. As its name implies, direct injection sprays fuel under very high pressure directly into the combustion chamber. Direct injection is more efficient and is also found on many modern diesel engines.

Fuel-injection systems use two basic types of airflow metering: speed density and mass air. Speed-density systems rely on manifold pressure, air charge temperature, and barometric sensors to calculate the volume and density of air entering the engine. Mass-air sensors typically use airflow over a hot wire to calculate air density and flow. Mass-air systems are more accurate and are used almost exclusively in port-type injection systems.

Throttle-body injection (TBI) systems control the air-fuel mixture more accurately than carburetors, are less prone to injector clogging, and cost less initially than port-type injection. However, with carburetors and TBI systems, the inner cylinders tend to get more fuel than the outer ones. This imbalance results in higher fuel consumption and exhaust emissions. Engine designers had to compensate by supplying the inner cylinders with extra fuel so that the outer ones don't starve and incur lean misfire. For these and other reasons, throttle-body systems were phased out of production.

Port-type fuel-injection systems spray fuel into the intake ports just upstream of the intake valves, making this system more efficient because each cylinder gets the same amount of fuel. The downside of port-type fuel injection is the higher cost and greater susceptibility to leaks and injector clogging. The smaller orifices (compared to throttle-body systems) may become partially clogged with fuel deposits, and the spray pattern slowly deteriorates, resulting in drivability problems.

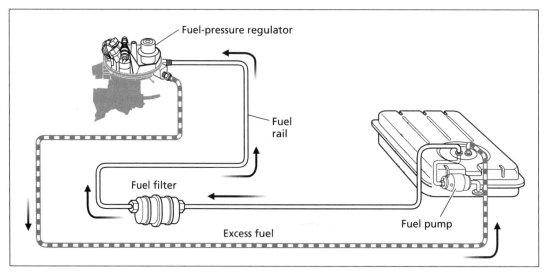

Figure 15.2
In single-point electronic fuel injection, used on vehicles in the late 1980s and early 1990s, fuel is injected at a throttle body on the intake manifold. Excess fuel is returned to the tank.

Port fuel-injection systems also have throttle bodies to control airflow; however, the fuel is not mixed with the air at that point.

Electronically Controlled Diesels

Due to increasingly strict emissions regulations, diesel engine manufacturers have had to introduce electronic controls, along with catalytic converters, to diesel engines sold in the United States. This trend in light trucks began with the 1994 Ford Power Stroke. The Cummins 5.9-liter engine in the Dodge Ram went to electronic controls in 1998 and General Motors' Duramax 6.6-liter engine in 2001. These engines use a "common rail" injection system that feeds all of the injectors from a single shared high-pressure fuel line, instead of individually from an injection pump as used in mechanical injection. Electronically controlled diesels use very high pressures (up to 21,000 psi) at the injector tips to thoroughly atomize the fuel, which improves combustion and driveability and reduces emissions.

As with a gasoline engine, the electronically controlled diesel engine's powertrain control module (PCM) electrically triggers the opening of the injectors, based on inputs from various sensors. On diesels, the sensors typically used are: accelerator position sensor (APS); camshaft position sensor (CPS); injection control pressure (ICP); manifold absolute pressure (MAP); engine oil temperature (EOT); intake air temperature (IAT); barometric pressure sensor (BARO); and exhaust back-pressure (EBP).

Electronically controlled diesels have self-diagnostic systems similar to their gasoline-fueled cousins. These systems can be accessed and diagnosed in the same ways, with scan tools.

Onboard Diagnostics

The first generation of electronic-feedback engine controls known as Onboard Diagnostics, Version 1, or OBD I, used oxygen sensors between the engine and the catalytic converter to monitor the fuel mixture and make running adjustments. These systems, which were introduced in the early 1980s, could only detect a limited number of malfunctions, like shorts or open circuits in the sensor and actuator circuits. They usually could not pinpoint the problem to a certain wire or sensor, only the circuit as a whole. When a problem is detected, a diagnostic trouble code (DTC) is stored in memory for a technician to read later.

As computerized engine and emission control systems continue to evolve and become

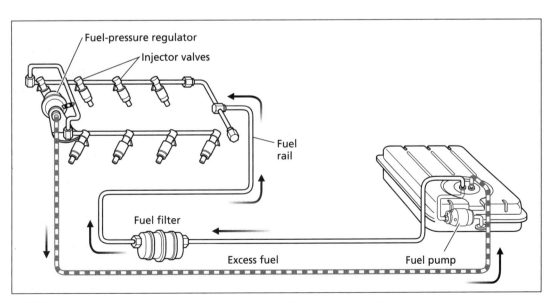

Figure 15.3
Multi-point electronic fuel injection allows precise metering of fuel at each cylinder.

more sophisticated, they've taken on control of more functions and provide more precise management. The latest generation of emission controls, Onboard Diagnostics, Version 2, or OBD II (see page 237 for codes), as it's usually called, was developed to address some of the shortcomings of the previous systems. Vehicles with OBD II were first sold to the public as early as 1994; during the 1995 model year coverage was extended and all cars and light trucks were OBD II-compliant by 1996.

Computerized engine controls have also brought with them a blizzard of acronyms and each manufacturer used its own, often different, names. OBD II regulations also standardize these acronyms.

Among the new features of OBD II is its ability to monitor the effectiveness of the vehicle's emission system in reducing pollution. OBD II goes a step further than OBD I by utilizing an additional oxygen sensor(s) downstream of the catalytic converter(s). The computer compares the signals coming from the upstream and downstream sensors. If there is no significant difference between the two signals, it indicates that the catalyst is not functioning.

Extremely accurate crankshaft position sensors allow the OBD II systems to provide misfire detection. It monitors the rate the crankshaft accelerates after each cylinder fires. If the crankshaft accelerates less from a particular cylinder, OBD II detects this and sets a trouble code.

OBD II also stores short- and long-term fuel-trim data. This means that a technician can see how the engine controls have been adapting to operating conditions and/or correcting for any malfunctions such as vacuum leaks. The exhaust gas recirculation (EGR) system, the air injection and the evaporative control system (EVAP) are monitored by OBD II. Components in these systems are run through a series of operational checks on a regular basis. The fuel tank is pressurized and if the filler cap is loose, for example, a DTC is set. This is a very common problem that often brings motorists into their dealers for "repair."

OBD II computers can also detect sensor readings that are out of range and ones that don't change readings as they should or when they should. They also can detect actuators that don't respond correctly.

On OBD I systems, each manufacturer had its own, completely different, sets of trouble codes and methods of accessing them. With OBD II, all manufacturers are required to use a set of more than 100 standardized "generic" trouble codes produced by the Society of Automotive Engineers (SAE). In addition, manufacturers can use additional codes for items of equipment that are specific to that brand.

The codes all have five characters. There is a letter followed by four numbers, such as P1234. A letter P indicates powertrain, B is for body, C is for chassis and U is for network communications. The second character says who wrote the DTC; 0 is generic SAE, 1 or 2 is manufacturer-specific. The third character identifies the subsystem; for example, 1 is for air/fuel control. The final two digits give the specific item.

Unfortunately, unlike OBD I, expensive, special scan tools are required for accessing OBD II codes. This prevents the average do-it-yourselfer from reading and using them for diagnosis. For advanced do-it-yourselfers, Actron, 9999 Walford Avenue, Cleveland, OH 44102; (800) 228-7667; www.actron.com, offers an OBD II scan tool for around $200.

B&B Electronics' AutoTap has a cable that plugs into your vehicle's diagnostic connector and into a COM port on a PC. It gives real-time data, such as sensor readings, rpm and trouble codes. AutoTap is available for 1996 and newer GM vehicles for $249.95 from B&B Electronics, 707 Dayton Road, Ottawa, IL 61350; (815) 433-5100; www.bb-elec.com.

Malfunction Indicator Lamp

The malfunction indicator lamp (MIL) is also variously known as the "check engine," "service engine soon," or "power loss" light. MILs, as this acronym suggests, illuminate only when there is a malfunction detected in the emission-control system.

If a problem is detected, a trouble code is set in the computer's memory, and the malfunction indicator lamp will be activated. Some DTCs will store as soon as a monitor check fails; others require two driving trips.

The light is connected to the vehicle's onboard computer and illuminates when one or more monitored functions are found to be outside of normal ranges. The light should also be activated briefly as a bulb check every time the engine is started.

If the problem goes away or is repaired, the computer is designed to shut off the lamp after a preset number of engine starts. Trouble codes can also be cleared by disconnecting the battery or removing the ECM fuse for several seconds. A listing of trouble codes related to the MIL for various vehicle brands appears later in this chapter.

When these lights stay on, owners often go scurrying through their operator's manual to find out what it means, only to be told simply to take the vehicle to a dealer. The books don't tell you whether it's safe to continue driving or if it's really necessary to tow it in. The MIL only monitors emissions-related problems. Generally, if the oil pressure and coolant temperature are within normal ranges and the engine isn't smoking, making unusual sounds, or running very rough, it's okay to limp in for service.

FUEL INJECTION COMPONENTS

Air Charge Temperature Sensor

The Air Charge Temperature (ACT) sensor (Figure 15.4) measures the temperature of air entering the engine. This sensor allows the computer to make minor adjustments to fuel mixture and ignition timing due to changes in the temperature of the air.

Barometric-Pressure Sensor

Weather and altitude (air density) changes require alterations in fuel mixture. The barometric-pressure sensor is used on some systems to inform the computer of changes in ambient air pressure so adjustments can be made to compensate for air density.

Camshaft-Position Sensor

Camshaft-position sensors measure the angular position of the camshaft. The ECM uses this information along with CAS readings to determine if a particular cylinder is on compression or exhaust stroke.

Crankshaft-Angle Sensor

A crankshaft angle sensor (CAS) measures the angular position of the crankshaft. The ECM

Figure 15.4
A sensor in the engine's air intake tract monitors air temperature.

uses this information to determine when to spray fuel (on sequential port injection only), when to fire spark plugs, and when to detect misfire (OBD II only). These sensors are mounted low on the engine and are prone to damage from road debris, water, and corrosion. Also, the wires and connections often get damaged or corroded. Owners can unplug and clean these terminals if a problem is suspected.

Coolant-Temperature Sensor

The coolant-temperature sensor (CTS) is a temperature-sensing resistor (thermistor) (Figure 15.5). It is usually located in the intake manifold near the thermostat, is screwed into a coolant passage, and has two wires connected to it. Essentially, the CTS exists because cold engines need more fuel than warm ones. The CTS tells the computer how cold (or warm) the engine is by changing resistance as the engine-coolant temperature changes. As the temperature goes down, resistance goes up. The computer uses the CTS readings to lengthen the "open" time of the injectors for a cold engine, which enriches the fuel mixture like a choke does on a carbureted engine. When the engine warms up, the fuel mixture is leaned out for best fuel economy and low emissions.

Detonation Sensor

The detonation (knock) sensor converts mechanical energy (vibration) into electrical signals (Figure 15.6). When the engine starts to knock or "ping," this block-mounted sensor generates a small voltage signal that tells the computer to retard the ignition timing and/or enrich the fuel mixture until the knock goes away. Then it will gradually return to the original setting until the sensor once again detects knock or ping. To check its operation, connect a timing light, and with the engine running, tap on the engine block with a hammer. If the timing retards, the knock sensor is working.

Electric Fuel Pump

Most electronically controlled fuel-injection systems have an electric fuel pump (Figure 15.7) mounted inside the fuel tank, combined with the sending unit for the fuel gauge. Tank-mounting the fuel pump reduces vapor lock tendency by pressurizing the entire fuel system. Additional pressure raises the vaporization point of the fuel. Some vehicles have an additional pump mounted on the chassis between the tank and engine.

If the engine won't start but has good spark, check the sound of the fuel pump. Listen for the characteristic whirring noise near the fuel tank while an assistant operates the starter. Remove the gas-filler cap to hear better, if necessary.

If the fuel pump doesn't run, check for voltage at the pump's electrical terminals while the engine is cranking. Also check the fuse, the

Figure 15.5
The electronic control system uses signals from the coolant temperature sensor to create proper air/fuel ratios for engine warmup.

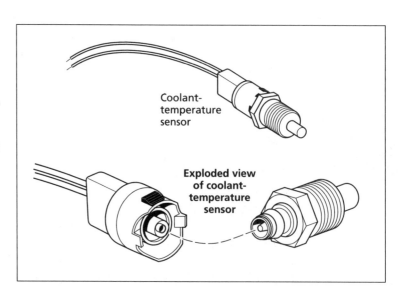

Coolant-temperature sensor

Exploded view of coolant-temperature sensor

Figure 15.6
A detonation sensor monitors the engine for spark-knock ("ping") and reduces spark advance as necessary.

inertia switch (if so equipped), and the relay(s) before you replace the fuel pump.

If your vehicle seems to be starving for fuel (surging, bucking, backfiring, etc.) or seems to be getting too much fuel (black, sooty spark-plug tips and/or exhaust, poor fuel mileage, etc.), perform a fuel-pressure test. Sometimes fuel gauges are inaccurate. Always double-check the fuel level by thumping on the bottom of the tank(s)!

On Dodge and General Motors throttle-body systems, connect a T-fitting into the fuel line going to the throttle body (the one with the filter). Don't connect it to the return line; you'll get a false reading.

On all Ford EFI systems and later Dodge and GM port injection, connect the gauge to the pressure-checking port on the fuel-injector rail. These ports appear similar to Shrader-type tire valves with dust caps; you must have the right fittings for them. Use a gauge designed for fuel-pressure testing that has a rating higher than the maximum pressure specified for your engine. Dodge TBI calls for 14.5 psi fuel pressure, most Ford port injection allows a range from 35 to 45 psi, and GM TBI requires 9 to 13 psi. GM central multi-point injection used on light trucks up to 1995 operates at 58 to 64 psi. GM's central sequential system used on Vortec engines starting in 1996 operates at 55 to 61 psi. The Dodge port injection typically uses 35 to 45 psi.

If the pressure is too high, check for a restricted return line. If the return line is open and unrestricted, replace the fuel-pressure regulator.

If the pressure is too low, look for a restricted line, hose, or fuel filter (don't forget the screen in the tank). The fuel-pressure regulator could also be at fault. Momentarily pinch the

fuel-return hose where it runs between the engine and frame. If the pressure rises rapidly, the regulator is probably bad. If the pressure doesn't rise with this test, the fuel pump is probably faulty.

Fuel Injectors

Fuel injectors are basically spray nozzles with electric solenoid-operated pintle valves (Figure 15.8). When the computer sends a ground signal to the fuel injector, the solenoid opens a path for the pressurized fuel to spray into the engine. When the current flow is shut off, the fuel flow is shut off.

Throttle-body injectors can be checked quickly by removing the air cleaner and looking at the injectors while an assistant turns the ignition key to "on" and cranks the engine. Fuel should spray out. If it doesn't, disconnect the wiring harness from the injectors and connect a common 12-volt DC test light (or special "noid-light" tester) to the terminals. The light should pulse when the key is turned on. This means the electrical portion of the system is working. A steady light or no light indicates electrical malfunctions.

Port-type fuel injectors can be electrically checked in a similar manner. However, you can't view the fuel spraying out as you can on a throttle body. Instead, remove a spark plug to see if it is dry or wet with fuel.

Specially formulated fuel detergents have been added to most brands of gasoline to combat deposit formation, and nozzle designs have been

Figure 15.7
The electric fuel pump creates pressure from 9 to 45 psi, depending on design of the system.

Precautions in Relieving Fuel Pressure

The fuel system is pressurized at all times. Be sure to read the following checklist before opening the fuel system:

✔ Remove the fuel-filler caps. With the engine idling, remove the fuel-pump fuse (on Fords, disconnect the wires at the fuel pump), and allow the engine to stall. Wrap a rag around the fittings to soak up any remaining fuel when you open them, and always wear eye protection!

✔ When working on fuel systems, always have a fire extinguisher rated for gasoline and electrical fires at hand. Read the instructions!

✔ Never smoke or allow open flames or unprotected light bulbs anywhere near the workplace.

✔ Never work in a closed garage or one with a gas-operated water heater or clothes dryer; the pilot light could ignite fuel vapors.

✔ Keep children and pets away from the work area.

✔ Remember to always wear eye protection when testing or disconnecting fuel-system components.

✔ Do not allow anyone near the driver's controls except a trusted assistant and only when needed during testing.

✔ Remove the keys from the ignition when they are not required for testing.

✔ Always relieve fuel pressure before disconnecting fuel lines and/or fittings.

✔ Never connect or disconnect jumper cables to the battery with the ignition key on.

✔ Before checking compression, disable the fuel-pump circuit by removing the fuse or relay.

✔ Never apply full battery voltage directly to any electronic component unless the service manual specifically directs you to.

✔ Never work under a vehicle supported only by a jack.

✔ Cover all open fittings to avoid contamination from dirt or moisture.

✔ Handle components with care; avoid heat and liquids. Never weld near electronic parts.

✔ Never touch the computer input or output terminals; static discharge could destroy the ECM in an instant!

changed to resist the tendency to clog. Several companies sell gasoline additives for your fuel tank that claim to unclog injectors. If all else fails, many repair shops have special injector-cleaning devices that chemically clean the nozzles on the vehicle. If you suspect that your engine is running rough because the injectors are clogged, have them cleaned and tested rather than replaced. Your wallet will thank you.

Fuel Filter

On fuel-injected vehicles, the fuel filter is especially important because the system is so sensitive to dirt and water (Figure 15.9). The slightest speck of dirt can plug an injector nozzle. The fuel filter is usually located under the vehicle along the inside of a frame rail near the fuel tank. Most manufacturers recommend filter replacement at least every 30,000 miles; however, towing is considered "severe-duty" operation and may require more frequent replacement.

Warning: The fuel system is under pressure, even when the engine is not running! Read the precautions in this chapter, and follow the procedure for relieving fuel pressure before loosening any lines. Wear eye protection. Always use the exact replacement filter; don't risk a fire by using a substitute.

When loosening fuel lines with threaded fittings at either end of the filter, use the proper line wrenches to avoid rounding off the hex shapes and use a backup wrench to prevent twisting the fuel line.

Pour the contents of the old filter from the filter inlet into a clean container (not glass) and check for water and other contamination. Note the arrow on the filter, which indicates the direction of fuel flow, and always check for leaks after startup.

Fuel-Pressure Regulator

The fuel-pressure regulator (Figure 15.10) keeps the fuel at a preset constant pressure to prevent fluctuations in the fuel mixture that would change the mixture. The regulator maintains a constant pressure by returning the excess fuel to the fuel tank.

Figure 15.8
When the ECM sends a voltage signal to the fuel injector, a solenoid inside the injector opens a path for the pressurized fuel to spray into the engine.

On Dodge and General Motors vehicles with TBI, the regulator is mounted in the throttle body; on Fords and other port-injected engines, the regulator is usually mounted at the downstream end of the fuel-injector rail. Some Chrysler models beginning in the mid-1990s have fuel systems with no returns, just a single fuel line going to the engine. On these, the regulator is at the tank.

On most port-injected vehicles, the fuel-pressure regulator has another function. Since fuel is sprayed into the intake manifold (or ports), a substantial difference between pressure at the ports and in the intake manifold must be maintained. This is accomplished with a vacuum line that connects the regulator to a source of intake manifold vacuum to compensate for the changes in manifold pressure due to engine load. This diaphragm may be checked with a hand-pump vacuum tester. Replace the unit if it won't hold vacuum.

Idle Air-Control Valve

The idle air-control valve (IAC) is a computer-controlled air bypass that allows the computer to adjust idle speed to a predetermined rpm. It consists of an electric motor connected to a variable orifice. The IAC increases the size of

Figure 15.9
Effective fuel filtration is essential for the close tolerances inside a fuel-injection system.

the air passage to raise the idle in response to signals from the computer. This occurs, for example, when the engine is cold, the automatic transmission is put in gear, or the air conditioning is switched on.

Idle speed is computer controlled and is not usually adjustable. If the idle speed is too fast, check for vacuum leaks around the intake manifold, leaking hoses, and throttle-body base gaskets.

Inertia Switch

The inertia switch shuts off the fuel pump in the event of an accident (Figure 15.11). Whenever the fuel pump is inoperative, the inertia switch (if equipped) should be checked and reset if necessary. See your owner's manual for procedure and switch location.

Manifold Absolute-Pressure Sensor

The manifold absolute-pressure sensor (MAP) keeps the computer informed of changes in

Figure 15.10
A fuel-pressure regulator maintains a specific pressure at the injectors, and allows excess fuel to return to the tank.

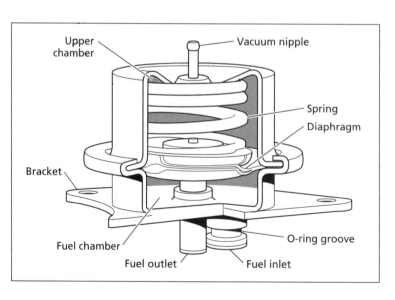

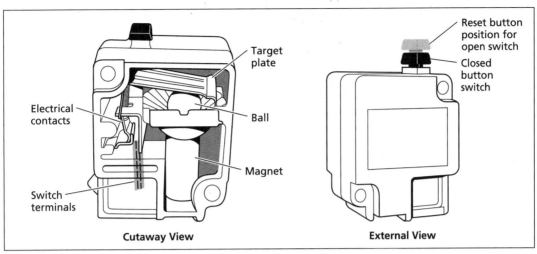

Figure 15.11
The inertia switch senses vehicle impact in an accident, and shuts off the fuel pump to lower fire danger.

intake manifold pressure (partial vacuum) by varying resistance in relation to changes in pressure in the manifold. As engine load increases, the manifold pressure increases (or conversely, vacuum decreases).

Manifold Air-Temperature Sensor

The manifold air-temperature sensor (MAT) sensor (now known as the air-charge temperature [ACT] sensor) monitors the temperature of the air coming into the intake manifold. Colder air is more dense and requires more fuel than hot air. Since the MAT sensor is a thermistor (resistance varies with temperature), it alters the voltage signal going to the computer in relation to the temperature of the incoming air.

Oxygen Sensor

Oxygen (O_2) sensors allow the computer to know what is coming out the exhaust and to make corrections based on that information (Figure 15.12). Every feedback or closed-loop system must have one.

Oxygen sensors are readily identified. They have a base similar in appearance to a spark plug and screw into the exhaust manifold or the exhaust pipe downstream of the manifolds. Earlier sensors are connected to only one wire; later models have two additional

Figure 15.12
The oxygen sensor, mounted in the exhaust pipe, relays data to the computer for control of combustion.

wires for a heating element that gets them working more quickly.

A zirconium element produces a small voltage in the presence of oxygen in the exhaust. This voltage, which will vary from 0 to 0.9 volts, with 0.450 volts indicating an ideal fuel mixture of 14.7:1, can be measured with an oxygen-sensor tester, or in some cases with a digital voltmeter (which has real-time graphing) probe inserted into the back of the oxygen-sensor connector. The voltage should constantly and rapidly vary with the engine running; if it doesn't, replace the sensor.

Most oxygen sensors require replacement every 30,000 to 50,000 miles. They are easily replaced, and you can save a considerable amount of money by doing it yourself. Be sure the threads are coated with an anti-seize compound (Loctite 771-64 or equivalent); the compound usually is applied to new sensors by the manufacturer. Refer to your owner's manual for the replacement interval recommended by the manufacturer of your vehicle.

Some vehicles have more than one oxygen sensor; V-type engines may have one in each bank. Beginning with OBD II emission systems, there are also oxygen sensors downstream of the catalytic converters.

Note: Oxygen sensors may be ruined by the use of certain automotive silicone sealers; read the labels to determine if they are compatible with oxygen sensors.

Throttle-Position Sensor

Throttle-position sensors (TPS) tell the computer the rate of throttle opening and how far the throttle is open; they work by changing resistance as the throttle opens and closes. This allows the computer to enrich the fuel mixture when the throttle is opened suddenly, preventing hesitation.

The most common symptom of a faulty TPS is hesitation when the throttle is opened quickly. Two quick checks may be made with an analog voltmeter. With the ignition on:

1. Test for a reference voltage at the TPS (usually 5 volts). If voltage isn't present, trace and repair the wiring.

2. Check for a smooth voltage change as the throttle is opened and closed. If the voltage changes abruptly and unevenly, the TPS is probably faulty.

The initial (or base) setting of the TPS is also critical for good performance. Normally the TPS doesn't require adjustment. However, whenever it is replaced or when diagnosis

indicates a problem, an adjustment should be performed following the factory-recommended procedure exactly. Since special tools may be needed that are beyond the scope of the home mechanic, have this work done by a dealer or fuel-injection specialist.

Mass Airflow Sensor

Mass airflow (MAF) sensors indirectly measure the mass of air entering the engine. These units, noted for their precision, are mounted in the intake tract between the air filter and throttle body. Typically, MAF sensors use the cooling effect of air flowing over a heated wire to calculate the mass of air flowing through them.

Faulty MAFs may cause drivability problems like hesitation and backfiring, or may prevent the engine from running. The most effective way to test a MAF is with an oscilloscope, using a printed-scope pattern from a known-good unit for comparison. A scan tool can also be used to check a MAF. However, here's one field test for a suspect MAF that is still functioning somewhat: Carefully check electrical connections, then tap on the housing of the MAF while the engine is idling. If the engine "coughs," replace the MAF.

Vane Airflow Meter

The vane airflow meter (VAF), used on certain port-type systems (some Ford trucks) only, measures the flow of air into the engine with an internal flap connected to a potentiometer, or variable resistor (Figure 15.13). Air temperature is also monitored by a built-in sensor.

The VAF meter is mounted between the throttle-control valve (or throttle body) and the air cleaner. A reference voltage is sent through the potentiometer and back to the computer. When the driver depresses the accelerator pedal, the increased volume of air entering the engine forces the flap to open wider, thus changing the resistance. The computer uses this information in determining how much fuel the engine needs.

Vehicle-Speed Sensor

Most computer-equipped vehicles are equipped with vehicle-speed sensors (VSS) that tell the computer how fast the vehicle is going. These sensors are usually mounted in the tailshaft of the transmission (or transfer case of four-wheel-drive models). When the vehicle is moving, a pulsing signal is generated. The computer uses the information provided by the speed sensor to control functions such as shift points and torque-converter lockup (on automatic transmission-equipped vehicles). Cruise control also uses this signal. The vehicle-speed sensors can be easily tested with a scan tool.

DODGE OBD I TROUBLESHOOTING

Fuel-injected Dodge trucks and vans prior to the introduction of the Magnum series engines use a throttle-body system. The computer (or SMEC) is usually located in the engine compartment adjacent to the left fender. Whenever the SMEC detects a problem, the "check engine" light on the dash is activated. This light may also be used as a diagnostic tool. By turning the ignition key on-off-on-off within five seconds (with the engine not running—do not activate the starter), electronically stored trouble codes may be accessed. The lamp should light for three seconds as a bulb check before displaying the trouble codes.

These codes are displayed as flashes of light. For example, Code 11 would appear as one blink, a short pause, another blink, then a long pause before the next code.

The computer will flash all codes stored in memory and then repeat them until the key is turned off. These codes represent problems detected by the computer in approximately the last fifty engine starts. Note: Missing code numbers are intentional by the manufacturer.

After repairs are made, disconnect the negative battery cable from the battery for five minutes to clear all stored codes. Reconnect the battery and drive the vehicle for about 10 miles to allow the computer to relearn the engine's characteristics. The engine may run roughly after first starting up.

FORD EEC IV

Ford trouble codes may be accessed with a special tester or an analog voltmeter. The procedures vary considerably with each engine option and model and are so complex that we recommend you take the vehicle to a qualified technician for these checks.

Before you throw in the towel, check all the usual problem areas we have listed. In addition, check the inertia switch, as this seems to be a common problem on Fords. Simply push the reset button as described in the owner's

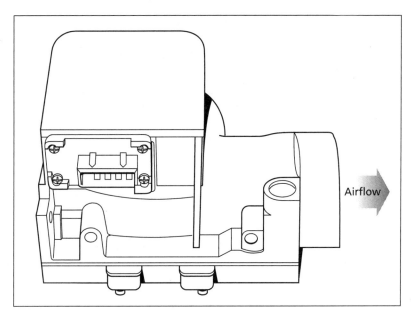

Figure 15.13
The amount of airflow entering the engine is measured by the vane airflow meter.

Airflow

manual. The inertia switch on F-series trucks is beneath the dash behind the left kick panel. On E-series vans, the switch is located under the right side of the dash under the heater-blower register.

GENERAL MOTORS FUEL INJECTION

General Motors OBD I computer trouble codes are displayed by the "check engine" light in the instrument cluster. They may be accessed by switching the ignition on with the engine not running. The "check engine" lamp should light as a bulb check. Then locate the 12-pin Assembly Line Diagnostic Link (ALDL) under the driver's side of the dash. Bridge the "A" and "B" terminals together with a special key or, in a pinch, use a bent paper clip or a short piece of wire.

These codes are displayed as flashes of light. For example, Code 12 would appear as one blink, a short pause, two blinks, then a long pause before the next code. (Missing code numbers are intentional by the manufacturer.) The computer will flash all codes stored in memory three times each and then repeat them until the tool is removed from the ALDL. After repairs are made, disconnect the negative battery cable from the battery for five minutes to clear all stored codes. Reconnect the battery and drive the vehicle for about 10 miles to allow the computer to relearn the engine's characteristics. The engine may run roughly at first. After testing, remove the bridging device from ALDL to exit code display mode.

"NO-CODE" DRIVABILITY PROBLEMS

Unfortunately, not all operational problems are covered by an OBD trouble code, nor do problems always trigger a trouble code. These problems are called "no-code" drivability complaints. Such faults are more difficult to track down, because you don't have a clear-cut starting point as you do when a code is set. In these cases you have to use basic mechanical sleuthing, just as technicians always did before there were trouble codes.

There's a tendency with computer-controlled engines to assume that problems are usually in the computer or its circuitry. However, don't forget that there's an engine under all that stuff, with pistons, valves, and gaskets. Always check the basics first: filters, plugs, cap and rotor, and ignition cables. Look for vacuum hoses that are cracked or disconnected and wires/cables that may be chafed through or cut. Battery and charging problems can raise havoc. Use a digital voltmeter to test battery voltage when the engine is running. If all these check out, test compression and cylinder leakdown rate to ensure that the engine is in good mechanical condition.

VEHICLE EMISSION CONTROL INFORMATION LABELS

The Vehicle Emission Control Information (VECI) label is required by federal law to be affixed to every emission-controlled vehicle sold in the United States and Canada. This sticker can usually be found on the radiator support, underside of the hood, fan shroud, or rocker-arm cover.

VECI labels provide important information on the specific vehicle you are working on, such as vacuum-hose routing diagrams and tune-up and emission specifications. If any discrepancy exists between the specifications shown in a service manual and the VECI label, trust the label.

TEST EQUIPMENT

To thoroughly test a computer-equipped vehicle requires thousands of dollars in special equipment, including an oscilloscope, exhaust-gas analyzer, scan tools, breakout boxes and even a chassis dynamometer. However, with standard hand tools and a few relatively inexpensive items, such as an analog and/or a 10-megohm impedance digital volt-ohmmeter, vacuum gauge, fuel-pressure gauge, and a little persistence, many maladies can be detected.

For specific information on wiring, component specifications, etc., refer to manufacturers' shop manuals.

EMISSION SYSTEM COMPONENT WARRANTIES

Most of the emission-control components are covered by a five-year/50,000-mile (whichever comes first) warranty against defects in materials and workmanship. Some OBD II components are covered for eight years or 100,000 miles. Many people overlook this coverage, which is available at any franchised dealer. Federal regulations require the vehicle manufacturer (for example, Chrysler, Ford, General Motors, etc.) to provide this warranty to the original and all subsequent owners of the vehicle.

These warranties generally include all of the major (expensive) parts of the fuel-injection and emission-control systems. Limited diagnostic time may also be included. Certain items, such as filters, are considered owner-maintenance items and are not covered. Components damaged due to modification, abuse, or improper service procedures are also not covered. Refer to your vehicle owner's manual or your dealer for specific details.

Electronic engine-control systems are made up of large numbers of components. Knowing the functions of the various parts helps one understand how the entire system works and where to look when a problem arises. We have listed the major components used in domestic light-truck electronic-fuel systems. The descriptions in this chapter are necessarily generic in nature since not all fuel systems use all of the items listed here. However, they are representative of the majority of the systems used in domestic motorhomes, trucks and vans.

OBD II Generic Codes

P0100 Mass or Volume Air Flow Circuit Malfunction
P0101 Mass or Volume Air Flow Circuit Range/Peformance Problem
P0102 Mass or Volume Air Flow Circuit Low Input
P0103 Mass or Volume Air Flow Circuit High Input

P0105 Manifold Absolute Pressure/Barometric Pressure Circuit Malfunction
P0106 Manifold Absolute Pressure/Barometric Pressure Circuit Range/Performance Problem
P0107 Manifold Absolute Pressure/Barometric Pressure Circuit Low Input
P0108 Manifold Absolute Pressure/Barometric Pressure Circuit High Input

P0110 Intake Air Temperature Circuit Malfunction
P0111 Intake Air Temperature Circuit Range/Performance Problem
P0112 Intake Air Temperature Circuit Low Input
P0113 Intake Air Temperature Circuit High Input

P0115 Engine Coolant Temperature Circuit Malfunction
P0116 Engine Coolant Temperature Circuit Range/Performance Problem
P0117 Engine Coolant Temperature Circuit Low Input

OBD II GENERIC CODES, Continued

P0118 Engine Coolant Temperature Circuit High Input

P0120 Throttle Position Circuit Malfunction
P0121 Throttle Position Circuit Range/Performance Problem
P0122 Throttle Position Circuit Low Input
P0123 Throttle Position Circuit High Input

P0125 Excessive Time to Enter Closed Loop Fuel Control

P0130 O2 Sensor Circuit Malfunction (Bank 1* Sensor 1)
P0131 O2 Sensor Circuit Low Voltage (Bank 1* Sensor 1)
P0132 O2 Sensor Circuit High Voltage (Bank 1* Sensor 1)
P0133 O2 Sensor Circuit Slow Response (Bank 1* Sensor 1)
P0134 O2 Sensor Circuit No Activity Detected (Bank 1* Sensor 1)
P0135 O2 Sensor Heater Circuit Malfunction (Bank 1* Sensor 1)

P0136 O2 Sensor Circuit Malfunction (Bank 1* Sensor 2)
P0137 O2 Sensor Circuit Low Voltage (Bank 1* Sensor 2)
P0138 O2 Sensor Circuit High Voltage (Bank 1* Sensor 2)
P0139 O2 Sensor Circuit Slow Response (Bank 1* Sensor 2)
P0140 O2 Sensor Circuit No Activity Detected (Bank 1* Sensor 2)
P0141 O2 Sensor Heater Circuit Malfunction (Bank 1* Sensor 2)

PO142 O2 Sensor Circuit Malfunction (Bank 1* Sensor 3)
PO143 O2 Sensor Circuit Low Voltage (Bank 1* Sensor 3)
PO144 O2 Sensor Circuit High Voltage (Bank 1* Sensor 3)
PO145 O2 Sensor Circuit Slow Response (Bank 1* Sensor 3)
PO146 O2 Sensor Circuit No Activity Detected (Bank 1* Sensor 3)
PO147 O2 Sensor Heater Circuit Malfunction (Bank 1* Sensor 3)

PO150 O2 Sensor Circuit Malfunction (Bank 2 Sensor 1)
PO151 O2 Sensor Circuit Low Voltage (Bank 2 Sensor 1)
PO152 O2 Sensor Circuit High Voltage (Bank 2 Sensor 1)
PO153 O2 Sensor Circuit Slow Response (Bank 2 Sensor 1)
PO154 O2 Sensor Circuit No Activity Detected (Bank 2 Sensor 1)
PO155 O2 Sensor Heater Circuit Malfunction (Bank 2 Sensor 1)
PO156 O2 Sensor Circuit Malfunction (Bank 2 Sensor 2)

OBD II GENERIC CODES, Continued

PO157 O2 Sensor Circuit Low Voltage (Bank 2 Sensor 2)
PO158 O2 Sensor Circuit High Voltage (Bank 2 Sensor 2)
PO159 O2 Sensor Circuit Slow Response (Bank 2 Sensor 2)
PO160 O2 Sensor Circuit No Activity Detected (Bank 2 Sensor 2)
PO161 O2 Sensor Heater Circuit Malfunction (Bank 2 Sensor 2)

PO162 O2 Sensor Circuit Malfunction (Bank 2 Sensor 3)
PO163 O2 Sensor Circuit Low Voltage (Bank 2 Sensor 3)

PO164 O2 Sensor Circuit High Voltage (Bank 2 Sensor 3)
PO165 O2 Sensor Circuit Slow Response (Bank 2 Sensor 3)
PO166 O2 Sensor Circuit No Activity Detected (Bank 2 Sensor 3)
PO167 O2 Sensor Heater Circuit Malfunction (Bank 2 Sensor 3)

PO170 Fuel Trim Malfunction (Bank 1*)
PO171 System Too Lean (Bank 1*)
PO172 System Too Rich (Bank 1*)

PO173 Fuel Trim Malfunction (Bank 2*)
PO174 System Too Lean (Bank 2*)
PO175 System Too Rich (Bank 2*)

PO176 Fuel Composition Sensor Circuit Malfunction
PO177 Fuel Composition Sensor Circuit Range/Performance
PO178 Fuel Composition Sensor Circuit Low Input
PO179 Fuel Composition Sensor Circuit High Input

PO180 Fuel Temperature Sensor Circuit Malfunction
PO181 Fuel Temperature Sensor Circuit Range/Performance
PO182 Fuel Temperature Sensor Circuit Low Input
PO183 Fuel Temperature Sensor Circuit High Input

PO2XX Fuel and Air Metering

PO201 Injector Circuit Malfunction-Cylinder 1
PO202 Injector Circuit Malfunction-Cylinder 2

PO203 Injector Circuit Malfunction-Cylinder 3

OBD II GENERIC CODES, Continued

PO204 Injector Circuit Malfunction-Cylinder 4
PO205 Injector Circuit Malfunction-Cylinder 5
PO206 Injector Circuit Malfunction-Cylinder 6
PO207 Injector Circuit Malfunction-Cylinder 7
PO208 Injector Circuit Malfunction-Cylinder 8
PO209 Injector Circuit Malfunction-Cylinder 9
PO210 Injector Circuit Malfunction-Cylinder 10
PO211 Injector Circuit Malfunction-Cylinder 11
PO212 Injector Circuit Malfunction-Cylinder 12

PO213 Cold Start Injector 1 Malfunction
PO214 Cold Start Injector 2 Malfunction
PO3XX Ignition System or Misfire
PO300 Random Misfire Detected
PO301 Cylinder 1 Misfire Detected
PO302 Cylinder 2 Misfire Detected
PO303 Cylinder 3 Misfire Detected
PO304 Cylinder 4 Misfire Detected
PO305 Cylinder 5 Misfire Detected
PO306 Cylinder 6 Misfire Detected
PO307 Cylinder 7 Misfire Detected
PO308 Cylinder 8 Misfire Detected
PO309 Cylinder 9 Misfire Detected
PO310 Cylinder 10 Misfire Detected
PO311 Cylinder 11 Misfire Detected
PO312 Cylinder 12 Misfire Detected

PO320 Ignition/Distributor Engine Speed Input Circuit Malfunction
PO321 Ignition/Distributor Engine Speed Input Range/Performance
P0322 Ignition/Distributor Engine Speed Input Circuit No Signal

P0325 Knock Sensor 1 Circuit Malfunction
P0326 Knock Sensor 1 Circuit Range/Performance
P0327 Knock Sensor 1 Circuit Low Input
P0328 Knock Sensor 1 Circuit High Input

OBD II GENERIC CODES, Continued

P0330 Knock Sensor 2 Circuit Malfunction
P0331 Knock Sensor 2 Circuit Range/Performance
P0332 Knock Sensor 2 Circuit Low Input
P0333 Knock Sensor 2 Circuit High Input

P0335 Crankshaft Position Sensor Circuit Malfunction
P0336 Crankshaft Position Sensor Circuit Range/Performance
P0337 Crankshaft Position Sensor Circuit Low Input
P0338 Crankshaft Position Sensor Circuit High Input

P0340 Camshaft Position Sensor Circuit Malfunction

P0341 Camshaft Position Sensor Circuit Range/Performance
P0342 Camshaft Position Sensor Circuit Low Input
P0343 Camshaft Position Sensor Circuit High Input

P04XX Auxiliary Emission Controls

P0400 Exhaust Gas Recirculation Flow Malfunction
P0401 Exhaust Gas Recirculation Flow Insufficient Detected
P0402 Exhaust Gas Recirculation Flow Excessive Detected

P0405 Air Conditioner Refrigerant Charge Loss

P0410 Secondary Air Injection System Malfunction
P0411 Secondary Air Injection System Insufficient Flow Detected
P0412 Secondary Air Injection System Switching Valve/Circuit Malfunction
P0413 Secondary Air Injection System Switching Valve/Circuit Open
P0414 Secondary Air Injection System Switching Valve/Circuit Shorted
P0420 Catalyst System Efficiency Below Threshold (Bank 1*)
P0421 Warm Up Catalyst Efficiency Below Threshold (Bank 1*)
P0422 Main Catalyst Efficiency Below Threshold (Bank 1*)
P0423 Heated Catalyst Efficiency Below Threshold (Bank 1*)
P0424 Heated Catalyst Temperature Below Threshold (Bank 1*)

P0430 Catalyst System Efficiency Below Threshold (Bank 2)
P0431 Warm Up Catalyst Efficiency Below Threshold (Bank 2)
P0432 Main Catalyst Efficiency Below Threshold (Bank 2)

OBD II GENERIC CODES, Continued

P0433 Heated Catalyst Efficiency Below Threshold (Bank 2)
P0434 Heated Catalyst Temperature Below Threshold (Bank 2)

P0440 Evaporative Emission Control System Malfunction
P0441 Evaporative Emission Control System Insufficient Purge Flow
P0442 Evaporative Emission Control System Leak Detected
P0443 Evaporative Emission Control System Purge Control Valve
          Circuit Malfunction
P0444 Evaporative Emission Control System Purge Control Valve
          Circuit Open
P0445 Evaporative Emission Control System Purge Control Valve
          Circuit Shorted

P0446 Evaporative Emission Control System Vent Control Malfunction
P0447 Evaporative Emission Control System Vent Control Open
P0448 Evaporative Emission Control System Vent Control Shorted

P0450 Evaporative Emission Control System Pressure Sensor Malfunction
P0451 Evaporative Emission Control System Pressure Sensor Range/Performance
P0452 Evaporative Emission Control System Pressure Sensor Low Input
P0453 Evaporative Emission Control System Pressure Sensor High Input

P05XX Vehicle Speed Control and Idle Control System

P0500 Vehicle Speed Sensor Malfunction
P0501 Vehicle Speed Sensor Range/Performance
P0502 Vehicle Speed Sensor Low Input

P0505 Idle Control System Malfunction
P0506 Idle Control System RPM Lower Than Expected
P0505 Idle Control System RPM Higher Than Expected

P0510 Closed Throttle Position Switch Malfunction

P06XX Computer and Output Circuits

P0600 Serial Communication Link Malfunction
P0605 Internal Control Module (Module Identification Defined by J1979)

OBD II GENERIC CODES, Continued

P07XX Transmission

P0703 Brake Switch Input Malfunction
P0705 Transmission Range Sensor Circuit Malfunction (PRNDL Input)
P0706 Transmission Range Sensor Circuit Range/Performance
P0707 Transmission Range Sensor Circuit Low Input
P0706 Transmission Range Sensor Circuit High Input

P0710 Transmission Fluid Temperature Sensor Circuit Malfunction
P0711 Transmission Fluid Temperature Sensor Circuit Range/Performance
P0712 Transmission Fluid Temperature Sensor Circuit Low Input
P0713 Transmission Fluid Temperature Sensor Circuit High Input

P0715 Input/Turbine Speed Sensor Circuit Malfunction
P0716 Input/Turbine Speed Sensor Circuit Range/Performance
P0717 Input/Turbine Speed Sensor Circuit No Signal

P0720 Output Speed Sensor Circuit Malfunction
P0721 Output Speed Sensor Circuit Range/Performance
P0722 Output Speed Sensor Circuit No Signal

P0725 Engine Speed Input Circuit Malfunction
P0726 Engine Speed Input Circuit Range/Performance
P0727 Engine Speed Input Circuit No Signal

P0730 Incorrect Gear Ratio
P0731 Gear 1 Incorrect Ratio
P0732 Gear 2 Incorrect Ratio
P0733 Gear 3 Incorrect Ratio
P0734 Gear 4 Incorrect Ratio
P0735 Gear 5 Incorrect Ratio
P0736 Reverse Incorrect Ratio

P0740 Torque Converter Clutch System Malfunction
P0741 Torque Converter Clutch System Performance or Stuck Off
P0742 Torque Converter Clutch System Stuck On
P0743 Torque Converter Clutch System Electrical

OBD II GENERIC CODES, Continued

P0745 Pressure Control Solenoid Malfunction
P0746 Pressure Control Solenoid Performance or Stuck Off
P0747 Pressure Control Solenoid Stuck On
P0748 Pressure Control Solenoid Electrical

P0750 Shift Solenoid A Malfunction
P0751 Shift Solenoid A Performance or Stuck Off
P0752 Shift Solenoid A Stuck On
P0753 Shift Solenoid A Electrical

For systems with single O_2 sensors, use codes for Bank 1. Sensor Bank 1 contains cylinder #1. Sensor 1 is closest to engine.

Chapter 16

ENGINE REPLACEMENT OR OVERHAUL

Weighing Priorities ■

Making the Right Engine Choice ■

Rebuilding Locally ■

Other Powertrain and Chassis Components ■

The RV Handbook

Owners of high-mileage tow vehicles and motorhomes realize they are facing a choice: trade up or decide to invest a sizable sum in an engine replacement or overhaul. Many factors must be weighed, including several that are purely personal:

1. Do you like your vehicle?

2. Does it serve your needs well (large enough, small enough, comfortable)?

3. Are its operating costs acceptable? If not, will a new vehicle reduce costs enough to help justify its purchase price?

Certainly, if you have doubts about your present vehicle, sinking more money into it doesn't make sense. The wise move would be to buy a later model.

Assuming, however, that you like the vehicle, the repair costs may be dramatically less than what you'd spend on a replacement vehicle—particularly if you're capable of doing some of the repair work yourself—-not to mention lower licensing fees (in some states) and insurance.

WEIGHING PRIORITIES

It's time to consider an overhaul when performance has dropped substantially and the engine uses more than a quart of oil every 500 miles. A check of cylinder compression and crankcase pressure will determine if valve repairs will suffice or if a complete overhaul is needed. If the results are bad, you must decide if you want to keep the vehicle or move on to a newer one.

Small-block engines tend to age gracefully, with performance gradually falling off as the motor reaches the end of its service life. However, large-block motors are occasionally subject to catastrophic failures. Therefore, it's best to analyze engine condition and take corrective steps before you're forced to do so under undesirable conditions.

MAKING THE RIGHT ENGINE CHOICE

If you decide to keep the vehicle and fix the engine, you'll face three choices:

Figure 16.1
New or remanufactured engines are available from auto/truck dealers and from a variety of other sources.

1. Purchasing a new replacement engine

2. Purchasing a remanufactured engine (which may be sold under either a private brand or that of the original vehicle's manufacturer)

3. Having your existing engine rebuilt by a local shop

Choosing a new or factory-remanufactured engine (Figure 16.1) over a shop rebuild has several advantages. It usually gets you back on the road much faster—often in a matter of several days. This is particularly important during a breakdown away from home. Furthermore, you can expect a reasonably accurate estimate of the total job cost, with no worries about discovering additional damage as the engine is disassembled. Finally, there's the security of having a nationwide warranty at an automotive dealership.

Nationwide warranties also are offered by the larger remanufacturing companies. All companies offer replacement engines for pickup trucks, and little is said about trailer towing. Unfortunately, some either don't offer engines commonly used in motorhomes, or will void the warranty of an engine that is installed in a motorhome. Owners of vehicles falling into this category can choose a rebuild offered locally, which allows personal observation of the quality of the work being per-

formed, as well as special arrangements with the rebuilder for components and machining procedures that may significantly improve the engine's performance and longevity.

In fact, the prospect of obtaining a superior-quality engine may make a local rebuild attractive for just about any RVer. Furthermore, a local rebuild may be less expensive than a new or remanufactured engine, especially if you're willing to handle some of the engine removal and disassembly tasks yourself. However, trouble away from home within the warranty period usually means you must handle it yourself and submit a repair claim to the shop that performed the work. It requires a considerable degree of confidence in the integrity of the shop. Be sure to get the warranty coverage in writing.

New Engines

Brand-new, stock replacement engines are available for some vehicles. Essentially, these are engines with many of the same strengths and weaknesses as the original engine, and they will deliver similar performance and service life. A major advantage is their relatively easy installation, with little likelihood of encountering fuel, electrical or emissions systems incompatibilities.

Although usually targeted at performance car and pickup enthusiasts, some of the more

Figure 16.2
GM Performance Parts offers the HT502 engine as a replacement for the Chevrolet/GMC 7.4L V-8.

detuned versions of these "crate" engines are suitable for RV applications as well. The prime example is the 502 cid HT502 Towing/Heavy Vehicle engine offered by GM Performance Parts (Figure 16.2), which is available as both a bare engine and as part of a complete retro-kit installation package for 1991-93 GM 10/20/30-Series pickups.

Ford Motorsports and Mopar Performance also offer crate engines, although their current products are not specifically identified as suitable for towing service.

When considering any crate engine, you need to make sure that it will fit your particular application with a minimum of installation headaches (including emissions controls), and that it has ample torque and drivability at the low speeds typically encountered in RV service (from idle to around 4,000 rpm). Be sure to choose one that does not require premium fuel, unless you regard the higher performance output as worth the cost.

Factory Remanufactured Engines

The remanufactured engines sold by new-vehicle dealers are produced by any of several sources, each of which must complete an extensive qualification program for both remanufacturing procedures and equipment. Sample engines are also periodically dynamometer-tested under severe service to verify durability. Most engines have a 36-month/50,000-mile fully-transferable warranty. For motorhomes, the warranty applies only to specifically approved applications.

The quality of engines available from other engine remanufacturers varies considerably due to the caliber of the inspection and machining processes, as well as the choice of bearings, pistons, rings and other engine components. In some cases, parts that should have been replaced may have been "reconditioned," and other parts may have been replaced with "off-brand" substitutes. This makes it advantageous to obtain a detailed list of which parts and procedures go into the engine, including the brands of all new parts installed.

Many of the reconditioning procedures for a quality factory-remanufactured engine are no different from those for an engine rebuilt by a local shop with a good reputation for quality. Thus, an examination of what goes into a good shop rebuild is useful for buyers of both engine types, and the important items are described later in this chapter.

AC Delco

AC Delco offers remanufactured engines for 45 engine families including most GM, Chrysler and Ford light truck applications and the three V-8 big-blocks: GM 7.4-liter (454 cid), Ford 7.5-liter (460 cid) and the old Dodge 440 cid V-8 engine that was popular until the late 1970s in Class A motorhomes. Most popular small-block engines also are offered.

A number of different remanufacturers are used, all of whom produce engines to an extensive set of Delco specifications. All engines include a new oil pump, intake and exhaust valves, flat lifters, brass or stainless freeze plugs, premium OE gaskets, oil filter, oil pickup screen and tube, and new or reclaimed oil pan and valve covers. Delco also performs a hot run test on every engine, which includes testing the oil pressure, compression and vacuum, as well as checking for air and fluid leaks. All engines have 36-month/36,000-mile nationally transferable warranties.

DaimlerChrysler

DaimlerChrysler's Mopar parts division offers 318 and 360 cid long-block remanufactured engines for both the early pre-Magnum and later Magnum series. All engines are rebuilt by outside sources to a detailed set of standards, which are periodically verified by engine teardowns, 100- and 500-hour durability tests and dynamometer and thermal shock testing.

All engines are built to original specifications, with all tolerances held to those of the original engine. All engines include new pistons, rings, bearings, timing chain and gears, and a complete gasket set. Other parts are reconditioned or replaced as required. All parts are either direct OEM replacements, or are purchased through OEM suppliers. The Magnum engines also include new valves, rocker arms, and either a new or repolished roller cam (where applicable).

All dealer-installed Mopar remanufactured engines have a 12-month/12,000-mile warranty, or a 12-month/unlimited mileage warranty when installed by an independent shop.

Cummins

Cummins Recon, a separate division of the diesel-engine manufacturing firm, stocks nearly 400 different engine configurations, which are remanufactured at the company's own facilities. All-new Cummins-brand parts include cylinder caps, rings, liners (if applicable), all bearings, bushings, seals, hoses, fuel tubes, fuel lines, filters, gaskets, plugs, and camshaft. The cylinder block, crankshaft, cylinder heads, rods, turbocharger, water and lube pumps, fuel pump, and injectors are typically replaced with Cummins-brand rebuilt components (Figure 16.3). In applications that permit it, the old engine can be replaced with a higher-power version, often at little or no extra cost. Cummins' motorhome warranty is

24 months/100,000 miles for both B- and C-Series engines, although some C-Series versions have an unlimited mileage warranty. Parts, labor, progressive damage, and maintenance items damaged by warrantable failure are covered.

GM

GM Goodwrench has both new and remanufactured engines for various GM products and more specifically addresses RV applications than does any other vehicle manufacturer. The aforementioned 502 cid HT502 Towing/Heavy Vehicle engine is the prime example. Emissions-legal in all states, the engine conversion kit is designed for 1991-93 Chevrolet and GMC 10-, 20-, and 30-series two-wheel-drive trucks equipped with 454 TBI engines and 4L80E automatic overdrive transmissions. The engine is rated at 515 lb-ft of torque at 2,800 rpm.

A full line of Goodwrench new and remanufactured engines is offered, covering all pop-

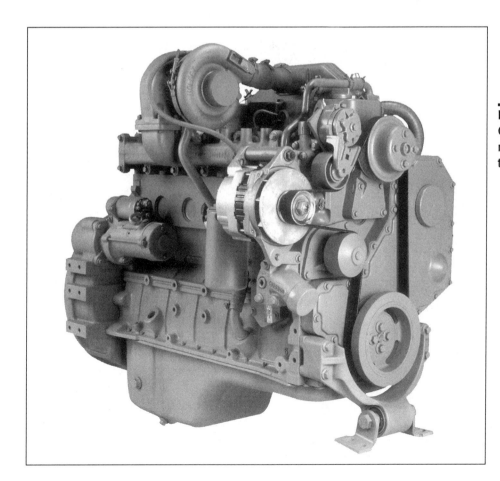

Figure 16.3
Cummins Recon offers remanufactured 5.9-liter turbo-diesel engines.

ular light truck engines. Warranty coverage is 36 months or 50,000 miles.

Ford

Ford remanufactured engines are built by outside sources to a detailed set of specifications, and are verified by periodic quality audits and warranty reports. The remanufacturing processes and parts used will vary considerably with the engine model and vehicle application. As an example, most 351 cid versions include new pistons, rings, valves, exhaust manifolds, oil pump, oil cooler, water pump, thermostat, gaskets, and in most cases, timing gears and chain. Remanufactured parts include the crankshaft, block, heads, valve covers, and oil pan.

Most 460 V-8 engines were, until 1999, supplied under a less-formal agreement with numerous independent remanufacturers, but are built under a single set of standards very similar to those for the 351.

All Ford remanufactured engines are individually hot-run, checked for leaks and compression-tested. A 2-year/24,000-mile warranty is standard for most applications except motorhomes, where no warranty is offered.

What to Expect in a Top-Quality Engine Rebuild

A top-quality engine rebuild or remanufacture should include:

- Thorough cleaning and magnetic inspection of all parts
- Boring each cylinder to match the individual piston assembly
- Cylinder honing with torque plates installed
- Moly-impregnated piston rings fitted precisely according to ring manufacturer's instructions
- Precision crankshaft grinding and polishing
- Connecting rods checked for trueness, pin-end roundness, cracks
- Cylinder heads, block, and intake manifold checked for warpage, cracks, excessive valve-guide wear
- High-volume oil pump
- Double-row timing-chain assembly (except Ford 460)
- New camshaft, selected for maximum torque and power below 4,000 rpm
- Deck heights (piston to top of block clearance) checked and corrected if necessary
- Rotating/reciprocating components balanced
- Spring-loaded Teflon valve seals, where applicable
- Valves and seats compatible with unleaded gasoline and resurfaced properly
- New valve springs

ATK

ATK is an engine remanufacturer that supplies local dealers across the nation. Remanufactured engines include new pistons, rings, main bearings, rod bearings, cam bearings, rocker nuts and swivels, timing chains, cam sprocket and crank gear, and all gaskets and seals required for installation. New or remanufactured parts include the valves, lifters, oil pump, and camshaft.

The engine block is line-honed, the crankshaft is magnafluxed, and the connecting rods are resized and balanced in sets. ATK/VEGE PowerTest engines are also hot-run for thirty minutes to check oil pressure, compression, coolant flow, and for leaks. ATK's standard warranty is 36 months or 60,000 miles; motorhomes with weight ratings over 11,000 lbs are excluded.

Jasper

Jasper is another nationwide supplier of remanufactured engines, supplying dealers and independent repair shops. The company's engines feature new pistons, rings, pins, pin bushings and lock rings, hollow push rods, timing gear or chain, intake and exhaust valves, valve springs, solid lifters, valve keep-

ers and seals, spring retainers, valve guides (as applicable), oil pump intermediate shaft, and gaskets. The camshaft and rocker arm assemblies are new or remanufactured as required, and the oil pump is remanufactured.

Jasper machines its crankshafts with no odd-size bearings or journals, and chamfers the oil passages for improved lubrication. Heads are checked for cracks with magnetic particle inspection and pressure testing. Every engine is hot-tested with recorded inspections of temperatures, oil pressure, vacuum pressure, and compression.

Light-duty truck engines have a 36-month/75,000-mile warranty except 1-ton and larger trucks, which are covered for 18 months or 75,000 miles.

Recon

Recon Automotive Remanufacturers Inc. offers a wide variety of domestic and import engines, all of which include new pistons, rings, and pins, timing gear and chain (except overhead cam engines), lifters, oil pump, rod and main bearings, gaskets and seals, freeze plugs, camshaft bearings, and push rods. Additional components that are either replaced or remanufactured to O.E. specifications include the

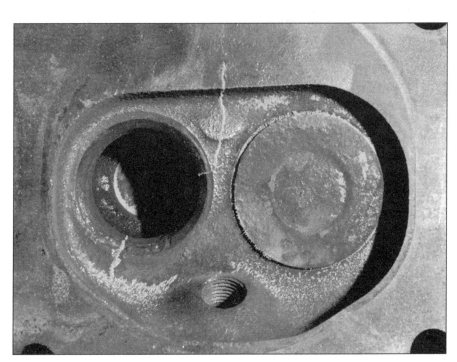

Figure 16.4
When magnetic force is applied, colored metal particles are attracted to any cracks on the surface—a cylinder head in this case.

crankshaft, valves, camshaft, valve springs, connecting rods, and valve guides.

A 12-month warranty applies to all vehicles except motorhomes and trucks 1 ton and above, which have a 6-month warranty. In both cases, replacement labor costs are covered up to $350.

REBUILDING LOCALLY

In having your engine rebuilt, the selection of an appropriate shop is crucial. A good shop uses quality parts and meticulous workmanship, and has the expertise to correct any faults in the original engine design. Many of these firms cater to the racing and marine markets, both of which demand considerable skill. If you cannot select a shop in which you have confidence, the warranty of a new or fac-tory-remanufactured engine may be a very strong point.

Cleaning and Inspection

Proper cleaning and inspection are essential in preventing dirty or defective components from being reinstalled, which could quickly lead to catastrophic failure. Typically, the block and heads are cleaned by soaking in a solvent-filled hot tank, air blasting with abrasive beads, or "cooking" in an oven for several hours.

The block, heads and most moving parts should be inspected for cracks (Figure 16.4) before reconditioning. Some shops also inspect them again prior to final assembly. Cracks in cast iron blocks and heads are sometimes reparable with pins or welding. Special welding processes are also often used to repair aluminum heads, although considerable skill is required to produce satisfactory results.

Figure 16.5
Cylinder boring must be in perfect alignment with crankshaft throws.

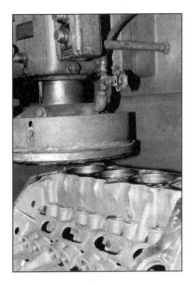

Figure 16.6
When one bank of a V-8 block is higher than the other, a special milling machine is used to create uniformity.

Some shops use pressure testing equipment to ensure that all cracks are fully repaired.

Machining Procedures

Boring is done when cylinder wear exceeds certain parameters, usually .009 inch. The number refers to taper—the amount of wear that occurs at the top of the piston's stroke (where maximum stress occurs), compared to the original bore, which is measured at the bottom of the cylinder. It's imperative that boring be done properly—that all cylinders are bored perfectly in alignment with the crankshaft throws—which requires very sophisticated equipment (Figure 16.5).

Although ignored by some rebuilders and remanufacturers, decking of the block is essential (Figure 16.6). In a factory engine, the distance between the top of the piston at the top of its stroke and the top of the block is often different on one bank than the other, causing imbalance and greater stress under heavy throttle. Decking corrects this deficiency by milling both sides of the block to a uniform deck height.

Some shops bolt torque plates to the cylinders during honing in order to simulate the cylinder wall distortion that normally occurs once the heads are installed and torqued to specs. This significantly improves ring sealing by producing a near-perfect cylinder shape.

Piston Selection

The choice of pistons is controversial, with some shops choosing cast pistons to lower cost, while others insist on the increased durability of forged pistons. A cast piston is created when molten aluminum is poured into a mold. A forged piston is created when a hot aluminum ingot is forced under pressure into a mold, creating a denser structure that withstands greater abuse.

In cast pistons, the use of factory-original parts is advisable (Figure 16.7), even though the cost is often greater. Most factory pistons are of a design that allows closer piston-to-cylinder wall clearances. When these pistons expand with heat, they maintain their original cylinder-wall clearance, while also providing increased strength. Some factory pistons, such as those in the Dodge 8-liter V-10, have a moly coating that helps reduce wear, particularly during break-in.

Forged pistons are considerably more expensive, but are worthwhile for high compression ratios or extremely severe service. However, they require additional cylinder-wall clearance, resulting in a little more piston noise. When combined with their typically shorter skirts, this may also reduce piston-ring life.

Another option is hyper-eutectic pistons, which use a special high-silicon aluminum alloy to produce greater durability than con-

Figure 16.7
Cast pistons can withstand more severe use.

ventional cast pistons, while retaining good cylinder wear and noise characteristics. For RVers desiring extra durability in their rebuild, hyper-eutectics can be a cost-effective alternative to forged pistons.

Piston rods should be inspected for cracks, bends, and bore distortions. Rods that pass muster are reconditioned, using a resizing machine. Installing new rod cap bolts is strongly recommended. Some newer engines like Ford's Triton series have powdered metal rods and "cracked" caps that lack a machined mating surface. Since any of these rods having elongated bores cannot be reconditioned by grinding the caps, the bores are instead cut to accept bearings with oversized outside diameters.

Most quality rebuilds use ductile iron piston rings with chrome facing and moly inserts. Unlike chrome-plated steel rings, they provide immediate seating, while still delivering considerably longer life than cast iron.

Fitting Components

Precision fit of piston rings to pistons is essential for proper durability, lubrication, and oil control. The ring manufacturer's specific instructions should be followed, including staggering the ring-end gaps to prevent combustion gases from leaking into the lower engine block (Figure 16.8).

Excessive clearance between crankshaft and piston-rod bearings and their journals will reduce oil pressure, and may also increase oil consumption by throwing excessive oil into cylinders. Plastigage should be used during assembly to assure proper crankshaft fit. Failure to lubricate the main cap bolt threads before assembly can also produce excessive clearance. Finally, crankshaft bearing selection has a significant effect on oil pressure, due to variations in eccentricity among various brands and part numbers.

Figure 16.8
Precision fit of piston rings is essential for proper wear and for oil control.

Figure 16.9
Valve seats should be machined at 70-, 45-, and 15-degree angles.

Most crankshafts are ground .010 inch smaller, which is called "10 under." Grinding 20 or 30 under is usually undesirable due to the loss of durability that often results. During crankshaft reconditioning, it's often beneficial to chamfer the oil holes in the crank journals, thereby improving oil flow to the bearings.

Valve Train Preparation

All replacement or overhauled engines should include hardened exhaust valves and seats. Proper valve and seat surface preparation is also essential, including machining at the three angles prescribed for the specific application, typically at 70, 45 and 15 degrees, bottom to top (Figure 16.9). The finished thickness of the valve head (edge of the valve) should be a minimum of ³⁄₆₄-inch exhaust and ¹⁄₁₆-inch intake, or the valve should be replaced.

Valve guide-to-stem clearances should be checked for excessive clearance, which would reduce valve life and increase oil consumption, even when improved valve guide seals are utilized. Factory specs on valve guide-to-stem clearance should be used. Bronze valve guides or sleeves are preferred over knurling, which in any case should not be used to take up guide-to-stem clearance in excess of .002 inch over factory specs, since the guide will soon return to its previous size.

New-Engine Startup

Before starting any replacement engine that hasn't been previously hot-tested, the lubrica-tion system should be primed. Typically, this is done by temporarily removing the distributor, allowing the use of an electric drill to rotate the oil pump shaft.

Some shops precisely measure the oil pressure during initial startup, comparing the readings to those of identical previously rebuilt engines. This provides confirmation that crankshaft bearing clearances are within acceptable limits, and that all major lubrication passages are clear.

Spark timing and air-fuel mixtures should be calibrated correctly for each mode of operation. Specific engine-oil and fuel-octane recommendations should be provided, along with a schedule for retorquing and periodic engine inspection.

Other engine-related components that should be checked, reconditioned, or replaced include the radiator, fuel filter(s), alternator, water pump, harmonic damper, motor mounts, and starter. A new transmission input-shaft seal should be installed while the engine is removed.

OTHER POWERTRAIN AND CHASSIS COMPONENTS

An automatic transmission will usually outlast the engine by a considerable margin, unless the transmission has been overheated. The transmission oil and filter should have been changed at least every 20,000 miles, or at 30,000 if one of the new long-life fluids has been used.

If the transmission shows signs of excessive wear, such as erratic shifting, slipping, or excessive metal and frictional particles in the pan, the cost of an overhaul must be included in the vehicle repair-or-replace decision. It's important to correct any factory defects or weaknesses, which are usually well known in the transmission repair industry, particularly among shops that cater to performance enthusiasts. Having the engine and transmission repaired simultaneously often minimizes labor costs and downtime.

Properly maintained rear axles and manual transmissions rarely fail until well after the 100,000-mile mark. Replacement of a clutch and throwout bearing might be considered as part of a vehicle rejuvenation program, due to its ease of access with the engine removed.

The vehicle's front suspension and brakes should be evaluated for wear. Front-suspension or brake repairs can be costly, particularly if linings or pads have worn enough to score the drums or rotors. Also consider having shock absorbers replaced.

Ultimately, the repair-or-replace decision usually involves more than finances. Often, there is a reluctance to part with a trusty vehicle that has provided many wonderful travel experiences. Few vehicles are so fraught with defects that they cannot be renovated at a fraction of the cost of a new one. So either decision—new or rebuilt—can be a satisfactory one.

Chapter 17

GETTING GOOD SERVICE

The most critical factor in maintaining your investment in an RV is proper care and maintenance. Following manufacturer-prescribed service recommendations not only adds to the usable life expectancy of your trailer, motorhome, or camper, it also preserves the warranty while assuring safe and pleasurable motoring. Eventual resale value is also sustained at an optimum level.

FINDING THE RIGHT SERVICE CENTER

Once this philosophy is accepted, the next important consideration is to put it into practice by locating a capable and knowledgeable garage for regular service and repairs. This is often a difficult task, for mechanics and garages that are set up to work on motorhomes and trailers just aren't around every corner. Larger motorhomes in particular require specialized mechanical knowledge and skills. Unlike automobile and light-truck garages, which can be found in even some of the smallest of rural towns, an RV service center may require effort to locate.

Quality of service is an ongoing concern among RV owners, dealers, and manufacturers. In this specialized field, it requires distinct training, experience, and know-how to work on vehicles that are both residential and automotive by design.

To assist dealer networks in improving and maintaining their abilities to deliver top-flight service, the Recreation Vehicle Industry Association (RVIA) provides one-week (forty-hour) clinics for experienced service technicians to refine their skills.

The Recreation Vehicle Dealers Association (RVDA) also maintains a program that provides formal certification and accreditation to service providers who have undergone and successfully completed an in-depth course of study.

A little preplanning and research can usually identify capable, certified repair facilities in your immediate area. Unfortunately for some, their RVs don't always cooperate by developing problems near one of these locations. It is therefore imperative that one also subscribes to a dependable and trustworthy emergency road service such as one operated by the Good Sam Club. Another "must" in finding repairs in unfamiliar surroundings is the annually updated *Trailer Life Directory*. This publication identifies RV service locations in the lower forty-eight states, Canada, and Alaska.

LEMON LAW PROTECTION

Honest and reliable RV service cannot always be assumed, however. As a result, consumers throughout the country have influenced the enactment of legislation in all fifty states known as automotive repair acts or "lemon laws." These statutes require dealers, technicians, and manufacturers of automobiles and automotive equipment to fulfill and uphold their warranty and service obligations.

Furthermore, they provide a system of arbitration between the consumer and the automotive concern that will settle disputes up to and including the buy-back of a vehicle by its manufacturer. Unfortunately for some RV owners, these laws vary from state to state and do not always recognize motorhomes or trailers; more information on lemon laws is included in this chapter.

ASSIGNING REPAIR RESPONSIBILITY

One issue still not completely resolved is which entity is responsible for repairs on a motorhome, the chassis or the coach builder? Over the past several years, the Recreational Vehicle Industry Association has been in the forefront of mitigating these contentious and often consumer-perplexing situations. To this end, the RVIA and certain motorhome manufacturers have entered into arbitration agreements to resolve warranty-related motorhome complaints. Although product disputes between motorhome and chassis manufacturers are infrequent, the arbitration process will help resolve most consumer grievances.

Under terms of these agreements where a motorhome and chassis manufacturer cannot resolve an owner's complaint covered by a state lemon law, either the coach or chassis manufacturer may invoke the arbitration process. This avenue is only open to chassis and motorhome manufacturers; consumers cannot initiate this particular action.

However, the existence of such pacts motivate manufacturers to promptly settle these issues because it allows them an informal and economical medium within which to negotiate the sharing of costs. Currently, the RVIA maintains separate agreements between chassis manufacturers such as Ford, Freightliner, and Spartan.

Trailers do not fall under lemon law statutes in most states and, as such, can leave unhappy owners with few sources for appeal. Fortunately, the RV industry is very competitive and will go to great lengths to keep its customers happy. As such, many manufacturers have developed responsive customer-relations departments within their organizations to handle warranty and service complaints. To further enhance this aspect, manufacturers consider service and adequate facilities as prime criteria in choosing dealers to market their product lines.

TIPS FOR IMPROVED SERVICE

State and federal regulatory agencies such as automotive repair bureaus and the Federal Trade Commission are usually "courts of last appeal" when seeking complaint resolutions. Improved customer relations are likewise only assurances rather than iron-clad guarantees that one will be skillfully and graciously accommodated. Refer to "A Checklist for Obtaining Better Dealer Service," page 260, for suggested guidelines to obtaining competent dealer service.

INDEPENDENT REPAIR SHOPS

Most RV owners would rather secure service from their original dealers or official manufacturer repair facilities. However, due to travel habits, people often find themselves far from these locations when mechanical failures occur. If you are faced with this very common dilemma, the guidelines listed in "Independent Repair Shops—Selection Guidelines," page 262, may assist you in securing necessary and reliable repairs from an independent repair shop.

CONSUMER RESPONSIBILITIES

Although providing capable and courteous service to customers is the primary responsibility of a dealer or manufacturer, the process is still a two-way street if it is to be successfully accomplished. This means the consumer has certain responsibilities as well.

One of the most prevalent complaints registered about RVers concerns a common practice of making service or repair appointments and canceling or failing to show up. This habit costs dealers and service centers untold income, especially during summer months, by encumbering already busy appointment calendars.

Another aggravating practice of many RV customers is to accidentally break or damage a component within their rigs before reading up on the item in owner manuals or product brochures. Instead of familiarizing themselves first, they embark on a trial-and-error process that ultimately leads to product damage.

In reporting these predicaments to their dealer, they subsequently become untruthful or defensive in attempting to have the damage repaired under the warranty. This doesn't set well with service centers and tends to undermine the basic tenet that "the customer is always right."

Another irritant has to do with RV owners who maintain unrealistic expectations of dealers and manufacturers in seeking resolutions or repair. A manufacturer is not likely to replace an entire motorhome because of defects that they deem repairable; likewise they are seldom open to fixing a situation at no cost to the customer that is long out of warranty unless there is a substantial, pre-existing paper trail.

Customer demeanor at repair facilities is another potential problem. Most dealers and garages that repair RVs understand that their owners are tied to their rigs—reluctant to leave them because of the value of their contents, even if the cost of staying in a nearby motel is not a financial burden. With a little negotiation and explanation up front, repair personnel will usually allow owners as much access to the coaches as is reasonably safe or prudent. However, shop personnel do not appreciate customers lurking over their shoulders either

A Checklist for Obtaining Better Dealer Service

✔ **Check the Dealer** Local reputation and first-hand examples of customer satisfaction are prime indicators for those purchasing a new or used RV. Checking out service bays beforehand and talking to a few customers may also speak abundantly for what might be expected in the future. Look for evidence of state, local, and industry certifications around mechanics' stations, waiting areas, and showrooms.

✔ **Check Your Warranty** Carefully read all warranty documents. Some warranties apply to specific components and are only covered by their respective manufacturer. Warranty exclusions are also important to note.

✔ **Get Written Estimates** Request printed work orders on all service, both warranty and nonwarranty. Get a written estimate on nonwarranty repairs and establish an understanding with the service representative that you must be notified if additional work is needed. Many states now mandate prior notification before work is performed beyond that which is originally agreed upon by the customer. For extra protection, be sure and have the service person provide a written confirmation that states you must authorize any additional repairs not noted on the original work sheet.

✔ **Verify** Replacement Parts Prior to work beginning, request that all old or defective parts which are replaced be returned to you for inspection. If preauthorized warranty work is performed at an independent facility, the manufacturer my also request an inspection of the item prior to reimbursement of your out-of-pocket expenses.

✔ **Resolve Problems** When problems arise, check first with the service manager. Nothing is to be gained by an insulting or aggressive approach. If this person is of no help, request to see the manager or owner of the facility or dealership. The next level of appeal is the vehicle manufacturer's customer-relations department. If all avenues have been fully explored without success, contact the state's consumer affairs or automotive repair bureau for any legal remedies, including small claims court, that are available in your case. At this point, you may also wish to contact one of several consumer advocacy agencies.

✔ **If you have received a check** for insurance coverage on your claim, don't sign it over to the dealership until you have inspected the work and have confirmed the quality of the repair. In effect, signing the check notifies the insurance company that the case is closed.

out of curiosity or mistrust. If you are that suspicious of the location, seek out another. If you are just mistrustful by nature, it is best to curb this tendency in the interests of speedy repair. Remember, a happy mechanic does much better repairs, especially if he does not have to carry on a conversation while working.

Even though the owner of an RV may be living in a vehicle that is set up in an RV park, most manufacturers are not willing to pay for service at the location; the unit must be brought to a dealership.

REPAIR SCAMS

With the large amounts of money spent annually in this country on vehicle maintenance and repairs, the field has become a very lucrative front for a small, though enterprising segment of con artists. These unethical people prey on motorists and RVers at one of the most vulnerable points in their lives: when they are experiencing mechanical problems far from home. Common practices of these predatory charlatans include puncturing tires with sharp objects, slicing fan belts, or squirting oil inside wheel drums. If people are not particularly wary when seeking help at unfamiliar service stations and independent repair facilities, they may be hoodwinked into unnecessarily replacing tires, belts, or brake cylinders among other things. The advice noted in "Guarding Against Repair Scams," below, should help consumers guard against such unscrupulous practices.

CONSUMER-WARRANTY RIGHTS

Every recreational vehicle comes with multiple warranties. As such, it may be difficult to sort out responsibility for repairs when something goes haywire. Motorhomes have two distinct warranties—one for the coach and

---

Guarding Against Repair Scams

❏ Be skeptical of pushy and overeager station attendants, especially in self-service stations. Avoid high-pressure sales tactics and be duly cautious of sales pitches that warn that it is "too dangerous to continue unless immediate repairs are undertaken." Above all else, demand proof before considering such advice.

❏ Never leave your RV unattended in a service or filling station. This invites sabotage, even if none was originally considered.

❏ Only allow under-hood inspections if you are present to observe. Slicing hoses and belts along with "short-sticking" engine oil are all familiar practices used to scam unwary travelers.

❏   If confronted with the need to buy parts, spend a few minutes to call around town for a price comparison. Small station markups are often opportunistic and exorbitant.

❏   When possible, pay for repairs with an oil-company credit card. These firms are often able to recover at least part of the money in a dispute between a customer and one of their dealer stations. Many credit-card companies also provide a "with hold of payment" for their customers until a dispute has been settled. When all else fails, small claims court may provide relief if you are close enough and have the time to access such help.

another for the chassis. All RVs also have specific warranties that apply to individual components as well. Overall, the terms, conditions, and duration of these contracts vary greatly.

While shopping for an RV, consider the warranty of a given unit as one of the most important points to study before buying.

Some manufacturers are more generous than others in this area. Once delivery is taken, the next thing is to become thoroughly familiar with the weighty stack of warranty documents included with a new unit. Time is often against consumers who only use their rigs once or twice a year. Prepare an outline of

Independent Repair Shops—Selection Guidelines

Check Your Warranty If your vehicle is still within the manufacturer's warranty period but you are unable to locate a manufacturer-authorized service center or garage, consult your owner's manual or warranty identification card for the company's customer relations department. Without prior approval for warranty repairs at an independent garage, a consumer is often left with the fruitless task of trying to recoup out-of-pocket expenses for repairs made outside warranty stipulations and guidelines. This is one of the most common problems RV owners experience with warranty issues.

Many dealers will not provide warranty service for vehicles purchased elsewhere, even if they are an authorized warranty station for the brand in question. You may be required to pay in advance. If so, make sure the manufacturer has provided a written approval for the work and for reimbursement.

Ask for Recommendations Those who ignore history are doomed to repeat it, especially when trading with incompetent or untrustworthy business establishments. With this caveat in mind, ask local campground managers for referrals to reputable and reliable service facilities.

Check Certification Look for visible evidence of a mechanic's skills in the form of training certificates and proficiency citations. Prominent display of such items often denotes the mechanic cares enough to be certified. Automotive manufacturers, trade schools, and oil companies all provide regular training to automotive service personnel. It's also a good indicator if a technician is schooled within the field you are seeking repairs, such as brakes, transmission, etc.

Check Accreditation Prominently displayed certificates from a state's Better Business Bureau or Automotive Repair Bureau are prime indicators that the establishment buys into a prescribed code of ethical standards.

Check Business History Ask locally how long a business has been in operation and, if possible, its reputation for competence and honesty. Be sure the establishment is capable of working on a larger RV, or at least the specific problem at hand. Most gas stations may not have the equipment and qualified personnel necessary to work on RVs.

products and time limits on the most important and costly items.

The Magnuson-Moss Warranty Act also bestows consumers in the United States with the right of prior review of warranties, regardless of the product. Dealers are required by law to post written notices in conspicuous locations such as showrooms, which tell consumers that copies of all warranties are available upon request.

If they are not on the premises, the dealer must provide information necessary to obtain the warranty for the manufacturer.

Check Alternative Shops Specialty facilities such as transmission centers and muffler shops may be better skilled and equipped to handle your particular situation if it falls within their field of expertise. They might also be considerably faster and cheaper in the long run.

Get a Written Guarantee Ask about guarantee terms on work performed and get a written verification. If work needs to be redone within the specified time frame, you will have some leverage in getting a refund.

Talk to the Mechanic Establish a clear understanding with the mechanic or service writer of just what work is to be accomplished.

Get a Written Estimate Obtain a written estimate before approving any repairs. If time and circumstances allow, use it to compare at other facilities in the vicinity.

Compare Rates Most automotive repair shops charge from pre-established rate tables in flat-rate manuals. These fees are established according to degree of job difficulty and average time necessary to perform a given operation. Other shops charge strictly by the hour. Determine beforehand how your repair cost will be estimated. If it appears your job might take less than the pre-established flat-rate time, try to negotiate a more equitable hourly fee.

Save All Receipts Keep copies of all receipts and work orders. Make sure all repairs along with a breakdown of individual charges have been noted. Parts and labor should be listed separately, while mileage of the vehicle and warranty terms should also be plainly spelled out. Retain all old parts until the warranty has expired.

Consider Emergency Service Programs Emergency response and towing programs such as Good Sam's Emergency Road Service (ERS) provide members with a nationwide, toll-free, twenty-four-hour number for towing any type of RV to the nearest Good Sam-approved repair facility. For additional information on Good Sam's ERS Program, write or call: Good Sam Club, 2575 Vista Del Mar Drive, Ventura, California; (800) 234-3450.

Spoken Warranties

Verbal promises by eager salespersons are sometimes offered to undecided buyers to sweeten an impending sale. These pledges can vary from offers of simple modifications or

---

RVDA CONSUMER SERVICE GUIDELINES

To assist RVers in gaining satisfactory service, the Consumer Care Commission of the Recreation Vehicle Dealers Association recommends the following guidelines:

- ■ Be open and capable of identifying the value of reliable products and good service.

- ■ Be willing to pay the necessary costs for reliable products and good service.

- ■ Accept responsibility for knowledge of all aspects of a vehicle's operation before leaving the dealership.

- ■ Become better informed about products by studying owner's manuals provided by manufacturers and suppliers.

- ■ Be more aware of realistic limitations of the vehicle.

- ■ Be prepared to accept responsibility for basic vehicle maintenance.

---

upgrades on the RV to free maintenance or extended service plans. Such commitments constitute spoken warranties. However, unless these promises are documented in writing on the sales contract, they are not binding. If a salesperson makes such an offer, insist that the terms and conditions appear on the sales agreement before signing. If the request is refused, it is doubtful you will receive what was offered.

Implied Warranties

Written warranties are not specifically required by law. However, implied warranties are, and can be found on the books in most states throughout the country. Just about every purchase one makes is covered by an implied warranty of some sort. The most commonly experienced version is known as a warranty of merchantability. This means a seller "implicitly" promises that a product will do what it is supposed to do. For example an air conditioner will cool, a heater will heat, a step will support, etc.

A warranty of fitness for a particular purpose is another type of implied warranty. This applies when you purchase a product on advice or declaration of a seller that it is suitable for a particular use. As an example, if an auto manufacturer assigns an explicit towing-capacity rating to a given vehicle and the dealer sells it as suitable for pulling your trailer, then the above-specified warranty would attach.

Items that do not expressly come under implied warranty protection are those marked "as-is" or "with all faults," which specifically draw a buyer's attention to the exclusion of all warranties. Sellers may also state in writing that no warranty is given. Several states do not permit "as is" sales.

If problems occur that do not relate directly to the manufacturer's written warranty, check to see if an implied warranty might exist within your state. Implied warranty coverage can last up to four years, but the length of coverage on individual items can vary by state. If you have questions on applicability of implied warranties or whether "as-is" sales are permitted in your area, check with your state consumer affairs office or the state attorney general's office for more information.

Resolving Warranty Disputes

Disputes over terms and conditions of a warranty can usually be resolved using suggestions listed in "How to Resolve Warranty Disputes," on page 266. However, if none of these actions resolves your problem or if a significant amount of money is at stake, you may wish to consider using an attorney to file a lawsuit based on the Magnuson-Moss Warranty Act.

This is the law that allows consumers to sue for damages or any other type of relief the court awards, including legal fees. Prospective litigants should note that in most cases, only the maker of the warranty can be sued.

However, some state laws allow dealers, distributors, or other associates to also be named in such actions. Your attorney should be able to advise you whether or not you have a valid claim under Magnuson-Moss.

Despite the fact that this law was enacted by Congress in 1974, many lawyers are still unaware of the array of remedies available under the act. When seeking counsel to represent you in such a case, it is wise to choose those persons with firsthand experience or who specialize in dealing with such issues.

Warranty Checklist

Federal laws also provide significant warranty guidelines and restrictions that have taken the fine-print complexity and a good deal of mystery out of the warranty process. Warranties must now stipulate the duration of coverage offered and items or practices which specifically exclude coverage. Following is a list of critical elements to consider when reviewing a warranty:

✔ Exclusions are one of the most important warranty elements to consider. Some are limited to replacement of parts only, while labor is not included. Modifications or addition of certain accessories will sometimes void powertrain or other warranties. Customary wear and tear such as tire tread, alignments, and brake pads are also usually excluded.

✔ Become thoroughly familiar with the consumer's responsibilities in obtaining warranty service. Are there specific mandates that the item must be serviced by the selling dealer or factory-authorized service center? Are service locations plainly spelled out on paperwork included with the product?

✔ What are the manufacturer's warranty obligations if the item is defective? Does the warranty specifically stipulate repair or replacement?

✔ Does the warranty cover consequential damages? Most do not, which means you won't be compensated for any damage caused as a result of the part or item failure or expenses incurred while seeking repair. For example, if your rig breaks down while on the road, you will not be reimbursed for motel expenses while it is laid up in a service facility. Likewise, if a refrigerator fails, it is highly unlikely that you will be compensated for spoiled food.

✔ What are the warranty's specified conditions and limitations? Most common prerequisites are proper use, care, and maintenance. If misuse or lack of service are evident or can be proven, the consumer is usually disqualified from coverage.

State Lemon Laws

One of the most disheartening experiences a person can have is paying thousands of dollars for a new RV or tow vehicle, only to find out later that it does not live up to prior expectations of performance, quality, or safety. However, since the early 1980s, all states have enacted one form or other of lemon law that allows consumers a relatively level playing field in seeking redress of their complaints.

Tow vehicle owners, especially, have the best of the situation as these laws usually provide fairly comprehensive coverage. Motorhome coverage is limited to chassis in some cases, and then only in states where such vehicles are recognized within lemon legislation.

In essence, lemon laws represent an extended warranty legislated by an individual state. Under most lemon statutes, a vehicle manufacturer is usually given a specific number of

How to Resolve Warranty Disputes

Read Become completely familiar with a product's warranty before buying. After purchasing, mail any required applications and proof of purchase within the prescribed time limits. File sales contracts and receipts with the factory warranty.

Discuss When problems occur, discuss them first with the original retailer. If a resolution cannot be reached, contact the manufacturer. Send any letters by certified mail and keep copies. Maintain a chronological history or paper trail.

Complain If the above steps do not bring results, contact local or state consumer protection agencies such as Better Business Bureaus or automotive repair oversight agencies. Manufacturers cannot legally stall a resolution of your problem until the original warranty runs out. If a problem exists before expiration of the factory warranty and there is a written record or history of complaint, the manufacturer is obligated to resolve the problem according to the terms of its warranty. Another avenue to pursue in lending weight to your appeal may be contacting a consumer-advocacy representative such as *Trailer Life's* "RV Action Line," *Highways'* "Good Sam Action Line," or *MotorHome's* "Hot Line." The magazines can be reached at 2575 Vista Del Mar Drive, Ventura, California 93001. These columns specialize in handling RV-related problems at no charge to readers and can be a good initial step in resolving a dispute. They may also save you from time-consuming and costly legal proceedings. (See page 268 for a sample complaint letter.)

Arbitrate Some manufacturers may be amenable to submitting a problem to a professional arbitrator rather than engaging in more costly legal proceedings. Inquire up front if the organization uses such methods. Be forewarned, you must abide by the arbitrator's decision once rendered.

Litigate Legal action is often the last resort, mainly because it can be very costly. Consider small claims court as an economical, do-it-yourself step to recover modest amounts. Generally speaking, filing fees are small and the court clerk will be able to provide you with instructions on how to proceed.

opportunities to remedy a defect within certain time frames before the law is triggered. Once this process is set in motion, it does not guarantee outright that the vehicle in question will be bought back or replaced.

Consumers must present their cases before a state-assigned arbitrator who rules on the merits and evidence within each pleading. Consequently, it is extremely important that comprehensive and detailed repair histories and records be maintained by the consumer as well as a timely and relentless pursuit of the problem.

Where do all the lemons go once bought back from unhappy customers? Obviously not into lemonade! To recoup some of the money lost in buying back unacceptable vehicles, manufacturers fix and recondition them to be marketed through various dealer networks. Because this practice is quite common and may still expose unwary consumers to inferior products, many states have now amended their lemon statutes to require that retailers provide buyers with a complete history on such vehicles. Many states also require branding of the term "lemon" on all titles, registration certificates, and sales documents.

Service Contracts/Extended Warranties

Buying a service contract or extended warranty can offer consumers an extra level of protection beyond normal warranty limits as well as peace of mind. Also considered breakdown insurance, these policies can cover repair costs of products and vehicles from minimal to the extremely expensive. Under the best of terms, these contracts can save consumers large sums of money when costly to replace items such as automatic transmissions and diesel engines act up. Many policies also include payment of motels and rental cars while the insured vehicle is laid up for repair. On the other hand, service contracts can be high-priced headaches for the unwary if not entered into under the right conditions and terms.

Service contracts are now offered by virtually all dealers and most manufacturers on products ranging from the entire motorhome or trailer to various components and appliances

within. Term lengths and amounts of coverage determine the cost of such a policy.

Not only do extended warranties vary considerably in what they cover or exclude, they differ widely in their reliability. These types of policies are also high-profit commodities for dealers, who usually market them aggressively. Although the industry has reputable underwriters who offer fair and worthwhile coverage, numerous others are shaky. Regardless of whether you are buying new or used, consider the following before entering into any service contract or extended warranty agreement.

What does the contract offer? Manufacturer warranties are generally included in the original price of a product; service contracts cost extra and are sold separately. Both provide repair and/or maintenance for a specified time period.

What is covered by the contract? Read all contracts carefully because they are usually very specific regarding parts and service coverage. If items or issues are not stipulated or listed plainly, they are not covered. No assumptions should ever be made when it comes to service contracts or any other for that matter. Service contracts and regular warranties alike will exclude coverage if an item is misused or not given required service and maintenance. Many consumers fail to realize that preconditions often exist whereby it is their responsibility to obtain preapproval before having an item repaired. This requirement can be especially vexing for those on the road, who often find themselves unable to make contact with an underwriter who lacks a twenty-four-hour telephone number because of a weekend or time of day.

What will the service contract give me that the manufacturer's warranty will not? Study your original warranty carefully before entering into an extended service contract. Be aware that service contracts usually overlap the warranty provided by the original manufacturer unless the RV is previously owned. Is the coverage really worth the added expense?

What other costs will I have? Most contracts have deductibles which must be paid up front. There may also be charges levied every time the coverage is used. Some expenses may be limited or excluded. For example, your contract may

How to Complain to a Dealer or Manufacturer

Following is a suggested format for writing a complaint letter to a dealer or manufacturer:

Date

John Doe, president
Acme RV, Incorporated
Address

Dear Mr. Doe:
I am writing concerning a problem I have with my (year, make, model), which was purchased on (date). The vehicle identification number is (#).

I experienced the first breakdown with my (vehicle) on (date) and have had repeated problems with it since then. My major concern at this point is (description). As a result of this problem, we have been unable to use our (vehicle) since (date), and have spent (amount) thus far trying to get it repaired and back on the road. I attempted to get help through (service manager, dealership) on several occasions, but the (vehicle) remains unrepaired and is not roadworthy. The following is a list of my repair attempts:

(date) (problem #1)
(date) (problem #2)

Attached are copies of work orders and receipts, plus receipts for (incidental expenses, towing, etc.). A reply at your earliest convenience would be appreciated.

Sincerely,

Your name and address

cc: Trailer Life "RV Action Line" (or)
MotorHome "Hot Line" (or)
Highways "Good Sam Action Line"

not cover towing or rental-car expenses. Additionally, you may have to pay transfer or cancellation fees if you sell the covered vehicle before expiration of the contract. If you are buying a used unit that has a transferable service contract, leave nothing to chance. While following through with the selling dealer, it is also wise to contact the insurance company directly to guarantee the transfer has been consummated. If a transfer fee is charged, be sure to get a written receipt.

Where can I get service? Some contracts may be restrictive in their service allowances, sometimes only available at the dealership where you bought the unit, but most allow the policyholder to arrange for service at any well-established service location. If the contract is restrictive, demand a list of specific locations where service may be obtained.

Who is responsible for the contract? If the contract is underwritten by a dealer, it may only be good if the dealer remains in business. Contracts offered by larger, independent companies and insurers are the best choices. Smaller companies with little or no proven track record seem to have a habit of disappearing. If in doubt, check with your state insurance board or Better Business Bureau before making any commitments.

Can I purchase a service contract later? Many companies allow buyers a reasonable amount of time after purchasing a product to obtain an extended service agreement. These time frames usually range from thirty days to one year, depending on the institution. If this is the case, take the extra time to get a copy of the contract and study it carefully before signing.

Secret Warranties

Manufacturers disdain the term "secret warranty," and would rather refer to these defect-repair issues as "good will programs" or "policy adjustments." The original reference stems from the fact that, in some cases, manufacturers rely on dealers to correct design problems undetected at the time of manufacture.

If a defect is not directly related to safety, it is the manufacturer's prerogative how consumer notification will be undertaken. Instead of issuing headline-grabbing recall notices, many companies rely on dealer networks to correct the problems at the customer's next service. Also, manufacturers may elect to issue a press release in the hope the defect will be widely circulated by the media. Because consumers are not notified directly and are only offered free repairs when and if they eventually learn of the defect, consumer advocates and state attorneys general have labeled this practice as the "secret warranty" program.

There is currently no federal law requiring auto companies to reveal their secret warranties. However, several states including California, Connecticut, Virginia, and Wisconsin have enacted such legislation while several more are considering it. Examples of past secret warranty brouhahas have centered around premature undercarriage rust-out, pulsating brake systems, cracked engine blocks, and peeling paint.

How does an unwary owner find out about a secret warranty issued on his or her vehicle? Usually by old-fashioned research and persistence. First, check technical service bulletins pertaining to your particular vehicle at your nearest dealer. A second way to detect secret warranties is by the existence of inconsistent dealer treatment of one consumer over the other for the same defect. This practice usually signals an accommodation-by-complaint-only approach, which is a prime indication. A good source to explore if you are having trouble on the local level is the National Highway Traffic Safety Administration (NHTSA). For a modest fee, this federal organization will send you a list of all the current service bulletins. Once you've selected one or more, you can purchase individual copies by the page.

What can one do in seeking redress under such a nebulous program? First and foremost, complain loudly and relentlessly. Press your case with the dealer first, and then the manufacturer. Small claims court is another avenue, although the statute of limitations on such cases is usually four years.

From the manufacturer's perspective, they admit a certain responsibility for correcting factory defects. However, they argue that they should not have to go to unreasonable lengths to mitigate such problems. Industry representatives have commented in the past that laws that would require formal notification of individual owners for every factory defect would be extremely costly and have questionable benefits. Costs for such a process would ultimately be passed on to consumers in the form of higher vehicle costs.

RECALLS

Recalls are usually safety-related defect notifications that come in two forms: voluntary and involuntary. A voluntary recall takes effect when a manufacturer of a vehicle or product discovers a defect and notifies owners by mail or through the media that such a process has been initiated.

An involuntary recall originates when complaints, breakdowns, or accidents occur in sufficient numbers to alert a government agency, such as the NHTSA or the Federal Trade Commission (FTC), that a problem exists in sufficient numbers to warrant further investigation. Because the investigative process can take considerable amounts of time, both the NHTSA and the FTC urge consumers who believe they have safety-related or other types of product defects to contact them as soon as possible with the pertinent information.

An important point to remember about recalls is that even though a factory defect has been discovered, there can be limitations regarding the company's legal responsibilities. Federal regulations do not permit companies to assign arbitrary cutoff dates on recalls, though a termination date is provided for in the law. In the case of a voluntary recall, a company's financial responsibility ends eight years from the purchase date of the product. If the recall is safety related, there is no cutoff date.

Appendix

TIRE RATING TABLES

Table A.1 Tire and Rim Association Ratings
Tire Load Limits (lbs) at Various Minimum Cold-Inflation Pressures (PSI)

		Radial Ply									
		35	40	45	50	55	60	65	70	75	80
		Diagonal (Bias) Ply									
TIRE SIZE	USAGE	30	35	40	45	50	55	60	65	70	75
LT205/75*15	Dual	1145	1260	1365	**1520**(C)						
LT205/75*15	Single	1260	1385	1500	**1655**(C)						
LT215/75*15	Dual	1225	1340	1460	**1610**(C)	1680	1785	**1930**(D)			
LT215/75*15	Single	1345	1475	1605	**1765**(C)	1845	1960	**2095**(D)			
LT225/75*15	Dual	1315	1440	1565	**1710**(C)	1800	1915	**1985**(D)			
LT225/75*15	Single	1445	1585	1720	**1875**(C)	1980	2105	**2205**(D)			
LT235/75*15	Dual	1390	1530	1660	**1820**(C)	1910	2035	**2150**(D)	2265	2375	**2535**(E)
LT235/75*15	Single	1530	1680	1825	**1985**(C)	2100	2235	**2335**(D)	2490	2610	**2755**(E)
LT255/75*15	Dual	1575	1730	1880	**2040**(C)						
LT255/75*15	Single	1730	1900	2065	**2270**(C)						
LT225/75*16	Dual	1365	1500	1630	**1765**(C)	1875	1995	**2150**(D)	2220	2330	**2470**(E)
LT225/75*16	Single	1500	1650	1790	**1940**(C)	2060	2190	**2335**(D)	2440	2560	**2680**(E)
LT245/75*16	Dual	1545	1695	1845	**2006**(C)	2125	2255	**2381**(D)	2515	2640	**2778**(E)
LT245/75*16	Single	1700	1865	2030	**2205**(C)	2335	2480	**2623**(D)	2765	2900	**3042**(E)
LT265/75*16	Dual	1740	1910	2075	**2270**(C)	2390	2540	**2755**(D)	2825	2965	**3085**(E)
LT265/75*16	Single	1910	2100	2280	**2470**(C)	2625	2790	**3000**(D)	3105	3260	**3415**(E)
LT285/75*16	Dual	1940	2130	2310	**2535**(C)	2660	2830	**3000**(D)			
LT285/75*16	Single	2130	2340	2540	**2755**(C)	2925	3110	**3305**(D)			
LT215/85*16	Dual	1360	1490	1625	**1765**(C)	1865	1985	**2150**(D)	2210	2320	**2470**(E)
LT215/85*16	Single	1495	1640	1785	**1940**(C)	2050	2180	**2335**(D)	2430	2550	**2680**(E)
LT235/85*16	Dual	1545	1700	1845	**2006**(C)	2125	2260	**2381**(D)	2515	2645	**2778**(E)
LT235/85*16	Single	1700	1870	2330	**2205**(C)	2335	2485	**2623**(D)	2765	2905	**3042**(E)
LT255/85*16	Dual	1745	1920	2085	**2270**(C)	2400	2555	**2755**(D)			
LT255/85*16	Single	1920	2110	2290	**2470**(C)	2635	2805	**3000**(D)			
7.50*15LT	Dual	1190	1310	1420	**1520**(C)	1620	1715	**1800**(D)	1870	1960	**2040**(E)
7.50*15LT	Single	1350	1480	1610	**1720**(C)	1830	1940	**2140**(D)	2130	2220	**2320**(E)
7.50*16LT	Dual	1430	1565	1690	**1815**(C)	1930	2040	**2140**(D)	2245	2345	**2440**(E)
7.50*16LT	Single	1620	1770	1930	**2060**(C)	2190	2310	**2440**(D)	2560	2670	**2780**(E)

*Indicates position where R (radial ply) or B (bias ply) designation will appear–i.e., LT215/85R16.
Letters and **boldfaced** tire load values indicate tire load ranges C through E.

Table A.2 Tire and Rim Association Ratings
Tire Load Limits (lbs) at Various Minimum Cold-Inflation Pressures (PSI)

TIRE SIZE	USAGE	65	70	75	80	85	90	95	100	105	110	115	120
225/70R19.5	Dual	2600(D)	2720	2860	**3000**(E)	3115	3245	**3415**(F)	3490	3615	**3750**(G)		
	Single	2755(D)	2895	3040	**3195**(E)	3315	3450	**3640**(F)	3715	3845	**3970**(G)		
245/70R19.5	Dual				3415	3515	3655	**3860**(D)	3940	4075	**4300**(G)	4345	**4540**(H)
	Single				3640	3740	3890	**4080**(D)	4190	4335	**4540**(G)	4620	**4805**(H)
265/70R19.5	Dual				3750	3930	4095	4300	4405	4415	**4675**(G)		
	Single				3970	4180	4355	4540	4685	4850	**5070**(G)		
N305/70R19.5	Dual				4540	4670	4860	5070	5230	5410	**5675**(H)	5770	**6005**(J)
	Single				4940	5130	5340	5510	5745	5945	**6175**(H)	6340	**6610**(J)
255/70R22.5	Dual				3970	4110	4275	4410	4455	4610	**4675**(G)	4915	**5070**(H)
	Single				4190	4370	4550	4675	4895	5065	**5205**(G)	5400	**5510**(H)
305/75R22.5	Dual							5840	6025	6235	6610	6640	**6940**(J)
	Single							6395	6620	6850	7160	7300	**7610**(J)
305/85R22.5	Dual				5355	5550	5780	6005	6215	6435	**6780**(H)		
	Single				5840	6100	6350	6610	6830	7070	**7390**(H)		

Radial Ply

			70	75	80	85	90	95	100	105	110	115	120

Diagonal (Bias) Ply

TIRE SIZE	USAGE	65	70	75	80	85	90	95	100	105	110	115
245/75*R22.5	Dual	3465	3615	3765	3915	4055	4195	**4300**(G)				
	Single	3470	3645	3810	3975	4140	4300	4455	4610	**4675**(G)		
265/75*22.5	Dual	3870	4040	4205	4370	4525	4685	**4805**(G)				
	Single	3875	4070	4255	4440	4620	4800	4975	5150	**5205**(G)		
295/75*22.5	Dual	4500	4690	4885	**5070**(F)	5260	5440	**5675**(E)	5795	**6005**(H)		
	Single	4500	4725	4945	5155	5370	**5510**(F)	5780	5980	**6175**(G)	6370	**6610**(H)
285/75*24.5	Dual	4540	4740	4930	**5205**(F)	5310	5495	**5675**(G)	5860	**6175**(H)		
	Single	4545	4770	4990	5210	5420	**5675**(F)	5835	6040	**6175**(G)	6440	**6780**(H)

*Indicates position where R (radial ply) or B (bias ply) designation will appear–i.e., 225/70R19.5.
Letters and **boldfaced** tire load values indicate tire load ranges D through J.

Table A.3 Tire and Rim Association Ratings
Tire Load Limits (lbs) at Various Minimum Cold-Inflation Pressures (PSI)

		Radial Ply												
		60	65	70	75	80	85	90	95	100	105	110	115	120
		Diagonal (Bias) Ply												
TIRE SIZE	USAGE	55	60	65	70	75	80	85	90	95	100	105	110	115
8*19.5	Dual	2230	2350	**2460**(D)	2570	2680	**2780**(E)	2880	2980	**3070**(F)				
	Single	2270	2410	2540	2680	**2800**(D)	2930	3060	**3170**(E)	3280	3400	**3500**(F)		
8*22.5	Dual	2490	2620	**2750**(D)	2870	2990	**3100**(E)	3210	3320	**3450**(F)				
	Single	2530	2680	2840	2990	**3140**(D)	3270	3410	**3530**(E)	3660	3780	**3910**(F)		
9*22.5	Dual	2960	3120	3270	3410	**3550**(E)	3690	3820	**3950**(F)	4070	4200	**4320**(G)		
	Single	3010	3190	3370	3560	3730	3890	**4050**(E)	4210	4350	**4500**(F)	4640	4790	**4920**(G)
10*22.5	Dual	3510	3690	3870	**4040**(E)	4200	4360	**4520**(F)	4670	4820	**4970**(G)			
	Single	3560	3770	4000	4010	4410	**4610**(E)	4790	4970	**5150**(F)	5320	5490	**5670**(D)	
11*22.5	Dual		4380	4580	**4760**(F)	4950	5120	**5300**(G)	5470	5630	**5800**(H)			
	Single		4530	4770	4990	5220	**5430**(F)	5640	5840	**6040**(G)	6240	6430	**6610**(H)	
11*24.5	Dual		4660	4870	**5070**(F)	5260	5450	**5640**(G)	5820	6000	**6170**(H)			
	Single		4820	5070	5310	5550	**5780**(F)	6000	6210	**6430**	6630	6840	**7030**(H)	
12*22.5	Dual		4780	4990	**5190**(F)	5390	5590	**5780**(G)	5960	6150	**6320**(H)			
	Single		4940	5200	5450	5690	**5920**(F)	6140	6370	**6590**(G)	6790	7010	**7200**(H)	
12*24.5	Dual		5080	5300	**5520**(F)	5730	5940	**6140**(G)	6330	6530	**6720**(H)			
	Single		5240	5520	5790	6040	**6290**(F)	6530	6770	**7000**(G)	7200	7440	**7660**(H)

*Indicates position where R (radial ply) or B (bias ply) designation will appear–i.e., 8R19.5.
Letters and **boldfaced** tire load values indicate tire load ranges D through H.

Table A.4 Tire and Rim Association Ratings, Flotation-Type Light-Truck Tires
Tire Load Limits (lbs) at Various Minimum Cold-Inflation Pressures (PSI)

	Radial Ply					
	25	30	35	40	45	50
	Diagonal (Bias) Ply					
TIRE SIZE	20	25	30	35	40	45
31×10.50*15LT	1400	1595	**1775**(B)	1945	2100	**2250**(C)
31×11.50*15LT	1455	1660	**1845**(B)	2020	2185	**2340**(C)
32×11.50*15LT	1575	1795	**1995**(B)	2185	2360	**2530**(C)
33×12.50*15LT	**1755**(B)	2000	**2225**(C)			
35×12.50*15LT	2015	2295	**2555**(C)			

*Indicates position where R (radial ply) or B (bias ply) designation will appear–i.e., 31 × 10.50R15LT.
Letters and **boldfaced** tire load values indicate tire load ranges B through C.

Table A.5 Tire and Rim Association Ratings, Trailer Tires
Tire Load Limits (lbs) at Various Minimum Cold-Inflation Pressures (PSI)

TIRE SIZE	15	20	25	30	35	40	45	50	55	60	65
ST155/80*13	540	640	740	815	**880**(B)	970	1040	**1100**(C)			
ST175/80*13	670	795	905	1000	**1100**(B)	1190	1270	**1360**(C)			
ST185/80*13	740	870	990	1100	**1200**(B)	1300	1400	**1480**(C)			
ST205/75*14	860	1030	1170	1300	**1430**(B)	1530	1640	**1760**(C)			
ST215/75*14	935	1110	1270	1410	**1520**(B)	1660	1790	**1870**(C)			
ST205/75*15	905	1070	1220	1360	**1480**(B)	1610	1720	**1820**(C)			
ST225/75*15	1060	1260	1430	1600	**1760**(B)	1880	2020	**2150**(C)	2270	2380	**2540**(D)
ST215/80*16	1090	1300	1480	1640	**1820**(B)	1940	2080	**2200**(C)	2340	2470	****2600**(D)
ST235/80*16	1270	1510	1720	1920	**2090**(B)	2270	2430	**2600**(C)	2730	2870	*****3000**(D)

*Indicates position where R (radial ply) or B (bias ply) designation will appear–i.e., ST155/80R13.
**Load range E/2910 lbs. @ 80 psi.
***Load range E/3420 lbs. @ 80 psi.
Letters and **boldfaced** tire load values indicate tire load ranges B through D.

Table A.6 Michelin Motorhome Tire-Load Ratings, Loads per Axel
Tire Load Limits (lbs) at Various Minimum Cold-Inflation Pressures (PSI)
2 Tires = Single; 4 Tires = Dual

TIRE SIZE		55	60	65	70D	75F	80F	85F	90F	95
*225/70R19.5	Dual	9290	9820	10,360	10,880	11,440	12,000	12,460	12,980	13,660
	Single	4950	5230	5510	5790	6080	6390	6630	6900	7280
**8R19.5	Dual	9150	9770	10,390	10,800	11,475	12,200	12,825	13,500	
	Single	4710	5035	5365	5600	5950	6340	6650	7000	

*XRV Tire
**XZA Tire

Index